V. G. KOROLENKO

THE HISTORY
OF MY CONTEMPORARY

V. G. KOROLENKO

THE
HISTORY
OF MY
CONTEMPORARY

Translated and Abridged by
NEIL PARSONS

LONDON
OXFORD UNIVERSITY PRESS
NEW YORK   TORONTO
1972

Oxford University Press, Ely House, London W.1

GLASGOW NEW YORK TORONTO MELBOURNE WELLINGTON
CAPE TOWN SALISBURY IBADAN NAIROBI DAR ES SALAAM LUSAKA
ADDIS ABABA BOMBAY CALCUTTA MADRAS KARACHI LAHORE
DACCA KUALA LUMPUR SINGAPORE HONG KONG TOKYO

ISBN 0 19 211702 5

English translation
© Oxford University Press 1972

Printed in Great Britain
by W & J Mackay Ltd, Chatham

Contents

Introduction

One day a local Jew came to see Korolenko with his son, aged about eleven. 'Here we are, Vladimir Galaktionovich,' he said. 'I told my son last year that if he worked at school and behaved himself, I would show him the best man in Russia. He has worked well for a whole year and his behaviour has been exemplary, so I've brought him to you.' (V. I. Frolov[1])

An acquaintance of mine said to me more than once:
'When I see Korolenko, I get to feel ashamed of my own existence . . .'
(S. Protopopov[2])

V. G. Korolenko has died in Poltava. The last embodiment of the conscience of the Russian people . . . has disappeared. (S. M. Dubnov[3])

Few writers have won such profound respect and admiration for their quality as men as has Korolenko. All his life he was a fearless champion of justice—a man who stepped forward to defend those who suffered innocently at the hands of the Tsarist government and police. Despite threats to his own life, he waged virtually a lifelong struggle against the virulent anti-semitism of the Russian government. In 1903, for example, a large-scale pogrom occurred in Kishinev. Korolenko went to investigate for himself, and the result was the article 'House No. 13', which denounced the complicity of the authorities. During 1905 there was a wave of pogroms in Southern Russia. Poltava, where Korolenko had settled in 1900, was one of the few towns of the Ukraine to escape, and it owed its escape very largely to the direct intervention of Korolenko, who, with a few brave associates, spent two whole days in the market-place reasoning with the crowds. The years 1911–13 were largely occupied with the notorious Beylis Case, in which a Kievan Jew, Beylis, was falsely accused of the ritual murder of a Christian boy. The trial finally took place in Kiev in the autumn of 1913, and Beylis was acquitted. He owed his acquittal in no small measure to the impact made upon society by Korolenko's articles.

[1] Quoted in Maurice Comtet: 'V. G. Korolenko et la question juive en Russie' in *Cahiers du monde russe et soviétique*, Vol. X, 1969, p. 253.

[2] S. Protopopov, 'Zametki o V. G. Korolenko', in *V. G. Korolenko v vospominaniyakh sovremennikov*, Moscow, 1962, p. 165.

[3] S. M. Dubnov, *Kniga zhizni. Vospominaniya i razmyshleniya*, Riga, 1934–5, Vol. 2, p. 356.

Korolenko's concern was by no means limited to the Jewish population of Russia. In 1892 a number of Udmurt peasants were accused of the ritual murder of a beggar. This case, like the Beylis Case, seems to have been started with the purpose of inflaming racial hatred. Korolenko wrote articles drawing attention to the irregularities of the trial, and eventually managed to bring about two re-trials, and even took a personal part in conducting the defence. He was largely responsible for the ultimate acquittal of the seven men originally condemned to hard labour. In all such cases Korolenko acted at considerable personal risk, motivated by his high ideal of justice, of a Russia in which men of all races would be free and equal citizens.

Korolenko's activity was many-sided. One has only to think of his work organizing relief for the victims of the great famine of 1891–2 or of intervention in Poltava during the Civil War on behalf of the victims of both the Bolsheviks and Denikin's troops to realize how total was his commitment to the society in which he lived. He was a true Man for all Seasons. As Gorky put it: 'He gave himself to the cause of justice with that rare, whole-hearted involvement in which the heart and the mind are in harmony and attain deep, religious passion.'[4]

Korolenko's works—stories, novelettes, essays, articles, *The History of My Contemporary*—present a broad and detailed picture of Russia during his lifetime. He was always a keen observer of his environment, and his best fiction is based upon autobiographical material, many stories having obvious echoes in the pages of *The History*. Thus, for example, the episode of the doll in Chapter 1 of this book served as the dramatic climax for the story 'In bad company'. The direct dependence of his Siberian stories—the best stories he wrote—on his experiences and impressions in exile is particularly obvious.

Korolenko was a convinced advocate of the social purpose of literature. 'Just as a man's legs carry him, let us suppose, from the cold and darkness towards habitation and light, so the word, art, literature help humanity in its progression from the past to the future.' He continually reminded young writers of their duty not only to portray life, but to portray it in its most characteristic guise, 'condemning or blessing'.

Given the nature of the man and the times in which he lived, it was inevitable that he should turn increasingly away from imaginative literature to journalism and non-fictional writing. 'Such a diversification may be right or wrong, but I never conceived of my literary work in any other way. It was second nature with me, and I could not do

[4] Gorky, 'V. G. Korolenko', in *V. G. Korolenko v vospominaniyakh sovremennikov*, Moscow, 1962, p. 162.

otherwise.' *The History*, which Korolenko came to regard as his 'most important task' and on which he laboured intermittently over a period of more than seventeen years, is a monumental work which crowns his career as a writer. It is at one and the same time a valuable historical document and a work of outstanding literary merit.

The History remained unfinished, for events in Russia continually took Korolenko away from it. The importance he ascribed to it can, however, be judged from the fact that he continued working on it even on his death-bed. He managed to reach the point where he settled in Nizhny-Novgorod in 1885 after his return from Siberia. As it stands, the work covers the first thirty-one to thirty-two years of his life.

The title of the work is somewhat curious, and stems from the fact that Korolenko did not regard the work as a simple autobiography. 'These notes', he wrote in the Preface to Volume I of the work,

> are not a biography, because I have not been particularly concerned about full biographical information; they are not a confession, because I do not believe either in the possibility or the usefulness of a public confession; they are not a portrait, because it is difficult to draw one's own portrait with any guarantee as to its likeness. . . . Here there will be nothing that I did not encounter in reality, nothing that I did not undergo, feel, or see. Yet I repeat: I am not trying to paint my own portrait. Here the reader will find only features from the history of 'my contemporary', a man better known to me than all other people of my time.

In a draft-version of this same Preface he had written that, while all the facts, impressions, thoughts and feelings set out in the work were facts of *his* life, were *his* thoughts, impressions and feelings, he had nevertheless only included those he considered bore some relation to things of general interest. In other words, the autobiographical material had been sieved, use being made only of what was judged to be significant. In this Korolenko was helped, as he realized, by the fact that he was separated from what he was describing by several decades. Enough time had elapsed for things to be seen in a truer and wider perspective. Unimportant things had had time to fade away.

The first volume, finished in 1905 but subsequently revised, covers Korolenko's childhood and schooldays in Volhynia, a part of S.W. Russia that had formerly belonged to Poland and where Polish, Ukrainian, and Russian elements were mixed. Volume II covers the years 1871–9—his years as a student, his first arrest and exile, his return to Petersburg, and the beginning of his second exile. Begun in 1909, the volume was completed only ten years later. The remaining two volumes are shorter and cover his years of exile, 1879–84. They are also different in character from the first volumes. In them Korolenko becomes more and more a *bytopisatel'*, a painter of the way of life of the peoples among whom he lived and worked. As the work nears its unfinished end, it becomes disjointed, a mere enumeration of events—witness to Korolenko's realization that time was running out. These last volumes, where Korolenko is separated from European Russia, are not included in this book (see Translator's Note, p. xiii).

The History covers virtually the whole of the reign of Alexander II—a reign that began with great expectations and ended with the Tsar's assassination at the hands of revolutionaries. In Volume I (the first two sections of this book) Korolenko shows the impact of some of the great events of the first half of the reign on provincial life. He writes at length of his recollections as a child of the Emancipation of the Serfs, of the ill-starred Polish Revolt of 1863. He also shows how his acceptance as a child of established ways of life, of the existing order, was replaced by a gradual critical awareness, which ultimately developed into a bitter consciousness of social injustice. His pictures of school-life in Russia in the 1860s are unique in Russian literature. Some are highly amusing (in 'The Yellow-Red Parrot' we are presented with an unforgettable portrait-gallery of his teachers), but there is always an undertone of seriousness, for these chapters also reveal the gradual stifling of all independence and initiative in education. Korolenko's early youth coincided with the emergence of Populism—the first revolutionary socialist movement in Russia. Volume II opens in 1871 with his first journey to Petersburg as a student. During the next few years (in Petersburg, then in the Petrovsky Academy just outside Moscow) he becomes caught in the ferment of Russian student-youth. His pictures of student life at this period are, again, very detailed and very finely drawn.

Korolenko's early life was fairly typical for a man of his background and generation. Although officially a *dvoryanin* (nobleman), he was more truly a *raznochinets*—a man with what one may loosely term a middle-class background. Not belonging to the privileged sections of society, many of the *raznochintsy* were radical socialists, and by the 1860s it was they who dominated the Russian Intelligentsia.[5] They constituted a

[5] The word 'Intelligentsia' was first used in the 1860s and acquired immediate currency, for it described what had become a distinct social category, made up of men who felt they had no place in the rigidly hierarchical and authoritarian social and political structure of Tsarist Russia. The 'Intelligentsia' of the 1840s had still been dominated by men who came from the gentry. By the 1860s the balance had shifted once and for all towards the *raznochintsy*, with the result that the Intelligentsia had become more radical. The Russian Intelligentsia has been compared to

vociferous extremist wing, and inevitably the government, seeking to protect its position, gradually resorted to repressive and reactionary policies. By the end of the decade a great gulf had opened between the government and the Intelligentsia as a whole. In the seventies Korolenko himself was twice the victim of extra-judicial arrest, imprisonment and exile—the victim of a government, frightened and unsure of itself, that had come to view every manifestation of independence as a hostile 'political' act. The story of his arrest at the Petrovsky Academy, his first exile, and his descriptions of Petersburg in the late 1870s throw interesting light on those troubled years. They reveal, among other things, how civilized, by comparison with twentieth-century dictatorships, was the treatment accorded political prisoners in Russia at this period. The Russian authorities could evince a certain self-ashamedness conspicuously absent in more modern police-states. This hint of self-ashamedness helped to produce an unsureness of touch, a deviousness of approach, that was very damaging to efficiency.

Korolenko comes to the conclusion that despite his exile for 'political unreliability', he was not by nature a revolutionary, but 'an observer'. Certainly he was opposed to the government, but, as he points out, so were all educated men of principle. Besides, fanaticism was alien to his nature. So was despair. This was a man who, on the road into exile in 1879, had written to his friend Grigoryev: 'You remember I was dreaming of a summer journey—well, I may be on a leash, but I'm journeying none the less.' He was a born optimist, who believed in the inevitability of gradual progress, and dedicated himself to improving the society in which he lived. Korolenko was a great liberal humanitarian, who refused to bind himself to any party or creed, and his *History* has the great merit of not being partisan: it reflects his sane and balanced personality, and breathes an urbanity and a deep compassion for men that give it a special and universal appeal.

The History is a many-sided work. As well as chapters devoted to important events, or to school-, student-, and prison-life, there are others which deal with such topics as his brother's short-lived career as a provincial correspondent, his own experiences as a proof-reader in Petersburg, or colourful individuals he met. These chapters are per-

---

a monastic order and to the crusading orders of the Middle Ages. It was a unique phenomenon—a 'class' held together by the bonds of radicalism, alienation, and an almost mystical sense of mission. The *Intelligenty* regarded themselves as the embodiment of the 'enlightened consciousness' of Russia. Comparatively few were, in fact, active revolutionaries, and many ultimately merged with society. The Intelligentsia always drew its greatest strength from the rising generation, as is, indeed, obvious from this book.

vaded by a gentle, indulgent, often wistful humour. The work contains a wealth of fascinating portraits, episodes, and anecdotes which are of great human interest, and offer a view behind the pages of history, a view of what life was really like in Russia in the reign of the Tsar-Liberator.

The work possesses, finally, one remarkable, underlying quality: Korolenko presents his reader with a constantly changing view of life. He was able to evoke with consummate skill the world of a child, a boy, a youth, and a man, and it is this artistic gift which makes *The History* much more than memoirs. It is literature, and worthy to stand with the autobiographical trilogies of Tolstoy and Gorky.

Translator's Note

This book is an abridged translation of Volume I and the first four of the five parts of Volume II of *The History*, covering Korolenko's life up to his exile in 1879. Material has been selected for translation according to what has been judged of interest for the English reader.

The chapters of this book rarely correspond exactly with the chapters of the original. Parts of chapters have been arranged as one chapter, and the titles of such chapters are the translator's. In chapters that correspond with original chapters it has been judged best to omit passages where Korolenko indulges in his occasional tendency to become excessively long-winded or sentimental. All this has been done in an attempt to present a version of the work which leaves no impression of incompleteness and incorporates what is best in the first two volumes.

Many of the people mentioned had Polish names, but—except in the case of famous historical figures—their names have simply been transliterated from the Russian. This has been done from considerations of consistency.

The rendering of place-names is often a headache, and the criterion adopted in this book has been what seemed to the translator most acceptable in English.

The translation is from Volumes V and VI of V. G. Korolenko, *Sobraniye sochineniy*, Moscow, 1954. Parts One and Two (Chapters 1–10) are from the following chapters of Volume V: 2, 3; 8, 9; 12; 14; 17, 18, 22; 20; 25; 26, 27, 28; 29; 34, 35. Part Three (Chapters 11–16) is from the following sections of the first and second parts of Volume VI: 1; 2; 3, 4, 5; 6, 1, 2, 3; 4, 7; 8, 9, 10. Part Four (Chapters 17–19) is from the following sections of the third part of Volume VI: 1, 4, 5; 7; 8. Part Five (Chapters 20–26) is from the following sections of the fourth part of Volume VI: 1, 2, 3; 4, 5, 6, 7; 9, 10; 11; 12, 14, 15; 16; 17, 18, 21, 22.

Some of the footnotes to the translation incorporate information contained in the notes to the above edition of Korolenko's works.

Finally I should like to thank Carol Buckroyd of Oxford University Press for her many helpful suggestions in reading this translation.

Neil Parsons
August 1971

PART ONE
Zhitomir

I
My Father and Mother

MY FATHER[1] STANDS OUT PERFECTLY CLEARLY IN MY
memory. He was a man of middle height, with a slight tendency to
fullness. As a civil servant of that time, he shaved very carefully; his
features were delicate and handsome: an aquiline nose, large hazel eyes,
and lips with strongly curved upper lines. It was said that as a young
man he had looked like Napoleon, especially when he wore the official
three-cornered hat *à la* Napoleon. But I found it hard to imagine
Napoleon lame, for my father always walked with a stick, dragging his
left leg slightly.

On his face there was always an expression of some secret sadness
and care. Only occasionally did it brighten. Sometimes he would have
us in his room, let us play about and crawl over him, draw us pictures,
and tell us funny stories and fairy tales. In his heart there must have
been a great store of good humour and laughter: he would even lecture
us in a humorous way, and at such moments we loved him very much.
But with the years these sunny moments became rarer and rarer still,
his innate cheerfulness became ever more thickly veiled with melancholy and anxiety. In the end he was concerned only that our education
should somehow be completed, and in our more conscious years there
was no real closeness between us and him. Thus he went to his grave,
little known to us, his children. Only long afterwards, when the carefree years of youth had passed, did I gather detail by detail what I
could of his life, and then the figure of that deeply unhappy man came
to life in my heart—both dearer and better known to me than before.

[1] Galaktion Afanasyevich Korolenko (1810–68).

He was a civil servant and so the objective history of his life was preserved in service records. He was born in 1810, and in 1826 became a clerk. He died in 1868 with the rank of an Aulic Councillor.[2] Such was the bare canvas on which were embroidered the patterns of a whole human life. Hopes, expectations, gleams of happiness, disillusionment. . . . Among his faded papers there was one which, strictly speaking, was of no use, but which my father had kept as a souvenir. It was a semi-official letter from Prince Vasilchikov[3] apropos of my father's appointment as District Magistrate in the town of Zhitomir.[4] 'This court', Prince Vasilchikov wrote, 'has with the addition of the magistracy acquired a wider and, consequently, more important sphere of activity, and requires a President who completely understands his appointment and can give legal procedure a satisfactory beginning.' With these considerations in mind the Prince proceeded to choose my father. At the end of the letter the grandee very kindly sympathized with the humble official for whom, as a family man, the transfer would entail real inconveniences, but at the same time pointed out that the new appointment greatly enhanced his future prospects and requested him to come as soon as possible. The last lines were written in the Prince's own hand, and the tone of the letter was respectful. It had to do with a modest reform, now forgotten and unsuccessful; but it had been a reform, and the illustrious Prince—a capricious, self-willed satrap, like all the grandees of that time, but a man who was nevertheless not without 'good intentions and noble impulses'—was summoning a humble official to collaborate with him. In this official he recognized a new man for a new job.

That had been in 1849. My father was being offered the post of District Magistrate[5] in a province-town. Twenty years later he died in the same post in a district-town.[6] Thus, he was obviously unsuccessful in his career. In my mind there is no doubt that this is to be explained by his quixotic honesty.

Society does not prize exceptions which it does not understand, and grows uneasy when it meets them. Every time my father went to a

[2] Seventh of the fourteen ranks in the Civil Service. It corresponded to the rank of lieutenant-colonel in the Army. The first eight ranks conferred the status of hereditary nobility.

[3] Governor-General of Kiev, Volyn and Podolsk Provinces, 1852–62.

[4] Principal town of Volyn Province, in south-western Russia.

[5] During the Governor-Generalship of Prince Vasilchikov the magistracies in all the towns of the South-West Region, except Kiev, were joined to the District Courts. The 'district' (*uyezd*) was an administrative subdivision of the 'province' (*guberniya*).

[6] Rovno.

new place the same scenes were repeated without any variation: 'by time-hallowed custom' representatives of the urban estates came to my father with presents. My father declined them calmly at first. The next day, however, the deputations would appear with gifts on an increased scale, and my father would now meet them uncourteously. The third day he would drive 'the representatives' away with his stick, and they would crowd in the entrance with expressions of astonishment and alarm on their faces. Later, when they had got to know my father in his work, they all came to feel great respect for him. Everyone admitted, from the smallest tradesman to the provincial authorities, that there was no force on earth that could make the judge act against his conscience and the law, but they still felt that if he would take moderate tokens of appreciation too, it would be more natural, simpler and generally more human.

When I was at an age to be aware of such things, there occurred quite a striking episode of this kind. A wealthy landowner, Count Yesky, had gone to law in the District Court with a poor relation, his brother's widow, I think. The landowner had influential connections and considerable means, which he made active use of. The widow was contesting the action by the right of poverty, paying no stamp-duty, and everyone forecast failure for her, since the case was an involved one and pressure had been brought to bear on the court. Before the end of the case the Count himself came to see us: his carriage bearing his coats of arms stopped outside our little house two or three times, and a lanky, liveried footman stood at our ramshackle porch. On the first two occasions the Count adopted the grand manner but acted cautiously, and my father merely pushed his approaches aside coldly and formally. The third time, however, he must have made a direct suggestion. My father suddenly flared up, called the aristocrat by some term of abuse and rapped his stick. The Count, scarlet with fury, left uttering threats and got quickly into his carriage.

The widow also came to see my father, though he did not particularly care for these visits. The poor woman, timid, depressed, dressed in mourning, her eyes red from weeping, would come to my mother, tell her something and weep. The poor soul kept on thinking there was something she needed to make the judge understand; very likely it was all unnecessary trifles which my father merely waved aside, pronouncing his usual sentence in such situations, 'Oh, that's not my province! Everything will be done according to the law.'

The case was decided in the widow's favour, and everyone knew that she owed this solely to the firmness of the judge. The Senate ratified

the decision with quite unexpected speed, and the humble widow became overnight one of the richest landowners not only in the district
but, very possibly, in the whole province.

When she again appeared in our house, coming this time in a carriage, everyone had difficulty in recognizing in her the former humble
petitioner. Her mourning was over, she even seemed to have become
younger, and radiated happiness and joy. My father received her very
cordially, with that benevolence we usually feel towards people greatly
indebted to us. But when she'd asked him for a conversation in private,
it wasn't long before she too came out of his room flushed and with tears
in her eyes. The good woman knew that the change in her position
had depended completely on the firmness and, possibly, even the
heroism of this modest, lame man. Yet she was not able to express her
gratitude to him in any real way.

This pained and even offended her. The next day she came to the
house when my father was at work and my mother happened to be out,
and she brought in quantities of various articles and fabrics, which she
spread over all the furniture in the drawing-room. She also called my
sister and presented her with a huge, magnificently dressed doll with
large blue eyes that closed when it was put down to sleep.

My mother was very alarmed to find all these gifts. When my father
came home from the court, one of the stormiest outbursts of anger I can
ever remember took place. He abused the widow, flung the fabrics on
the floor, blamed my mother, and only calmed down when a cart
appeared before the door, on to which all the presents were heaped to
be sent back. At this point, however, an unexpected difficulty cropped
up. When it was the doll's turn, my sister started protesting vehe-
mently, and her protests assumed such a dramatic character that after
a few attempts to take it away my father finally gave in, though very
unwillingly.

'Through you I've become a bribe-taker', he said angrily, going off
to his room.

Everyone looked upon this as pointless crankiness.

'Please tell me what harm there is in a bit of gratitude', one virtuous
court-official, who didn't take bribes, said to me. 'Just think: the case is
over and done with, a person thinks she owes everything to you and
comes with a grateful heart. And you almost set the dogs on her. Why?'

I am almost certain that my father never considered the question
from the point of view of its direct harm or otherwise. I suspect that he
had started out with high and, probably, not altogether usual expectations for those times. But life had given him no chance and he prized,

like a last treasure, that trait of character which distinguished him not only from the throng of notorious bribe-takers, but also from the men of the golden mean of that time. . . . And the harder it became for him with a large and growing family, the more keenly and jealously did he guard his moral independence and pride.

In the main my father's attitude to local officialdom was very good-humoured: he guarded from corruption only the small circle on which he had direct influence. I recall several instances when he came home from the court deeply distressed. Once when my mother, looking with anxious sympathy into his upset face, had given him a dish of soup, he took two or three spoonfuls and pushed the dish aside.

'I can't eat it', he said.

'Is the case over?' my mother asked quietly.

'Yes. . . . Hard labour. . . .'

'Lord above!' my mother said in alarm. 'And what about you?'

'Oh, what's the use!' he replied with irritation. 'Me! What can I do?' But then he added more softly, 'I did what I could. . . . The law was clear.'

He didn't eat any dinner that day nor lie down to sleep as he usually did after dinner, but walked about his room for a long time, tapping his stick. When my mother sent me into his room two hours later to see if he had gone to sleep, and if not to tell him to come and have some tea, I found him kneeling by his bed. He was praying fervently before the icon, and his whole rather stout body was shaking. He was weeping bitterly.

But I am sure that these were tears of pity for a victim of the law, and not a gnawing consciousness of guilt as its instrument. In this respect his conscience was always unshakeably clear, and when I think about it now the basic difference between the outlook of upright men of that generation and people of our days becomes clear to me. He acknowledged himself responsible only for his individual activity. A bitter feeling of guilt for the injustices of society was completely unknown to him. God, the Tsar, and the law stood for him on a height beyond the reach of criticism. God is omnipotent and just, but on earth there are many triumphant scoundrels and much suffering virtue. This enters into the mysterious plans of Higher Justice—and that was all there was to it. The Tsar and the law were also beyond human judgement, and if sometimes when the law was applied one's heart almost turned over from pity and sympathy, this was a natural misfortune, not subject to any general conclusions. One man died from typhus, another—from the law. An unhappy fate! The function of a judge was to see that the law, once set in motion, was applied correctly. If it was not, if bribable officials were distorting the law in favour of the strong, he, the judge, would fight within the limits of the court with every means at his disposal. If it were necessary to suffer for this, he would suffer, but in Case No. such-and-such every line written by his hand would be free from falsehood. And in this form the case would go beyond the District Court to the Senate and, perhaps, higher still. If the Senate agreed with his considerations, he would be sincerely glad for the right side. If the Senators too had been suborned by power and money, it was the affair of their consciences, and some day they would answer for it, if not before the Tsar, then before God. . . . That laws can be bad, that again was the responsibility of the Tsar before God. He, the judge, was not responsible for that any more than for the fact that lightning sometimes kills an innocent child.

Yes, it was a well-rounded outlook, a kind of stable equilibrium of the conscience. Its foundations were not shaken by the habit of analysis, and men of integrity in that period did not know the deep disharmony of mind stemming from a consciousness of individual responsibility for the whole order of things. I do not know if this roundness of outlook exists any more in the mind of even a single civil servant in such a complete and inviolable form. I do not think it does. The days of such an outlook have gone for ever, and even my generation in its very youth was seized by the gnawing, heavy but creative awareness of general responsibility. . . . My father died early. Had he lived longer, we young people, consumed with the spirit of criticism, would doubtlessly have heard from him more than once his usual formula, 'That's not our province!'

And, of course, he would have had in mind those high and determining factors which, in his opinion, had to stand beyond criticism. What this clash would finally have resulted in remains now a mystery about which I often think sadly, with regret.

My father had his own reasons for the deep sadness and remorse, which coloured the whole of his life as it was known to me. As a young man he had been very handsome and had enjoyed enormous success with women. He had, apparently, directed his abundant and perhaps unusual energies to various undertakings and adventures in that sphere, and this had gone on until he was past thirty. His own practical experience instilled in him a deep mistrust of womanly virtue, and, when his thoughts eventually turned to marriage, he conceived an original plan to safeguard his domestic happiness.

My mother's father had a large family (four daughters and two sons).

One of the daughters was still a minor, thirteen years old, a mere child who went about in short dresses and played with dolls. It was upon her that my father's choice fell. In a family in which he could count on traditions of moral integrity, he was choosing as a wife a girl who was still half a child and would bring her up so as to avoid the period of girlhood coquetry. My grandfather was against the marriage, but gave way before the entreaties of his wife. The formal obstacles stemming from the bride's minority were removed by the witness of fifteen residents; the toys were taken out of my future mother's room, the short dresses replaced by a wedding dress, and the marriage took place.[7]

Summing up human lives is a very difficult task. Happiness and joy are so interwoven with unhappiness and grief that I don't know to this day whether my parents' marriage was a happy or an unhappy one. At any rate, it was very hard for my mother to begin with. At the time of her marriage she was a sickly girl, with a thin and not fully developed figure, a thick, flaxen braid, and lovely, starry grey–blue eyes. Two years after the marriage she gave birth to a daughter, who died after a week, leaving a deep scar in her young heart. My father turned out to be terribly jealous, and his jealousy showed itself in strange and harsh ways: every glance a man gave his young wife seemed unclean to him, and her girlish laughter at some joke in company appeared inexcusable flirting. It reached the point that when he went away he used to lock his wife up, and the young woman, almost a child, sitting under lock and key, would weep bitterly from childish distress and a deep sense of injury to her dignity as a woman.

The third or fourth year after his marriage my father went away somewhere in the district on official business and stayed the night in a cottage where he was poisoned by charcoal fumes The following morning he was carried out unconscious in his underclothes and laid on the snow. He came round, but half his body was paralysed. He was brought to my mother almost incapable of movement, and, despite all measures, remained a cripple for the rest of his life. And so my mother's life was linked at the very beginning with a man more than twice her age, whom she was as yet unable to love because she was only a child, who had tormented and humiliated her from the very first days, and who had, finally, become crippled. And yet I cannot say whether she was unhappy.

Even I was old enough to remember the question of the dissolution

[7] In 1847. In view of the bride's extreme youth she was left with her parents for a year. Korolenko's mother was Polish. Most of the aristocracy and the urban middle class of the region were Polish in origin.

of this marriage, after someone's report, and my father was very alarmed by it. Men in brass-buttoned uniforms whom we had never seen before began appearing in our house. My father welcomed them, had them to dinner and arranged card-evenings for them. Of this collection of consistorial officials I especially recall a secretary, a shortish man in a long-tailed uniform, the flaps of which almost trailed along the floor. He had an unclean face, which put one in mind of red blotting-paper with ink blots on it. His eyes were small, glittery and quick. Before sitting down at the dinner-table, he would usually walk round the drawing-room, examining and touching various objects, and I noticed that the objects on which his sharp little eyes fell with special attention would soon disappear. So disappeared, incidentally, the family's prized possession—a large telescope in which father showed us the moon. We were very sorry about that telescope, but my father said with sad humour that the long-coated official could make it so that he and mother would not be married, and would become a monk and nun. And since unmarried people, and monks and nuns as well, could not have children, it meant that there wouldn't be us either. We realized, of course, that it was a joke, but we couldn't help feeling that our whole family depended in some strange way on that man with the metal buttons and a face like an ink-blot.

On one occasion about this time I ran into my mother's bedroom and saw that my father and mother had been crying. My father had bent down and was kissing her hand, while she affectionately smoothed his head and seemed to be reassuring him about something, like a child. I had never seen anything like this between them before, and my little heart leapt with a presentiment. It turned out, however, that the crisis had passed safely, and soon the consistorial figures who were frightening us disappeared. But I remember even now the moment when I found my father and mother so moved and filled with love and pity for each other. It meant that by this time they had settled down together and loved each other quietly, but well. It is this atmosphere of mutual respect and friendship that I remember during the whole of that period of my childhood, when the world seemed still and unchanging.

My father was a deeply religious man and, apparently, in his misfortune he saw a righteous retribution for the sins of his youth. Moreover, it seemed to him that his children would also have to pay for his sins; they would inevitably be weak and he would not manage to set them up in life. Therefore one of his chief concerns was treating himself and us. Since he was a man who got bees in his bonnet and believed in wonder-working universal remedies, we had to suffer the beneficent action of incisions behind the ears, cod-liver oil with bread and salt, blood-purifying syrup, Morrison's pills, and even a certain Bonscheit's skin-puncturer, which was supposed to increase the circulation through hundreds of small pricks. Then a homoeopath appeared in our house—Doctor Chervinsky, a round man with a thick stick in the form of a caduceus. One day my elder brother, who had a very sweet tooth, got to the homoeopathic medicine-chest when my parents were out and ate at one go the entire store of pills containing arsenic. My father was very frightened at first, but when he had satisfied himself that my brother remained in perfect health, he had his doubts about homoeopathy.

After this, Hahnemann's[8] profound works disappeared from father's table, and in their place appeared a new book in a modest black binding. On the first page was a vignette with a verse (in Polish):

> If you want to be strong and live many years,
> Take baths and showers, and drink cold water.

To stress the point, the vignette showed three naked men of superb physique, one of whom was standing under a shower, another sitting in a bath, and the third pouring a huge mug of water down his throat with obvious pleasure.

We children examined the vignette with total unconcern, only realizing its true significance the following morning, when my father ordered us to be got up and brought to his room. In the room stood a wide tub full of cold water, and father, who had previously gone through the whole procedure himself, made us stand in the tub in turn and, scooping up the icy water in a pewter mug, began douching us all over. It was a barbaric act, but it did us no harm, and we soon became so hardened that, barefoot and in nothing but our night-shirts, we would hide in the mornings in an old carriage where, shivering with cold (it was autumn, the time of the morning frosts), we waited until father went to work. My mother promised him each time that she would dutifully perform the act of douching when we came back, but— God will forgive her, of course—she sometimes deceived father in this. And as we used to spend the whole day outside, no matter what the weather, virtually without supervision of any kind, even father's mistrustfulness soon yielded before our invariably blooming appearance and apparent invulnerability.

This faith in books and science was a generally noticeable and touch-

---

[8] Samuel Hahnemann (1755–1843), a German doctor, was the founder of homoeopathy.

ing feature of my father's character, though at times it led to unexpected results. One day, for example, he bought a brochure somewhere, the author of which affirmed that with the help of borax, saltpetre and, I think, flowers of sulphur one could feed horses amazingly
well with exceptionally modest portions of usual horse food. At the
time we had a pair of grown geldings on whom my father began
experimenting. The poor horses grew thin and weak, but my father
believed so strongly in the validity of this scientific method that he
completely failed to notice this, and to my mother's anxious remarks:
what if this science killed the horses, he would reply, 'I don't know!
They're putting on flesh, and you talk nonsense. Isn't that right, Filipp?
They're putting on flesh, aren't they?'

'They certainly are', the cunning coachman answered.

The judge's horses became known all over the town for their unusual leanness and the avidity with which they would gnaw at their
halters and at fences, but my father noticed only an improvement
until one of them died without any apparent reason. I remember the
expression of pained surprise and remorse on his face as he stood over
the corpse of the poor martyred beast. He immediately ordered the
other horse to be fed on oats and hay without the scientific admixture
and then, apparently, he sold it. Still, it later turned out that it was not
science alone that was to blame for the failure, but also the coachman,
who had sold the small quantity of oats allowed the horses to buy
drink, leaving the horses on borax and saltpetre alone. Be that as it
may, the experiment was not renewed.

Clearly, some of his early plans lingered on for a long time in my
father's mind, and he strove to break out of the strong clutches of dull
official routine. At one time he would acquire a telescope and works on
astronomy, then he would start studying mathematics, or buy Italian
books and dictionaries. The parts of his evenings that were not taken
up with the writing of documents and decisions, he devoted to reading
and would sometimes walk about the house, thinking deeply over what
he'd read. At times he would share his thoughts with mother, and occasionally, if she was not at hand, he would even turn with touching,
even childlike openness to one of us children.

I remember I was once alone with him in his room when he put
down a book, walked thoughtfully up and down for a while, then
stopped by me and said, 'Philosophers claim that man cannot think without words. As soon as man starts to think, then inevitably—understand?
there are words in his head. Hmm—what do you say to that?'

Without waiting for an answer he began walking from corner to corner, tapping his stick and dragging his left leg slightly, obviously completely engrossed in trying out this psychological question on himself. Then he stopped by me again and said, 'If that is true, it means a dog doesn't think, because it doesn't know words . . .'

'Spot understands words', I answered with conviction.

'What do they amount to? Not much.'

I was just a child then, and hadn't even started school, but the simplicity with which my father had put the question and his deep thoughtfulness infected me. While he walked about, I too tried to analyse my thoughts. Nothing came of this, but later on as well I tried many a time to catch those formless movements and vague images of words which pass like shadows on the background of the consciousness, without finally assuming definite forms.

'I see that the English', my father said another time at dinner, when we were all present, 'are offering a lot of money to a man who makes up a new word.'

'There's not much to that!' my elder brother said cockily. 'I'll make one up straight away.' And without pausing for thought he blurted out some utterly preposterous word. We laughed.

'Fool,' said father, clearly peeved at such a frivolous attitude to the scheme of the English scholars. But we all took my brother's side.

'Why a fool, when he really has made one up?'

'Made one up, indeed! And what does it mean?'

'Mean? . . .' My brother was rather taken aback, but immediately answered: 'It doesn't mean anything, but it's new.'

'That's why you're a fool! It must mean something, it must make sense, and there mustn't be another word with exactly the same meaning. Anyone can make up any amount of your sort of words! Scholars are no more stupid than you and don't say things for a joke.'

'Still', he added a little later, 'I think one could make one up . . .'

'Certain philosophers,' he said on another occasion when we were at table, 'think that there is no God.'

'Oh, what nonsense!' said my mother. 'Why on earth do you repeat foolish words?'

'I can't understand it', my father answered. 'It's not fools who say so, but learned men . . .'

'Who created the world and man, then?'

'There's an Englishman who contends that man came from the monkey.'

'And where did the monkey come from?'

We all laughed, including my father.

'That, of course, is an error of reason', he said, and added convincedly and rather solemnly: 'There is a God, children, and He sees everything . . . everything. And punishes severely for sins.'

I don't remember whether it was then or on another occasion that he said with special emphasis, 'In the Scriptures it says that parents are punished in their children to the seventy-seventh generation. That may well seem unjust, but . . . perhaps we do not understand. . . . All the same, God is merciful.'

Only now do I understand the meaning that verse had for him. He was afraid that we would be punished for his sins. And his conscience rose up against the injustice of the punishment, while his faith demanded submission and gave hope.

2

Omens of Change

IN OCTOBER 1858, THAT IS WHEN I WAS FIVE YEARS OLD, the young Tsar, Alexander II, came to Zhitomir.

The town had made grand preparations for this visit, and an enormous triumphal arch had been built on the square, near the Church of the Bernardine Fathers. We had looked at it the evening before, and I had been struck then by the size, strangeness, and apparent superfluousness of this wooden structure in the square. After that I vaguely remember crowds of people, a terrible roar of human voices and something unseen, passing quickly somewhere in the depths of that human sea—after which the people, as if they'd suddenly lost their heads, rushed to the centre of the town. Everyone said that it had been the *Tsar* passing.

I remember the impression of the evening illuminations much more distinctly. There were long chains of lights stretching to the square, where over everything hung the enormous arch, glowing like a bonfire. Crowds of people were moving about below like black streams, and above the sky was blacker still. Shouts of 'Hurrah!' broke out from time to time, which were taken up and grew stronger, passing along the streets into the distance, rolling, echoing, booming. I took a firm grip of some woman's skirt, people were pushing me, and the servants had a hard job getting us out of the crowd. When my mother met us she was in a state of alarm and angry at the servants. Then my father, in his uniform and wearing his sword, and my mother in an evening gown drove off somewhere or other.

We had been told to go to bed, but we couldn't sleep. We lived in a quiet cul-de-sac, but a muffled roar from the town still reached our ears and the sense of excitement filtered into our bedroom. When our old nurse had taken our candle into the next room, we thought we could see a glow through the chinks in the shutters. We all got on to one bed by the window, our faces stuck to the panes, looking through these chinks, listening to the noise and exchanging our impressions— over which towered imperiously, like the fiery arch over the town, one awesome word: the *Tsar*!

My elder brother was, of course, the most knowledgeable among us. For a start, he knew a song for the occasion:

> Far from his own land
> The white Russian Tsar,
> Our Sovereign of the true faith
> Rode to gain glory.

We liked the song, but it didn't explain much. My brother also added that the Tsar went about clothed in gold, ate with golden spoons from golden plates, and, most important, 'could do everything'. He could come into our room, take what he liked, and nobody could say anything to him. And that was nothing: he could make any man a general and cut off any man's head with his sword, or he could order it to be cut off and it would be cut off immediately. Because the Tsar has the right. The Tsar departed, but echoes of his visit constituted the most important element in our lives for a long time after.

We had a distant relation, Uncle Pyotr, an elderly, tall and rather corpulent man with unusually alert eyes, a smooth-shaven face and pointed little moustache. When he twitched the ends of this moustache we would laugh till there were tears in our eyes, and when he spoke the grown-ups would often laugh too; he was, in a word, a man with the established reputation of a wit. After the Tsar's visit he told a few

stories. One of them in particular has stuck in my mind: just before the
Tsar was due to pass by, the police noticed a cow in a side-street.
When the policemen rushed towards it, it got frightened, and when the
'Hurrahs!' broke out the cow became completely frenzied and rushed
into the crowd, scattering people with its horns. In this way it apparently got through to the empty space that had been left for the passage
of the Tsar, and got there at the very moment the Tsar's carriage sped
by. The cow hurtled straight after the carriage and arrived triumphally
at the Governor's house, while behind it came two panting and dreadfully alarmed policemen.

This story made a strange impression on me. The Tsar and suddenly—a cow. That evening we talked about the occurrence in our
room and made conjectures about the fate of the poor policemen and
the owner of the cow. The supposition that they had all had their heads
cut off seemed quite plausible. Whether this was good, or cruel, or
just—such questions did not occur to us. There had been something
tremendous, that had passed by like a storm, and in the middle of this
thing had been the Tsar, who 'can do everything'. What did the fate of
two policemen matter? Though, of course, it was a pity.

There must already have been talk at this time of the emancipation
of the peasants. On one occasion Uncle Pyotr and someone else we
knew expressed doubts as to whether 'the Tsar himself' could do everything he wished. 'Nicholas—he was a real Tsar. Everything trembled
before him. Yet how did he end?' My father replied with his usual
saying, 'Hmm. . . . It's way beyond us. If the Tsar wants to he'll
do it.'

One year passed, and another. Rumours increased. It was as if a
splinter had penetrated the peacefulness of life, giving rise to vague
anxiety and colouring all events with a special tint. And now came an
omen: lightning struck 'the old figure'.

This was a big crucifix, which stood in the garden of our neighbour
Pan Dobrovolsky, at the intersection of our lane and two other streets.
It stood among bushes of acacia, elder and guelder-rose, which grew
in wild profusion around its pedestal. They said that the souls of the
departed, whose bodies were transported almost every day to the
Polish and Lutheran cemeteries, would give the owner of the farm no
peace to sleep, and so he had erected the figure in defence. That had
been a long time ago; since then the owner himself had been transported along that same sandy road; the figure had become weather-
beaten, blackened, cracked, completely covered with multi-coloured
lichen—all in all, it had assumed the appearance of respectable, slum-

bering old age. Whoever had occasion, even once, to bury a close friend or someone he had known remembered for ever the dark old crucifix, hanging solemnly right at the turning to the cemetery, and all the surrounding area took its name from it: of us it was simply said that we lived in the Kolyanovskys' house, near the old figure.

One night a bad storm broke out. With the evening, clouds had moved in from every quarter, striking ominously against each other and flashing lightning. When night had fallen, flashes followed one another continuously lighting up the houses, the pallid green of the garden, and the old figure as if it were daytime. Deceived by this light, the sparrows woke up and with their puzzled twittering increased the sense of alarm hanging in the air; the walls of our house shuddered every now and then from the rolling thunder, while the window-panes jingled quietly and plaintively after each clap.

We had been put to bed but didn't sleep. We listened timidly to the noise of the storm and the frightened twittering of the sparrows, and looked through the chinks in the shutters, lit up by the blue reflection of the lightning. When it was already far into the night, the storm seemed to be abating a little, the claps of thunder passed into the distance, and only a steady downpour on the roofs could be heard. Then, suddenly, somewhere very near, a solitary thunderbolt struck, which made the very ground shake. The house was in alarm, my mother got out of bed, took down the big thunder candle from behind the icon and lit it. We didn't go back to bed for a long time, awaiting with an uneasy feeling some sign of God's special anger. The following morning we got up late, and the first news we heard was that the last thunderbolt had smashed the old figure.

Our whole courtyard and kitchen were, of course, full of stories of this amazing occurrence. Only the night-watchman, whose box was right next to the figure, had witnessed it. He had seen a snake of fire come down from the sky straight on to the figure, which burst into light. Then a terrible cracking was heard, the snake jumped across to the old stump of a tree, and the figure slowly keeled over into the bushes. When my brother and I ran to the end of the lane, there was already a considerable crowd of people there. The figure was broken. The splintered base still stuck up fairly high in the air, and among the dense, crushed foliage of the bushes and shrubs could be seen the scorched arms of the cross with the crucified figure. The picture was full of some special meaning. From time to time the foliage, pressed down by the weight that was on it, yielded a little, a branch cracked, and the top part of the figure shuddered, as if it were alive, and moved down. Then not only we children, but, apparently, the whole crowd fell silent in superstitious fear.

That year the coachman Petro was working at our place. He was quite an old man who went about in a sheepskin coat winter and summer alike. His face was wrinkled, and his thin lips under a small moustache preserved an expression of some unexplainable bitterness. He was unusually taciturn, never took part in the talk and tittle-tattle of the servants nor took from his mouth the short pipe in which he occasionally poked burning tobacco with his calloused little finger. I think it was actually he who first said, looking at the broken figure, 'Hmm. . . . Something's going to happen.'

After that this sentence became the backcloth of my impressions of that time perhaps, partly, because after the destruction of the figure there followed another related occurrence. In one village a phantom started appearing. . . . About twenty-five miles from our town, behind thick, almost uninterrupted forest—perhaps little remains of it now—was the locality of Chudnov. The lodges and cabins of the foresters were scattered about the forest, and in places near the river there were whole settlements.

I don't recall exactly which one of our servants, though I think it was Petro, had relatives in those parts, who came to our town from time to time. It must have been they who brought the news that in one of the forest settlements around Chudnov a '*mara*' had started appearing. It appeared, of course, at night, the other side of the river, opposite the village—tall and white. In its huge head burned two fiery eyes and its mouth belched flames. Appearing suddenly on a steep rise the phantom stood facing the village, striking terror into everyone, and shouted in a voice from beyond the grave, 'O-o-oh, something's going to happen, o-o-oh . . .' After this the eyes dimmed and the phantom would disappear.

Later my father, who at the time apparently circuited the county as examining magistrate, told us the end of this story when he came back from one of his trips. According to him, a soldier, who was either on leave or discharged, was passing through the village and decided to rid the people of the *mara*. For a comparatively cheap reward in vodka he crossed the river at dusk and concealed himself below the steep rise. When the tall figure with fiery eyes appeared at the usual time everyone naturally thought the foolhardy soldier had perished. But then, at the very first sounds of the ominous moaning, a sort of rumpus suddenly occurred, a shower of sparks issued from the *mara*'s head and it vanished. After a little time had passed the soldier called quite unconcernedly for the boat. However, he didn't tell the frightened villagers anything, but only assured them that 'there won't be anything any more'.

My father gave us his own explanation of this mysterious event. According to him, foolish people were being frightened by some local joker, who stood on stilts, draped himself in sheets, and on his head put a bucket of coals in which he had made openings to represent eyes and a mouth. The soldier, it would seem, had seized him from below by the stilts, so that the bucket fell down amid a shower of coals. The rascal had then paid the soldier to keep silent. We liked this humorous explanation, which dispelled the terrible picture of the wailing phantom, and we would often ask our father to tell us the story again. It always ended in merry laughter. But this sober explanation made not the slightest impression in the kitchen. The cook Budzinskaya, and others with her, explained the affair in a still simpler way: the soldier himself consorted with the devil; he had met the *mara* as a friend and it had agreed to go away to another place. So the moral of the whole episode remained unweakened: 'Something's going to happen . . .'

Then they started talking about 'golden decrees', which had appeared no one knew how on roads, and in fields, and on hedges, apparently from the Tsar himself, and which the peasants believed but the squires did not, which gave the peasants courage but made the squires afraid. . . . Next followed the striking story of the horned priest.

This story consisted of the following: a peasant was ploughing a field and ploughed up an iron kettle containing gold coins. He carried the money quietly home and buried it in his garden, not saying a word to anyone. However, he couldn't endure the secret alone and confided in his wife, making her swear that she wouldn't tell anyone. His wife naturally swore not to, but she wasn't strong enough to bear the weight of an unshared secret. So, she went to the priest and when he'd freed her from her oath she spilled the whole thing out.

The priest proved to be cunning and greedy. He killed and skinned a bullock, put on its hide with the horns, his wife sewed him up with thread, and at midnight he went to the peasant's hut and knocked on the window with a horn. The peasant looked out and fainted. The next night the same thing happened, only this time the devil uttered the categorical demand, 'Give up my money.' The peasant was terrified and before the third night dug up the kettle and brought it into his hut. When the devil appeared again with his demand, the peasant, at his order, opened the window and hung the kettle by its iron handle on the horns of his terrible visitor. The priest ran home joyfully to his wife and, lowering his horns, said, 'Take the money off'; but when his wife tried to take the kettle off, it seemed to have stuck fast to the horns. 'Well, in that case, cut the seam and take it off with the hide.' But as soon as his wife started cutting the seam with scissors, the priest shouted in a voice that was not his own that she was cutting his sinews. It turned out that the gold coins had stuck to the kettle, the kettle had stuck to the horns, and the bullock's hide to the priest.

Naturally, like everything else unusual, the matter 'reached the Tsar', who conferred with his elders, and it was decided that the priest should be led over the whole land, through the towns and villages, and exhibited in the squares. And everyone should come and try to take the kettle off, because the treasure was probably stolen or had had a spell put on it. Robbers had probably killed a man and buried the money in the earth, or somebody 'knowing' had buried it with a spell. And if the heirs of the man whose money this had rightfully been could be found, the kettle would yield and could be taken off the horns, and the bullock-hide be taken off the priest.

My father had told us this story himself, laughing and adding that only fools believed it, as it was simply an old fairy tale; but the simple, uninformed peasants believed it, and in certain places the police had had to disperse crowds which had gathered at rumours that the horned priest was being brought to them. In our kitchen the priest's itinerary was followed: it was reported with absolute exactitude that the priest had already been in Petersburg, Moscow, Kiev, even in Berdichev, and that now he was being brought to us.

My younger brother and I wavered between doubt and belief, but we now had a new pastime at any rate. We would climb on to the high posts of the fence at the corner of the street and look out along the high-road. We would sit there for hours on end, motionless, sometimes with a stock of pieces of bread, looking into the dusty distance, gazing at every dot that appeared. A sort of constant inertia of expectation held us in our uncomfortable position exposed to the sun—until our heads ached. Sometimes we wanted to go away, but from behind the horizon on the narrow line of the road by the cemetery dots would appear which rolled down the slope, grew larger and turned out to be the most prosaic objects, but others took their place and once again it seemed that this must be what everyone was waiting for.

Once somebody shouted in the yard, 'They're bringing him!' There was a commotion, the servants came running out of the kitchen, and the stablemen and neighbours down the street came out too. At the cross-roads could be heard the beating of drums and a drone of voices. My brother and I also ran out. But it turned out that it was a prisoner being taken for execution in a high cart.

This foolish fairy tale merged with the falling of the figure, the *mara* and the general mood of expectation: 'Something's going to happen!' What exactly would happen wasn't known. The golden decrees, peasant riots, murders, the horned priest . . . it was something unusual, disturbing, unprecedented—and formless. Some people believed one thing, others—something else, but everyone felt that something new was coming into our stagnant life, and every trifle was met anxiously, fearfully, keenly. By this time no trace remained of my childhood impression of the immobility of the existing world. On the contrary, I felt that not only my own little world, but also the reaches far beyond the boundaries of the yard and the town, even Moscow and Petersburg, were expecting something and were anxious about it.

A newspaper in the depths of the provinces was a rare thing then, and in place of informed news there were rumours, opinions, guesses, in a word false interpretations. Somewhere in the highest quarters a reform was being prepared, and the future cast a wide shadow across society at large and the people; in that shadow phantoms rose up and moved about, and uncertainty became the very backcloth of life. The overall features of the future were not known and mere trifles assumed the proportions of important events.

It was at this time that they brought the telegraph line through our town. First of all they brought fresh poles of uniform length and stacked them at intervals along the streets. Next they dug holes, one of them right at the corner of our lane and Vilna Street, where the shops were. Then they set the poles in the holes and brought up big drums of wire in carts. An official in a new telegraph uniform was directing the work; the workmen climbed up on to the poles on ladders and, holding on with their feet and one hand to the hooks that had been driven into the poles, pulled the wire along. When they had got it taut in one place, they would trundle the cart to the next pole, and by the evening three or four parallel lines of wire hung in the air, the poles carrying them far along the high-road which stretched to the horizon. The workmen were in a great hurry, not stopping work even at night. The following morning they were already far beyond the turnpike, and a few days later it was reported that the wire had reached Brody and been linked with the foreign lines. In our town there remained a dead body: a workman had fallen off a pole, caught his chin on a hook and had his head split open.

I never recall hearing such a loud sound from the telegraph wires as in those first days. I remember one clear evening particularly well. For some reason it was especially quiet in our little street; the rumbling of carriages along the cobbled streets of the town was also subsiding, and because of this the unusual ringing sound stood out more clearly. It somehow made the flesh creep hearing that unceasing, unvarying, and incomprehensible cry of dead iron stretching through the air from somewhere in the mysterious capital, where the Tsar lives. The sun had gone right down, only between the far-off roof-tops, in the direction of the Polish cemetery, did a fiery red streak of light still linger. And the wire, as it cooled, cried out louder and louder, filling the air with its groans and sobs.

Later on they must have made the wire tauter, because the sound became less loud: on ordinary days when there was no wind the telegraph would only vibrate quietly, as if the shouting had changed to an indistinct muttering.

Those first days one could often see inquisitive people standing with their ears to the poles, listening intently. The rumour of the day anticipated the invention of the telephone by a long time: it was said that people talked along the wire, and as the wire had been taken to the frontier there arose the natural supposition that it was for our Tsar to discuss affairs with foreign rulers. My brother and I also spent a long time standing by the poles. The first time I put my ear against the wood I was struck by the diversity of the sounds running through it. It was not a single, even, light metallic ringing; it seemed a whole river of sound was overflowing through the wood—complex, indistinct, alluring. And at times the imagination actually caught something like a distant muttering.

One fine day this muttering was finally translated into ordinary speech. Someone came into our kitchen with the news that the retired official Popkov had deciphered the telegraph conversation. Popkov was reputed to be an unusually knowledgeable man: he had been kicked out of his job no one knew exactly what for, but as a token of his former position he wore an old uniform with regulation buttons, and as a token of his present misfortunes he sometimes wore bast shoes. He was very short, with a freakishly large head and unusual forehead. He lived by writing petitions and complaints for people. As a known pettifogger he was not supposed to do this, but his papers only enjoyed the confidence of simple folk all the more; they thought he had been forbidden to write precisely because his every paper possessed such power that even the highest authorities were unable to wrestle with it. Even so, he lived a life of extreme penury, and in times of great difficulty when all other sources had dried up, he got along by buffoonery and performing feats of strength. One of these feats consisted in breaking nuts with his forehead.

And now they said that this man, who had lost his job because he knew too much, was able to listen in to the secret conversations between our Tsar and foreign rulers, mainly the Frenchman, Napoleon. Foreign rulers were demanding of ours that he set everyone free.[1] Napoleon III would speak loudly and haughtily, and our Tsar would answer him courteously and quietly.

This, apparently, was the first completely clear form in which I heard of the impending emancipation of the peasants. The alarming, yet vague prediction of the Chudnov phantom—'Something's going to happen'—was assuming the shape of a definite idea: the Tsar wanted to take the peasants away from the landowners and set them free. . . . Was this good or bad? In our kitchen, as far as I can remember, they didn't expect anything good—perhaps because its membership was to some extent aristocratic. The cook was *pani* Budzinskaya, the chambermaid *pani* Khumova, a woman with delicate, refined features, who always spoke Polish, and the man-servant Gandylo would naturally have been very offended if he had been called a peasant. Of all our servants only our old nurse and Budzinskaya still wore village dress and head-scarves, but they too didn't look like villagers any longer. Only the coachman Petro, in his eternal sheepskin coat and heavy boots with turned-down tops, had the look of a real peasant. But he was a very tactiturn man, who only smoked and spat continually, never expressing any general judgements. His face remained perpetually stern, enigmatic and gloomy.

A man generally measures his position by comparison. This whole group lived quite nicely under my mother's lenient régime, and in the evenings in our kitchen, well heated and saturated with the smell of rich borsch and warm bread, there gathered a company of people who on the whole were contented with their lot. . . . The noise of the cricket could be heard, the tallow candle burned dimly above the stove, the spinning wheel hummed, and interesting stories were told one after another until someone, satiated and sleepy, got up from the bench and said, 'It's late . . . time to go to bed.'

Among these evening stories there would also be tales of cruelty by the landowners, but generalizations were not made. In the world there were good squires and cruel squires. God punished the cruel ones, some-

[1] I also heard the legend of the interference of foreign powers in the Emancipation many years later in Arzamas District, Nizhegorod Province. (Korolenko's note.)

times very harshly. But the peasant had to know his place, since all this had been laid down by God. To these people God had apportioned comparatively easy work, complete freedom from hunger and a fair amount of leisure in the warm kitchen. The unknown, that was now near at hand, thus seemed to them in part alarming. 'Something's going to happen'—but whether it would be good or bad wasn't known. Anyway, it was disturbing.

Such, however, was not the mood of our kitchen alone. Early one morning a large crowd of peasants appeared in our courtyard. They were in long coats and sheepskin caps, and had just come from their village; many had bark or canvas bags slung over their shoulders. From the crowd, gathered around the wide stairway of the big house, rose a low buzz of conversation, and even at some distance the rather heavy peasant smell—a mixture of sweat, tar, and sheepskin—could be detected. Soon from above, from the lady's house, two old men without hats came down and said something to the crowd which had anxiously moved towards them. From the peasants there arose a quiet, apparently contented murmuring, and then the whole crowd knelt down: at the top of the stairway Mrs. Kolyanovskaya had appeared, supported by attendant maids. She was a stout, stately lady, with very alert black eyes, an aquiline nose and a very obvious little black moustache. At the top of the steps, high above the kneeling crowd, surrounded by her staff, she seemed a queen among her subjects. She said a few gracious words, to which the crowd replied with a roar in which could be felt devotion and joy. At midday they put up tables in the yard and regaled the peasants before their return journey.

I learned from the conversations of the adults that these were serfs of Kolyanovskaya, who had come from the distant village of Skolubov to ask that they be left as of old—'we are yours, and you are ours'. Kolyanovskaya was a good mistress. The peasants had sufficient land, and during the winter months almost all the workmen dispersed to various jobs. They, too, obviously lived better than their neighbours and 'something's going to happen' evoked in them the fear that this impending but unknown thing would 'equalize' them.

That same summer the Kolyanovskys took me with them to their estate. This visit has remained in my mind exactly like a picture from a wonderful dream: the big manor-house and not far away a line of peasant cottages, peeping out from the hillside with their thatched roofs and white painted walls. In the evenings the large windows of the manor-house were lit up, and the little cottages glimmered somehow affectionately and meekly with their little lights scattered in the darkness. And it all seeemd so peaceful, friendly, and full of harmony. In the cottages lived the peasants, those same peasants who had once taken down our old porch and built us a new one—strong, clever men. In the house were the masters, good and kind. At Kolyanovskaya's table gathered distant relations and employees, quiet, obliging, gentle people. On everything there lay the special imprint of a firmly established way of life, in which there were no contradictions and no dissonances. I remember a stranger appeared one evening at dinner in a smart frock-coat, starched shirt, and gold-rimmed spectacles—a figure whose very appearance was glaringly at odds with all this rusticity. He started trying to demonstrate that the peasants were oxen, slackers, drunkards, that they couldn't do anything properly. Kolyanovskaya quietly objected: take the house in which we are sitting—it, and everything inside it down to the last chair, had been made by her peasants. They had also built her house in the town, and a clever old peasant had taken charge of everything. One might ask what foreign architect could build stronger and better? Her poor relations and attendants expressed agreement with a sense of real conviction. It was as if there was nowhere for the opinion of the stranger to squeeze in to this complete and irreversible conviction.

I felt that Kolyanovskaya was right too. The unfamiliar world of the village, a world of strong, clever, humble people, seemed good and beautiful in its humility. In the evenings young lads and girls with garlands of cornflowers, and carrying rakes and scythes on their shoulders, would return from work past the house, singing happily. . . . When they took the first sheaf of corn from the field, they brought it solemnly to the squire's yard. The sheaf swayed above the heads of the lads in sheepskin caps and the girls in garlands of cornflowers. And it seemed that the sheaf was consciously taking a silent part in this joy of work. This was called *zazhinki*. With even greater solemnity they brought the last sheaf to the *dozhinki*, and there in the yard stood tables of food, and the lads and girls danced till late at night in front of the porch, on which sat the squire's whole family, kindly disposed and good. Then the crowd sang its way from the illuminated manor-house to the humble lights on the hill and as the singers dispersed into their cottages, the song melted away until it finally died altogether in the unseen far end of the village. Everything seemed peaceful, beautiful, perfect and indestructible. And I remember it all as an old-time idyll, a little place, illuminated by the soft rays of the setting sun.

One day, when my father was at work and my mother was chatting with my aunts and some friends over a piece of work, there was a rumbling of wheels in the yard. One of my aunts looked out of the window and said with dismay, 'Deshert!'

My mother got up from her chair and hurriedly gathered up her work from the table, saying distractedly, 'Jesus, Mary, Saint Joseph . . . this is awful! And my husband isn't at home.'

Deshert was a landowner and a very distant relative of ours. In the family there were whole legends surrounding his name with an aura of terror and darkness. They spoke of terrible tortures to which he had subjected his serfs. He had many children who were divided into liked and disliked. The latter lived in the servants' quarters and if he happened to encounter them he flung them out of his path like dogs. His wife, a hopelessly cowed creature, could only weep in secret. One daughter, a good-looking girl with sad eyes, had run away. A son had shot himself. All this had apparently had no effect whatever on Deshert. He was an out-and-out serf-owning type, who recognized nothing apart from himself and his own will. He didn't like the town: here he was aware of certain limits, which provoked a perpetual deep seething of anger within him, ready to explode at any moment. And it was this that was particularly unpleasant and even frightening for his hosts.

This time, getting down from his *britska*, he categorically announced to my mother that he was dying. He was a terrible hypochondriac, and at the slightest indisposition had everybody rushing about all over the place. Now, without so much as asking leave, he occupied my father's room, and from there his groans, calls, orders and oaths carried through the whole house. When he came home, my father found his room cramfull of basins, compresses, lotions, and medicine-bottles. The dying man was lying on his bed, now quietly groaning, now swearing as loud as a colonel at his regiment on drill. My father shrugged his shoulders and submitted.

The few days this original character spent in our house I remember as a kind of nightmare. Nobody could forget for a single moment that in my father's room lay Deshert, huge, terrifying, and 'dying'. At his rude summons my mother would shake all over and hurry as fast as she could. At times when the shouts and groans had ceased, it became even more terrifying: from behind the locked doors came the sound of giant snoring. Everyone walked on tiptoe, and my mother sent us outside.

This illness ended rather unexpectedly. One day my father brought Uncle Pyotr, the humorist, home with him. Pyotr's eyes, when he greeted my mother, were laughing, his moustache-ends twitching. In a perfectly natural voice, such as had not been heard in our house for several days, he asked, 'Well, where's your patient?' My mother looked apprehensively and implored, 'For God's sake . . . what do you want to do? No, no, please don't go in there'.

But my father, who was fed up to the teeth with all this and had been put out enough, opened the door and they both went in. Pyotr went up to the bed without any precautions and said loudly in Polish, 'I hear you are dying! I've come to say good-bye to you.' The sick man groaned and started complaining that he had a pain in his side, that he had no stomach left and felt generally very bad.

'Well, there's nothing for it', said Pyotr. 'I see myself that you are dying. We all die sooner or later. You today, me tomorrow. Go and fetch the priest; let him prepare himself as a good Christian should.' Deshert groaned. Pyotr stepped back a couple of paces and started taking visual measurements of the man from head to foot. . . .

'What are you looking at me like that for?' asked Deshert plaintively and querulously.

'Nothing, nothing at all', Pyotr reassured him, and then, paying no attention to him, said to my father in a business-like tone of voice, 'I tell you, you'll need *some* coffin . . . whoah!'

These words hit Deshert like a bombshell. 'My horses!' he shouted so loud that his coachman rushed out of the kitchen without a second's delay to carry out his order.

Deshert started dressing, shouting that he would rather die on the road than stay a minute longer in a house where they laughed at a dying relation. Soon Deshert's horses were brought up to the porch and, all swathed and muffled up, he sat down in his carriage and drove away without saying good-bye to anybody. The whole house seemed brighter straight away. In the evening they talked in the kitchen of what life was like for the people under such a squire, and cited examples of squires' inhumanity. Deshert wasn't seen in our house for a long time, only now and again rumours reached us of new examples of his cruelty towards his family and serfs.

About a year must have passed. The feeling that 'something's going to happen' was growing, and the thing itself was unfolding and taking shape. My father was now working on certain new committees, but little was said—and only very guardedly—of the nature of this work.

One day I was sitting in the drawing-room with a book, and my father was reading *Son of the Fatherland* in the soft armchair. It must have been after the evening meal, because he was in his dressing-gown and slippers. He had read in some new book that sleeping after dinner wasn't good for one, and was trying to break the habit; but at times sleep would still suddenly overcome him in the chair. Such was the case now: all was quiet in the room, only the occasional rustling of the newspaper or my father's quiet snoring could be heard.

Heavy, hurried footsteps suddenly sounded in the next room, the door was opened violently and on the threshold appeared the thin, tall figure of Deshert. He appeared like a ghost. His face was pale, his moustache straggly, his hair standing straight up, and his eyes burning darkly. He strode into the room, stopped, and then started walking from corner to corner, as if trying to stifle the rage boiling up within him. I huddled in my corner, trying not to be noticed, but at the same time something stopped me slipping out of the room. It was fear for my father: Deshert was huge and vicious, and my lame father seemed weak and defenceless. After he had made a few quick turns, Deshert suddenly stopped in the middle of the room and said, 'Listen! So it's true, then?'

'What?' asked my father. There was a glint of amusement in his attentive eyes. Deshert gave a start of impatience and answered, 'All the devils take you! You know, what they're shouting from all the roof-tops now. Even the lousy serfs are shouting it about.'

My father, continuing to peer at him with curiosity and amusement in his eyes, nodded his head slowly. Deshert uttered something between a groan and a bellow, strode around the room again and then, stopping dead, declared, 'So! Well, let me tell you . . . while they are still mine . . . while you are cooking up your rotten plans . . . I'll . . . I'll . . .' He stopped, as if anger was preventing him speaking. In the room it was quiet and tense. Then he turned towards the door, but at that moment from my father's chair came the sharp rap of his stick on the varnished floor. Deshert looked around; I too looked involuntarily at my father. His face seemed calm, but I recognized the light in his expressive eyes. He made an effort to get up, then sank back in the chair and, looking straight at Deshert, said in Polish, obviously struggling to keep his temper, 'Listen, you . . . what's your name? . . . If you . . . now . . . so much as touch a single man in your village, I swear to God you'll be brought to town under guard.'

Deshert's eyes became round, like those of a wounded bird of prey. Profound surprise was visible in them.

'Who . . . who would dare?' he said hoarsely, almost choking.

'You'll see', said my father, now calmly taking out his snuff-box. Deshert stood looking at him dumbfounded a few seconds longer, then turned and walked across the room. The clothes on his thin body seemed to have sagged. He didn't even slam the outer door and disappeared unusually quietly. . . .

My father remained in the armchair. Under his unfastened dressing-gown his snuff-besprinkled shirt was shaking slightly. He was laughing the usual inward laugh of a somewhat stout man, and I looked at him with delight and admiration. In my young heart glowed a special feeling of joyful pride. My mother ran into the room and asked anxiously, 'What's up with him? Has he gone? For God's sake what happened in here?'

When my father had briefly outlined what had in fact taken place, she clasped her hands. 'Jesus, Mary! What'll happen now? Those poor people!'

'He won't dare', said my father with certainty. 'Those times have gone.'

Writers, when they write about that time, usually end with an apotheosis of emancipation. Joyful and deeply moved crowds of people, incense, a prayer of thankfulness, hopes. . . . I personally did not see anything like that, perhaps because I lived in a town. I certainly remember some official celebration—either on the occasion of the emancipation, or the announcement of the conquest of the Caucasus. Representatives of the peasants had been driven to town to hear the manifesto read, and the evening before the streets were full of long peasant coats. There were a lot of peasants with medals, and also many women and children. This last circumstance is to be explained by the fact that an ominous rumour had spread among the people: the landowners had got the better of the Tsar, and again there would be no freedom. They were driving the peasants into the town and would shoot with field-guns. Among the squires, on the other hand, it was being said that it was unwise to gather such a mass of people in the town at such a time. This was discussed in our house too the day before the celebration. My father shrugged as usual. 'That's not our province.'

On the day of the celebration troops were positioned in the form of a square in the centre of the town. On one side shone a row of brass cannon, and the 'free' peasants lined up facing them. They gave an impression of sombre resignation to fate, and now and again would sigh heavily or start to lament. When, after the reading of some document or other, blanks were fired from the guns, hysterical shouts came from the crowd, which gave rise to a scene of great confusion. The women had thought they were starting to shoot the peasants. . . . The old times had bequeathed to the new a part of their sad inheritance.

3

The Time of the Polish Uprising

IT BROKE OUT, AS EVERYONE KNOWS, AT THE BEGINNING OF 1863, but there had been muffled unrest and demonstrations earlier on.

One day—it must have been in about 1860—my father came home from work serious and preoccupied. After talking something over with my mother, he called us together and said, 'Listen, children, you are Russians and must speak Russian from now on.'

After this, colloquial Russian was used in our Polonized family for the first time. We accepted this reform fairly light-heartedly, and, I dare say, even with pleasure—it was something new—but the reasons that had provoked it remained unknown to us. Rumours were already reaching us of events in Warsaw, and then in Vilna (where quite serious demonstrations took place as early as 1861). But all this was somewhere far away, in an unknown, almost unreal world, and did not interest us. In our world[1] an unruffled calm still reigned.

Polish was the dominant language in Rykhlinsky's boarding-school,[2] but there wasn't the slightest national discord there. Rykhlinsky managed for a long time to maintain an atmosphere of mutual tolerance. There were some pure Russians there, among them the two Sukhanov brothers, the elder of whom always headed his class. On one occasion there was an incident involving him or another Russian pupil: a young Pole, learning that his Russian schoolfellow had taken communion the day before, started making fun of the Orthodox ritual. He made a chalice out of paper, made faces at it and finally spat in it. The Russian had held himself in check for a time, but finally hit out, catching the boy across the cheek with such a slap that the sound rang through the whole hall and was heard by Rykhlinsky. When he'd found out what had happened, he called both of them out and asked the Pole in front of the

---

[1] Korolenko lived in Volhynia, in the Western Ukraine. Most of the so-called 'right-bank Ukraine' (west of the Dnieper) had remained Polish until the Partitions in the reign of Catherine the Great. Korolenko tells us that in the country the landowners, and in the towns the middle estate were Polish or, at any rate, people who spoke Polish. In the villages the people spoke an Ukrainian dialect that had undergone the influence of both Polish and Russian. Some civil servants (like Korolenko's father) and army men spoke Russian.

[2] The school Korolenko attended as a day-boy before entering Zhitomir High School.

whole school, 'What would you have done if he had made fun of the "Host" [the Catholic communion] in the same way?'

The Pole hesitated, but then said, looking down, 'I would have hit him.'

'And so he hit you. Go and get on your knees over there.'

The boy, completely scarlet, knelt down in the corner and remained there a very long time indeed. We guessed what old Pan Rykhlinsky was waiting for us to do. After conferring we chose a deputation, at the head of which was Sukhanov, and went to ask that the punished boy be forgiven. Rykhlinsky received the deputation solemnly and then went out into the hall on his crutches. Sitting down at his usual place, he told the boy to get up and suggested the two enemies shake hands.

'Good, now it's over,' he said, 'and forgotten. But,' he added, staring at us fiercely and extending his sinewy hands, his short fingers spread open, 'if ever I hear of anyone making fun of someone else's faith again, I'll br-reak every bone in his body.'

And once more we lived amicably, not ascribing any significance to differences of nationality.

Meanwhile, events far away were getting hotter and hotter and, like gusts of wind, their hot breath began to carry to us. More and more often we heard of events in Warsaw and Vilna, of certain victims, but our elders still tried not to speak about it in front of the children.

On one occasion my mother and father stayed out very late at the Rykhlinskys'. Eventually I heard through my sleep the rumbling of our *britzka* in the yard, and some time later woke up completely with an unusual sensation: my mother and father, both still dressed, were standing in the bedroom and arguing about something heatedly, obviously forgetting the time and their sleeping children. Their conversation went something like this:

'All the same,' my mother was saying, 'you must agree: there was before, even in Nicholas's reign. . . . There are still people alive who remember.'

'Well, what of it,' objected my father, 'there used to be, but there isn't any more. It existed in Alexander's reign, Nicholas took it away. They shouldn't have revolted.'[3]

[3] This conversation alludes to the Constitution granted to the Kingdom of Poland by Alexander I in 1815. The Kingdom of Poland was that part of former Poland acquired by Russia not by the Partitions of Catherine's reign but by the settlement of 1815. Unlike the territories gained by the Partitions, the 'kingdom' was not integrated into the Russian Empire, but had its own government, army, and system of finance. After the Revolt of 1830–1 these 'privileges' were taken away. Thus, in the Uprising of 1863 the Poles had no army of any kind to serve as a nucleus. In 1864 the very name 'Kingdom of Poland' was replaced by the purely administrative designation 'the Vistula Region'.

'But tell me honestly, is that fair?'

'That's not my province! What's fair, what's unfair . . . you weren't asked. You took the oath, and that's all there is to it!'

'No, wait . . .'

'No, you wait.'

'Will you just let me say . . .'

I had never heard such a heated argument between them, and particularly at such a time of night. I sat up in bed, quite amazed. Noticing an unexpected listener, they both turned to me.

'Here we are. Let the child decide,' said my mother.

'All right then. Listen, my boy: let's suppose you had promised your mother you'd always obey her. Should you keep your promise?'

'Yes, I should,' I answered fairly convincedly.

'Wait', interrupted my mother, 'now listen to me. Over there lies your new coat. [There really was a new coat, which I'd carefully laid out on the chair that evening.] If some stranger came in and grabbed it, would you try and take it back?'

'I'd take it back,' I answered still more convincedly.

'What's the use!' said my father irritably, feeling that the judge was leaning to the other side. 'And I suppose he'd give it back, just like that! What if he's stronger . . .'

'There we are, there we are . . .' my mother cut in hotly. 'He's stronger, and so he takes it away. You hear! You hear?'

'Oh, nonsense!' said my father, annoyed that his chances were getting even slimmer. 'But if you'd given it away yourself? And had promised never to demand it back? And then you shout "Give it back?"'

'Given it away yourself!' my mother interrupted bitterly. 'Tell me: would you give it away yourself? Of course, if they put a knife to your throat . . .'

At this point my little sister started to cry in her sleep. They remembered where they were and broke off the argument, displeased with each other. My father, leaning on his stick, flushed and excited, went to his room, while my mother took my sister on her knees and started reassuring her. Tears were running down her face. Surprised by this unusual scene, I didn't get to sleep for quite a time. I was aware that the quarrel was not a personal one. They had been arguing, and my mother had been crying not from any personal insult but about something that had once existed but did not exist now. She had been crying about her own country, where there had been kings in crowns, hetmen, beautiful clothes, and an incomprehensible but fascinating 'freedom'. . . . Now there was nothing of that. My father's people had taken it away. They were stronger. My mother had been crying because it was unjust; they had been humiliated.

The next morning my first thought was about something important. My new coat? It was lying in the same place as the evening before, but there was much else that was not in its place. In my mind lay the seeds of new questions and new moods.

'Something's going to happen' was now taking on new forms. The atmosphere was becoming red-hot. Women and girls of our acquaintance were now appearing in black clothes of mourning. For this the police began prosecuting: women demonstrators in black dresses and especially if they wore emblems (a heart, an anchor and a cross) were taken off to the police-stations where reports were drawn up. On the other hand, acid was poured on light-coloured dresses and they were cut with knives in the Catholic churches. . . . Catholic priests delivered impassioned sermons.

In September 1861 the town was astounded by an unexpected event. One morning, on the main square by the Church of the Bernardines, in an area enclosed by a small palisade, people on their way to market were surprised to see a huge black cross with a white border of mourning, a garland of fresh flowers and the inscription: 'In memory of the Poles tortured in Warsaw'. The cross was about ten feet high and stood right by the police-box. The news flew through the town with the speed of lightning. The townspeople began crowding to the place where the cross had appeared. The authorities could think of nothing better than to dig the cross up and take it away to the police-station.

Through the town broke the news that the cross had been jailed. Throughout the day crowds of people gathered outside police head-quarters. In the Catholic church the women formed a council, refused to admit the Chief of Police, and after midday a crowd of women, all in deep mourning, moved off towards the Governor's residence. The small one-storeyed house of the Governor on Kiev Street was besieged. My father, driving past, saw this crowd and the old grey-haired Chief of Police, who was standing on the front steps and trying to persuade the women to disperse. Troops were called out. The crowd was still not dispersing as the evening approached, and at dusk it was broken up. In the town this produced the impression of an explosion. Stories were told of women hurling themselves into backyards and doorways, and fleeing into shops in an effort to escape from their rough-handed pursuers. And the arrest of the cross provoked consternation even among the Orthodox population, accustomed to the fact that they recognized the same sacred symbols as the Catholics.

From that time patriotic excitement and demonstrations overflowed in a great torrent. Martial law was proclaimed in the town with the beating of drums. One day our street was occupied by a detachment of soldiers. They went from house to house, taking away arms. They didn't by-pass our house either: on a wall-rug above my father's bed hung an old Turkish pistol and a curved sabre. They took them as well. This was the first search I was ever present at. The procedure seemed unpleasant and frightening to me.

All this served to increase the general excitement and, of course, it was reflected in the hearts of us children. And as I was neither a Russian nor a Pole, or, more correctly, was both the one and the other, the reflections of these tumults moved over me, like the shadows of shape-less clouds driven by a strong wind.

On one occasion my mother took me with her to the Catholic church. We used to go to church with my father and occasionally to the Catholic church with my mother. This time I stood with her in a side chapel, by the sacristy. It was very quiet, as if everyone were waiting for some-thing. The priest, young and pale, with burning eyes, uttered Latin exhortations in a loud and excited voice. Then a deep and uneasy silence enveloped the gothic arches of the Church of the Bernardines, and amid the silence came the sounds of the patriotic hymn: 'Boże, coś Polske przez tak długie wieki . . .'[4]

Quietly, at different moments and from different places in the crowded church there rose first of all just a few individual voices, which gradually came together like streams. Nearer, stronger, louder, more harmoniously, and in the end under the arches of the church a single, thousand-voiced choir resounded and rolled forth wave upon wave, accompanied by the deep roar of the organ somewhere in the heights above. My mother was kneeling and weeping, covering her face with a handkerchief. This outburst, which had united the whole crowd in a single transport of emotion, wide as the sea, made a truly stunning impression upon me. It seemed that something had caught hold of me and was carrying me aloft, rocking me and evoking strange visions.

'Cossaks', said someone near by. The word was clearly whispered farther on and was then drowned in a sea of sounds.

When he heard of the demonstration my father was very displeased. A few days later he said to my mother, 'The Chief of Police was telling me that your name has been taken too.'

[4] 'God, Thou who for so many centuries hast surrounded Poland with the radiance of might and glory . . .', the first lines of a hymn that was especially popular in Poland at the time of the Uprising of 1863. It is not known who wrote it.

'Well, what can I do?' my mother said. 'I didn't sing myself and I didn't know that there would be singing.'

'And if you had known?' my father asked.

'Then . . . I would not have taken the child', she answered. 'After all, I can't not go to church.'

From then on she always kept herself apart from the activity of the exalted patriots and devotees of her sex, but she went to church as before, regardless of whether she would be noticed or not. My father was on edge and anxious both about her and his own position, but as a sincerely religious man he recognized the right of another faith.

Troops passed through the town. On one occasion the rumour spread that Bashkirs were coming. Wild, not understanding a word of Russian or Polish, they only gabbled in their own tongue and beat people. This evoked an almost superstitious terror. And, indeed, a few days later a detachment of strange soldiers on small horses passed through the streets. They wore sharp-pointed caps with shaggy sheepskin edgings, had high cheek-bones and small eyes, and sat astride their mounts in a wild sort of posture. On seeing a crowd of curious people, one of them suddenly spurred his horse and swung his whip. There was a hysterical shriek, but the Bashkir had ridden past, his dark face grinning, revealing white teeth; then the others rode by, raising dust with their horses' hoofs, and laughing too. It seemed strange to me that they were laughing like ordinary people, and I pictured with horror an attack by these swarthy savages. They passed through and disappeared beyond the western turnpike in the direction of Poland, where, it was said, blood was already flowing; and other detachments entered the town.

In our stable there also stood three or four Cossack horses. The Cossacks settled themselves in the same place, by the horses, while infantrymen were quartered in the kitchen and the shed. These lodgers didn't get much of a welcome: the householders and their tenants had long arguments with the billeters, were unwilling to allot them premises, and went off somewhere or other to complain. But we children soon got on friendly terms with them. The Cossacks would sometimes put us on their horses and take us to the river to water them. The soldiers would condescendingly allow us to clean the buttons on their uniforms with a piece of rag and chalk, and the thin cabbage-soup they brought back in pots from the company kitchen seemed unusually tasty to us.

I remember one soldier particularly well. He was already an old man, with a lined face, a bristly grey moustache, and a ring in his left ear. When he'd settled himself in the shed, where he hung up his accoutrements on nails and carefully stood his gun in the corner, he leaned his shoulder against the doorpost, and watched for a long time in silence, with an air of serious attention, as we carried out drill in the yard with wooden guns. After a time he could no longer endure the role of an onlooker; he walked up in front of us, took a 'gun', and began to demonstrate the real method, impressing us with the precision and elasticity of his movements. It seemed that with every movement springs knocked and clanked inside the soldier.

'Here I am teaching you Polacks, and then you'll go and rebel and kill me', he said in conclusion, half-jokingly, half-angrily.

After a time there were excellent relations between us and him. We spent many hours together on summer evenings on Afanasy's soldier's mattress, which smelled of sweat, leather accoutrements, and sour soldiers' soup, until his company went off somewhere in the District after bands of insurgents. For us parting with him was very unpleasant, and the old soldier, too, evidently did not feel himself. Long service in Nicholas's army had already taken all his life[5] and broken all family ties, and the old soldier's heart was nourished only by temporary attachments formed in the places where he was stationed.

Among the Cossacks a sergeant with curly brown hair stands out particularly clearly. His face was pitted from smallpox, but that didn't prevent him passing as really handsome. It was a real delight for us to watch him fly on to his horse's back almost by magic, without any preliminaries at all. Occasionally he got drunk and then, his eyes flashing, he would shout in the yard, 'Oh, you Polacks! What are you rebelling for! Just see: some day the Don will give Mother Moscow a shaking, and what a shaking. . . . Not your sort.' He would clench his fist and shake it above his head, as if Mother Moscow were really squashed within it. Our friend, the old soldier Afanasy would shake his head reproachfully and say, 'The Cossacks are a desperate lot. A thieving lot too: when there's something to steal, their fingers start itching. For them army life's different too. It's easy. We'd be made to run the gauntlet[6] for something, but they get off light. Their sergeant will give a man a lash or two, and that's all there is to it. And that's not for the stealing. It just means: don't get caught!' The Cossacks only laughed at these serious words from Afanasy.

Insurgent bands had now appeared in our region too. An ominous shadow hung over the life of the town. Every now and again we heard

---

[5] Before the Milyutin reforms (see p. 118, note) the length of service in the Russian army was twenty-five years.

[6] The offender would be made to run between two lines of soldiers who beat him with sticks.

that one or another young man we knew had disappeared. He'd gone 'to the woods'. Girls would ironically ask those who remained, 'Are you still here?' Several youths from Rykhlinsky's school had gone to the woods too.

One day at dinner my mother said to father, 'Stasik has arrived. They've asked us over this evening.' My father looked at her in surprise and then asked, 'So all three sons have come?'

'Yes, all three,' my mother replied with quiet sadness.

'You've all gone out of your minds!' my father said, angrily putting aside his spoon. 'You've all gone out of your minds—the old ones as well!'

Rykhlinsky's three sons, students of Kiev University, had apparently come to say good-bye and ask their father's blessing before going off to join a rebel band. One was a final-year student in the Faculty of Medicine, another was, I think, in his third year, while the youngest, Stasik, about eighteen, had only finished high school the year before. He was everyone's favourite, a rosy-cheeked cheerful lad with sparkling dark eyes. After an evening spent among the family and close friends, all three knelt down for their old parents' blessing, and in the night they rode away.

'I'd have given that Stasik a leathering and locked him up,' my father said angrily the next day.

'Even children are going off to fight for their country,' mused my mother with tears in her eyes. 'What's going to happen?'

'What'll happen?—they'll all be caught like chickens,' my father answered bitterly. 'You've all gone out of your minds.'

In the beginning the mood of Polish society was elated, confident. There was talk of victories, of some Rujhitsky who was going to lead the Volynian detachments, and that Napoleon would send help. In the boarding-school the Polish pupils passed round these pieces of news, which Marynya, the Rykhlinskys' only daughter, used to bring. She had big eyes, like Stasik, and they sparkled with joyful animation. I too believed in all these successes of the Poles, but the feeling they evoked in me was a very complex one.

One night I had a vivid and distressing dream. It all seemed to begin with a game of 'Poles and Russians', which had at that time replaced all our other games. We usually divided up not by nationality, but by lot, so that Russians would find themselves on the Polish side and Poles on the Russian. I can't remember now whose side I was on in the dream, I only remember that the game soon turned into real war. There was a wide expanse of field through which wound a little river, overgrown with rushes. In one place there was a fire, in another horsemen in sharp-pointed caps were riding past in dust and smoke, and somewhere else shots were rattling out, the wind bearing away white puffs of smoke as from a soldiers' shooting-range. I was running from someone and hiding under a steep river-bank.

And suddenly it turned out that it was not actually I who was hiding, but a platoon of Russian soldiers. Frightened and pathetic, they had concealed themselves under the bank in the rushes, up to their knees in water. Foremost of all and nearest me stood old Afanasy in his round peakless cap and with a ring in his left ear. He was giving me a serious, rather harsh and reproachful look, and my heart was wrung with anguish and fear. There, in the field, triumphant Poles were galloping about in smoke. Suddenly on top of the bank appeared Stasik Rykhlinsky on horseback. His merry dark eyes were sparkling and he was smiling in his lively boyish way. I froze in anticipation, and it seemed to me that there was nothing in the world more terrible than that nice young lad, who was about to discover Afanasy and the soldiers hiding in the rushes. These people were now close and dear to me, and I felt sorry for them, as for my own kith and kin. 'That,' I thought, waking up in a sweat and with my heart thumping, 'is because they are Russians and I am Russian.' But I was making a mistake. It was only because they were people. And soon my sympathies changed.

Two or three weeks later came rumours of encounters around Kiev. These were pathetic ventures, the insurgents being quickly dispersed by Cossacks and peasants. The Rykhlinsky family was weighed down with anxiety. Once we were having a lesson in Marynya's room. She used to teach the younger pupils French, and on this occasion was called to her father's room. She returned flushed, her eyes red from crying, but tried to go on with the lesson. Suddenly, however, she jumped up, threw herself on to her bed and started sobbing. I rushed to get water, but she pushed the glass aside and said through her sobs, 'Go away, all of you. I don't need anything.'

It soon became known in the school that all three of her brothers had been captured in a minor action. The eldest had been wounded in the neck by a Cossack lance. Old Pan Rykhlinsky came to breakfast and dinner, and administered justice exactly as he'd done before. His wife ran her side of things just as sedately, Marynya taught us French without giving further expression to her feelings, and the whole family proudly bore its grief, awaiting fresh blows from fate.

The uprising had no success anywhere, Napoleon didn't come, peasants even in Poland joined unwillingly, and in other places dealt cruelly with the rebelling squires. One day I saw a convoy of captured insurgents.They were sitting crowded in long, high-walled carts, such as are used for transporting sheafs of corn; some of them had bandaged heads and arms in slings. The faces of the wounded were pale. On the bandages of one of them spots of blood were to be seen. Up in front sat peasants, urging on the horses, while alongside rode the escorts—also peasants. The sympathy of the majority of the townspeople was on the side of the prisoners. Young servant-girls spat at the conquerors wheeling on their sorry-looking mounts, while they in turn derisively shook their forelocks and cocked their sheepskin caps. The prison, situated on narrow, congested Chudnov Street, was soon crammed full of these prisoners, and premises were rented from private citizens for the detention of the suspicious and unreliable. The triumph of the conquerors and the settling of accounts was beginning.

One day a hired two-horse open carriage drew up outside our home, and from it stepped a young officer, who asked for my father. He was in a fresh, new-looking, dark blue uniform, on which white aiglets stood out to effect. His spurs jingled pleasantly with every step. 'H-how handsome!' said my sister. And my brother and I were also very taken with him. But my mother, on seeing him, suddenly became alarmed, and went hurriedly to my father's study. When my father came out into the drawing-room, the handsome officer was standing by a picture, on which was depicted rather crudely in oils the figure of a bearded Pole in a red Polish surcoat, with a sabre at his side and a hetman's staff of command in his hand.

The officer bowed, jingled his spurs and, pointing to the picture asked, 'Mazeppa ?'[7]

'No, that's Zolkiewski,'[8] my father replied.

'Ah-ah', the officer drawled, looking as though he disapproved of them both equally, and then went off into the study with my father. A quarter of an hour later they both came out and got into the carriage. My mother and my aunts watched discreetly but anxiously from the windows as the two men drove away. Apparently, they were afraid my father had been arrested. To us it appeared strange that such a handsome, clean-looking and pleasant figure could evoke anxiety. That evening my father related that, as they were passing the prison, the

[7] Mazeppa (1644–1710), a Hetman of the Dnieper Cossacks who in 1708 declared against Peter the Great and joined Charles XII of Sweden. After Charles's defeat at Poltava, Mazeppa fled with him to Turkey.

[8] Zolkiewski (1547–1620), a Polish general who in 1610 commanded the armies of Poland in their intervention in Muscovy.

prisoners, looking from the windows, also thought the judge had been arrested, and started loudly abusing the gendarme.[9] By virtue of his office my father sat on the Commissions, of which the handsome officer with the pleasantly jingling spurs was one of the most harshly exigent members. Other officials, with local ties, were more leniently disposed.

Once, when he'd come home after a sitting, my father told my mother that one of the people 'under suspicion' had arrived before the beginning of the hearing and, throwing a letter he'd just received on to the table, said with despair, 'I'm not defending myself any longer. Do what you like. My son went off to join a detachment and . . . has been killed.'

The gendarme and the Prosecutor had not yet arrived. My father, glancing at the remaining members of the Commission, gavĕ the letter back to the old man and said in an official tone of voice, 'The Commission is not yet in session, but personal conversations are out of place here.' A few minutes later the gendarme walked in, but the old man had already composed himself and hidden the letter. His particular case ended favourably, and the family was saved from confiscation of property and ruin.

In our town there were three executions, if I'm not mistaken. Sentences of death were passed on the so-called 'hanging gendarmes',[10] and officers in service in the Russian army who had joined the uprising. I only remember one execution: that of a former officer whose name, I believe, was Stroynovsky. He was young and handsome, had got married not long before, and had a brilliant career in front of him. He had been captured on the field of battle, and—'the law was clear' . . . . I don't know whether my father's signature was among those on the sentence or not, but nobody felt any bitterness towards him on that account anyway. Indeed, Stroynovsky, after sentence had been passed, asked for my father to visit him before his execution. At this meeting he gave my father certain things to attend to, and also his last greetings to his young wife. At the same time, he spoke bitterly of his former detachment: when he had wanted to fall back, they had noisily demanded battle, but when peasants with scythes and Cossacks had appeared before their barricades on the forest road, they had turned tail, and he had been taken. He died with bitterness and regret, but manfully and proudly.

The romanticism which had nourished the mood of the young Poles

---

[9] A member of the political police in Tsarist Russia.
[10] The name given to men who caught and executed people whom the secret Central Committee saw as enemies of the uprising.

who had revolted was a poor military school. They had been inspired
by the dead past, by the shadows of life, not by life itself. The crude,
prosaic advance of a crowd of peasants and Cossacks was not at all
reminiscent of fine battle-scenes—and poor Stroynovsky paid for his
faith in historical romanticism.

It was a bright clear day in June or July. In the morning it became
known that a black stake had been set up and a hole dug on some wasteland by the slaughter-house beyond the Kiev turnpike, and therefore
everything that day seemed specially sad and solemn, and oppressively
significant. In the middle of the sunny afternoon a short, dull sound rang
out heavily and clearly—just as though you'd been hit in the ear by a
compact round lump of earth. And with this sound something in the
clear day seemed to open out, like a cloud opens from heat-lightning.
There was no cloud, there was no lightning, the sun was shining. And
yet something had nevertheless unfolded, and for one moment something mysterious, hidden, and usually unseen looked out from behind
the clear day. That was the moment when all of us became aware that a
human life had ceased. It was said afterwards that Stroynovsky had
asked for his eyes not to be covered and his hands to be left unbound,
and that it had been allowed. He was also supposed to have given the
soldiers the order to fire himself. On the other side of the town his
mother was at the house of friends. When the sound reached her,
she collapsed, as if she'd been cut down.

I repeat: I do not know even now whether my father's signature was
on the sentence of the Court-Martial Commission, or whether it was a
field-court composed only of army men. Nobody spoke about it and
nobody considered it important. 'The law was clear.'

4

Zhitomir High School

IT WAS A TIME OF GREAT CHANGE IN THE EDUCATIONAL system. Popular elementary education and the use of the birch were being discussed in the press and in society at large. The Director of Education[1] for the Kiev District was the famous Pirogov.[2] Not long before (in 1858) he had published a series of brilliant articles, in which he had come out decisively against the birch. Dobrolyubov[3] had welcomed these articles, especially as they came from the pen of a man with practical experience in the field of education, and from them he had drawn the conclusion that in the Kiev District the birch was already a thing of the past. It turned out, however, that such hopes were premature. The following year (1859) Pirogov called a conference in which, besides the Director and his Assistant, a number of professors, high-school headmasters, senior masters, and prominent teachers took part. The Conference came out in favour of gradual reform and retained the birch, merely deciding to regulate its use. Not only did Pirogov not disassociate himself from this decision, but actually added his own justification for the regulations,[4] famous in their day, by which all kinds of school offences were painstakingly weighed, categorized, and allocated

---

[1] A very approximate equivalent of the Russian *popechitel' uchebnogo okruga*.

[2] Nikolay Ivanovich Pirogov (1810–81), physician and educationalist. The articles alluded to appeared in 1856 (not 1858). Pirogov's views on education were, in fact, too enlightened for the government, for in March 1861 he was retired from his post, and the following year was given an appointment which took him abroad. While abroad he operated on the wounded Garibaldi.

[3] Nikolay Aleksandrovich Dobrolyubov (1836–61), one of the most influential radical critics of the nineteenth century. In 1856 he joined Nekrasov's *Contemporary*, and the following year took over the post of chief critic, which he held until his early death. In 1857 he published in *The Contemporary* the article 'A few words about education' (*'Neskol'ko slov o vospitanii'*), in which he welcomed and developed the ideas expressed in Pirogov's articles.

[4] 'Regulations concerning offences and punishments of pupils in the high schools of the Kiev Educational District.' These were first published in *The Journal of Education* (*Zhurnal vospitaniya*), No. 11, 1859. It was prescribed that birching should be administered as seldom as possible and in strict accordance with the seriousness of the offence. It could only be administered 'on the decision of the Staff Council with a three quarters' majority in favour in closed ballot'.

various degrees of punishment. A table with these categories was to hang on the wall, and a boy who'd committed an offence was to find it himself in the appropriate column. It was supposed that this would contribute to developing a sense of legality. Among the offences inevitably involving corporal punishment was, incidentally, religious fanaticism.

It was a compromise between theory and practice, and a very unsuccessful one at that. The regulations did not last more than a few years. The spirit of the times was sweeping the birch away, but in places where conservative usages still held firm, the recognition of corporal punishment in principle came as very convenient. Dobrolyubov reacted to the appearance of the regulations with a very severe article,[5] full of bitterness and sarcasm apropos of Pirogov. The entire press was divided into two camps: for and against Dobrolyubov, the 'moderate liberalism' of the time being for the Director and gradualism, and against the journalist with his radical demands. In this dispute the Zhitomir High School acquired a certain notoriety. It transpired that in the number of birchings there it had left all other schools far behind: in 1858 290 boys out of 600 had been birched. This was seven times more than, for example, in the Kiev Second High School, and thirty-five times more than in the Kiev First. The simple-hearted old-school teachers, led by Kichenko the headmaster, had put down this eloquent figure in their reply to Pirogov's questionnaire, obviously not foreseeing the effect that it was destined to have.

At the time I was too little and do not remember to what extent echoes of this dispute in the press penetrated to the pupils themselves. They had their own literature, which was memorized and passed round in manuscript form and through albums. It was invariably satirical in tone. I recall a long and apparently quite well-written poem which said, *inter alia*, that in Zhitomir 'human teachers' could not live among 'animal teachers'. By some law of fate the 'humans' were taken away by the devil:

> Devils have taken Trofimov,
> They'll take Dobrashov too

wrote the anonymous author, sparing nothing in his description of the teachers remaining in the staff menagerie. From the very tone of these works, full of anger and bitterness, one could judge what feelings of

---

[5] The article 'Russian illusions, destroyed by the birch' (*'Vserossiskiye illyuzii, razrushayemye rozgami'*) appeared in *The Contemporary*, No. 1, 1860.

gratitude the schools of the time evoked and the mood in which their pupils went out into life.

All of us in the boarding-school dreamed, of course, of entering the high school and were interested in advance in everything the high-school boys brought from class. We knew of the terrible Kichenko, the old teachers, the supervisor[6] Zhuravsky, and the caretaker Mina, whose wife treated boys to excellent cakes in the break at one and a half kopecks each; he himself treated the same boys to the birch in the punishment-room. If, despite all this, we dreamed of the high-school uniform, it was something like the ambition of a young soldier going off to war.

Finally, at the end of June 1858, in a uniform with a red collar and brass buttons, I set off for the first time to lessons in the new high-school building. After the entrance exam I'd caught a fever and had missed almost a quarter of the year. The enormous state institution was running without me at full steam, and I felt insignificant, pitiful and at fault in advance. At fault because I'd been ill, because I didn't know anything, because I was so small and unlike a high-school boy. I was going defenceless to meet Kichenko, Mina, harsh customs and punishments.

In the large and noisy classroom I didn't feel at all at home, and I felt particular consternation on seeing the familiar figure of the old school-boy Shumovich. He was a chap of about eighteen, broad-shouldered and squat, with the walk of a young bear and a serious, almost morose look. For two or three years now he had gone almost daily to school past our yard. If I or my younger brother happened to cross his path, he would grab us in his bear paws, squeeze and pummel us, twist our noses, box our ears and, finally, turning us so that our backs were towards him, he would propel us forward with a deft knee-blow in the small of the back. He would then unhurriedly wend his way. If we caught sight of him a long way off, we would hide behind the wicker-gate, but when he'd passed, something drew us after him. We would run behind, shouting 'Shumovich! Shumovich!' He would turn and measure the distance between us.

It so happened that the reform which prohibited a boy remaining more than two years in the same class came only at the second stage of his lengthy school career. This giant turned out to be my classmate, and I thought with terror what he'd do to me during the break. However, he gave no indication that he remembered our out-of-school relations. No doubt, such memories did not give him any pleasure either.

I felt completely lost and when during the first lesson the teacher of

[6] *Nadrizatel'*, an under-teacher, assistant.

natural history suddenly called my name, I froze with fright. My heart started thumping, and I looked round helplessly. The boy sitting next to me nudged me with his elbow and said, 'Go out to the desk', adding in a loud voice 'He's been ill. He hasn't prepared.'

'He's been ill, been ill . . . hasn't prepared!' droned the whole class. I took heart from this friendly solidarity behind me. I went up to the desk, stopped, and looked down.

'He's been ill, ill, ill . . . i-i-ill . . . not pre-e-e-pa-a-a . . .' fifty voices were droning.

The teacher Prelin was not, in fact, frightening. Young, handsome, with fair hair and blue eyes, he asked me what I knew, and on being told that I didn't know anything as yet, he invited me to come to see him at home. I sat down, encouraged and won over by the warm and serious look he had given me.

'He's all right . . . a nice fellow,' said my neighbour, Kryshtano-vich. At this point the door swung wide open, and a big stout man came into the class with a decisive, almost military step. 'The Headmaster Gerasimenko,' my neighbour whispered timidly. Hardly bowing to the teacher, the headmaster opened a register and said in a sharp, almost barking voice, 'Marks for the first quarter-year. Listen! Abramovich . . . Balandovich . . . Buyalsky . . . Varshaver . . . Varshavsky . . .'

He scattered surnames, subjects, and marks as from a bag. Every now and then short comments would break from this stream: 'well done', 'the Council expresses disapproval', 'threat of the birch', 'a thrashing for the wretch'. Calling out my name he added, 'A lot has been missed—must try hard.' When he'd barked out his last comment he quickly closed the register and went out just as swiftly as he'd come in.

An anxious hubbub filled the class. Behind me someone started crying. Prelin, red-faced and seemingly embarrassed, was bent over his register. My neighbour, a blue-eyed and very pleasant boy in a tight uniform, nudged me with his elbow and asked simply, though with rather a worried look, 'Listen, what did he say about me: "threat of the birch" or "a thrashing for the wretch"?'

'I didn't notice.'

'Swine. Don't you care about your mate?'

'But you didn't notice yourself.'

'No, the Devil only knows what he's saying . . . barks like a dog.'

'What did he say about Kryshtanovich? Anyone notice? . . .' boys started asking. ' "A threat", wasn't it?'

'No, "a thrashing for the wretch". I heard it,' said someone behind.

'Is that right?' Kryshtanovich asked, turning round.

'It's right, old chap, I'm afraid.'

I looked at him sympathetically, but he merely tossed his tousled, flaxen forelock and said, 'To the devil with them! What about you? Are you going to work hard?'

'How d'you mean?' I asked naïvely.

'You've missed a lot. You won't catch up anyway. They'll thrash you. I don't work at all. I want to go into the telegraph.'

Prelin rapped his pencil, and the talking stopped.

In the break that followed I didn't walk out, but was carried out as by a raging torrent. And immediately I was whirled round like a chip of wood. I was a new boy. It was obvious, and I was pinched, pushed, and boxed on the ears from all quarters. Some of the older boys had attained considerable skill in the art of boxing the ears so that there was a crack like a firework going off. Besides, I had short-cropped hair and rather sticking-out ears and, while I looked round helplessly, something like machine-gun fire was going on around my head. It was stopped only by the impetuous interference of Olshansky, a boy I knew. He was a stout, exceptionally happy-go-lucky and sturdy fellow, who threw himself into the attack with reckless courage and soon pulled me out of the maelstrom. True, he himself didn't come out of the fight unscathed, and twice even rolled with his opponents in the grass. He then jumped up and shouted, 'Run after me!'

We ran into the second yard. Trying to get away from a lamp-post of a boy who'd caught up with me, I grabbed hold of a young tree. It rocked and cracked. My pursuer stopped, and another shouted, 'He's broken a tree, he's broken a tree! I'll tell Zhuravsky!'

Meanwhile the bell had been rung from the steps, and all the boys rushed into the building with the same speed. Olshansky, who liked the role of my protector, pulled me along by the arm. Running up to the step where the short caretaker was shaking a big bell, he suddenly stopped and poked the bellringer with his finger, saying, 'This is Mina!'

The famous Mina was a small, squat man with long arms like a monkey's and a sunburned face, on which his very fair beard stood out somehow incongruously. His long straight nose seemed to be sinking in his broad, light-coloured moustache. Stopping his ringing, he looked at my happy-go-lucky protector and said, 'What are you laughing for? Watch out, Olshansky—it'll soon be Saturday. I don't suppose you've learned your lessons again?'

Olshansky unconcernedly poked his tongue out at Mina and disappeared in the corridor. Just before the lesson, when we were all seated at our desks, the supervisor Zhuravsky came in. He looked round for someone and his eyes stopped on me, 'You, new boy, stay behind after class.' I was astonished. The other boys were curious too. Kryshtanovich slapped me on the back and said, 'Well done, new boy! You'll get the birch straight away. . . . That's pretty good!'

I felt so innocent that I wasn't even scared. It turned out, however, that I was, in fact, guilty.

'Did you break a tree?' a boy who'd come up from a back desk asked me.

'No, but . . . I bent it.'

'There we are. I heard Dombrovsky telling Zhuravsky.'

'For a tree—they can thrash you.' Kryshtanovich surmised.

An exchange of opinions ensued. Although tree-breaking had hardly been envisaged by the Pirogov table of punishments, these trees had only just been planted in the new school, and damaging them was considered a serious offence. Even so, the majority of opinions were favourable to me: 'They won't birch without the agreement of the parents.'

This was yet another form of the 'gradual' compromise: the parents were given the choice of whether a boy should be birched or suspended. As far as Olshansky, Kryshtanovich, and certain others were concerned, the school had been given *carte blanche*, and thrashings were administered without further formalities. 'It's time to teach Dombrovsky a lesson', said Kryshtanovich. 'This isn't the first time.'

'Mm—yes . . .' someone else said very significantly.

When classes were over, I and a few other boys went to Zhuravsky. I got off fairly lightly. My new friends submitted that I was still a new boy, who had only recently recovered from illness and that I hadn't actually broken the tree. Towards the end of this chat another group of boys came up, and seemed to make a special point of engaging in a talk with the supervisor. Zhuravsky reprimanded me and let me go. As we were going down the corridor, Dombrovsky dashed out of an empty classroom. He was red and there were tears in his eyes. Kryshtanovich told me with a smile that an 'execution' had just been carried out on him. After classes, when he was collecting his books, one of the 'veterans', seemingly Shumovich, crept up behind him and threw his hood over his head. Then they pulled him on to a desk, Kryshtanovich took off his leather belt and gave the 'goat' fifteen strokes. When the operation was over, the executioners had rushed out of the classroom and, while Dombrovsky was freeing himself of his hood, they had tried to attract Zhuravsky's attention, so as to have an alibi. Thus the boys had closed ranks and punished a traitor. Later on I met the same thing in prisons. The forms, of course, were more cruel, but the basis was the same.

This episode immediately introduced me, a new boy, into a new society with the rights of a full member. I walked home with the proud awareness that I was now a real high-school boy, that the whole class knew me, and that because of me an important act of social justice had been carried out. 'You're a good chap, you're beginning well!' Kryshtanovich encouraged with patronizing earnestness. In his eyes I now only lacked the punishment-room and a birching.

The next Saturday my friend and champion Olshansky seemed rather preoccupied. To my questions as to what was the matter he did not reply, but during the break he slipped past Mina shamefacedly and unobtrusively. Kryshtanovich, with whom I now walked home from school every day, was also in a dismal frame of mind and before the last lesson he said, 'Umm, today . . . umm, they're going to give me the birch. . . . Wait for me.' Then, unconcernedly flicking back the lock of hair on his forehead, he added, 'It won't take long. I'll ask them to do me first.'

'You aren't scared?' I asked sympathetically.

'It's nothing. Where I come from, old chap, in Belaya Tserkov, they didn't do it like here. It was hellish. My father's pretty good with the birch too, the swine!'

After school, when the mass of boys had quickly streamed out, only a sullen group of the doomed remained in the empty and eerily quiet corridor. Zhuravsky came out with the register in his hands, and behind him ambled Mina. On seeing me, Zhuravsky stopped.

'Ah, the new boy!' he said. 'You've got here too. I told you you would, didn't I?'

'No, I'm with him,' I answered.

'Aha, with Kryshtanovich! You're in good company. You'll go a long way. Fifteen for you today, Kryshtanovich.'

'Sir, I'd like to ask . . .'

'I can't. You should ask the Council.'

'No, I don't mean that . . . I want to be done first. My aunt has come, sir . . . from Kiev.'

'Ah! So you want to delight her as soon as possible. Well, all right, all right, that can be arranged.' And, calling out the register, he put the others in classrooms and said, 'Now then. Let's go, Mr. Kryshtanovich. Auntie is waiting.'

And the three of them—Mina, Zhuravsky, and my friend—went off to the punishment-room like men going to a business meeting. When the door of the room opened, I caught sight of a wide bench, two birches and Mina's assistant. Then the door slammed shut again, swallowing up, as it were, Kryshtanovich's handsome figure in his short-waisted uniform. The stillness in the corridor became even more unpleasant. My heart thumping, I expected to hear through the door a commotion, entreaties, and shouts. But there was nothing of the kind. There was only a tense stillness, and a peculiar whistling, ticking sound. I had scarcely realized what it was when it stopped, and Mina appeared from behind the solid door. He ambled in his bear-like way to one of the classrooms and opened the door with his key. At that moment from the room there came a terrific roar, which reverberated through the whole building. Mina was dragging the resisting Olshansky by the arm. My cheerful friend's mouth was wide open, his plump cheeks were smeared with tears and chalk, he was yelling at the top of his voice, trying to hold on to the doorposts, and then even trying to get a grip on the smooth walls. But Mina, indifferent as fate itself, was taking him without any noticeable effort to the punishment-room, from which Kryshtanovich was now emerging, doing up his braces under his tunic. His face was a little redder than usual, but that was all. He looked with curiosity at the floundering Olshansky and said to me, 'There's a fool. What will he gain by that?'

A derisive light came into his eyes. 'Mina'll let him have it now. Wait,' he added, holding me back and listening. Mina had disappeared behind the door with his victim. A minute later there came the sharp sound of a blow—zh-zhik—and a wild shriek. We were coming up to the school gates when Olshansky shot out of the corridor like a cannon-ball; he was dropping books, looking back and finishing dressing himself as he ran. Still, the following Monday he was once more his cheerful, happy-go-lucky self.

In 1866 echoes of one event of high politics reached us. On 4 April 1866[7] in Petersburg Karakozov had fired at the Emperor Alexander II. In the June of that year, after the examinations, the annual Speech Day took place. First, we gathered in the school and were then taken two-abreast to the Gentry Assembly Hall.[8] The special solemnity of

[7] 16 April 1866 (New Style). Karakozov had been connected with a group of radical students, among whom the murder of the Tsar had been discussed, but dismissed. Karakozov was unbalanced, and his act was entirely his own. The attempted assassination, however, served to harden the reactionary tendencies of the government. The Liberal Golovnin was replaced as Minister of Education by Count D. A. Tolstoy, an extreme reactionary, and the government henceforth looked with great suspicion on the students.

[8] There was a Gentry Assembly Hall—*dvoryanskoye sobraniye*—in every province-town for meetings of the provincial nobility. It also served as a club.

the occasion was apparently to be explained by the fact that the school was going to display its own poet before the authorities and local society. First of all, the teacher of literature, Shavrov, made a speech which I cannot remember at all, and then on to the platform stepped a short boy with a big, curly head. In a strained sort of voice he read with sharp barks and a strong accent a poem which spoke of 'a miraculous deliverance'. The poem was high-flown and pretentious. It began with a question like 'Whither flow our people's noisy waves?'—and then informed us that:

> Terrible news runs through Russia
> Of an evil design on our Tsar . . .
> A miracle took place before our eyes,
> Our crowned Sovereign was saved from harm.

When he'd finished, the poet presented a scroll of his poem to the Governor's wife, and the bishop kissed the Jewish schoolboy on the head.

As far as I can remember, Karakozov's attempted assassination did not at that time awaken any questions in me or in my immediate contemporaries. The Tsar was something colossal, far removed from us, one of nature's elements! And people who shot at him also seemed elemental. It was something unreal and far away from our daily life. And so a ceremony about it was an official ceremony, it was for show, it was artificial—we sensed this clearly. Leaning over the rails of the high gallery, we watched with ironic curiosity as the poet Varshavsky walked up to the bishop's hand and the bishop touched his rough, curly head with his lips. On the boys' faces there was either indifferent curiosity or derision.

The poem appeared in the school magazine, which was permitted to be printed in the provincial printing-works. I think two or three numbers appeared. The Provincial Chancellery and the editing-board of teachers were killing the free flight of school poetry, and it languished. In this magazine sanctioned by the authorities the school Muse appeared as if on an official visit, constrained, tense, ill at ease, whereas at home she was much more interesting.

Varshavsky's poetic talent, which had begun its flight with solemn odes and presentations to people in high places, was not destined to bloom. In the school magazine another poem of his appeared, not so solemn in content this time, entitled: 'The Cap'. It was about the school cap which, according to the poet, decorated curly young heads thirsting for knowledge and attracted to them 'the eyes of the belles'. Another boy, Iordansky, wrote a sharp criticism of it, in which he refuted all the poetic suppositions of Varshavsky point by point. 'The poet asserts that the cap attracts pretty girls', he wrote in a very energetic style. 'But I say: on the contrary!'

Coming one day to see my brother, the critic read his article out and when he said, 'But I say: on the contrary!' his eyes flashed and he banged his fist hard down upon the table. For some time after this I imagined 'critics' as people angry at authors for something and telling them 'on the contrary'.

The literary venture of the Zhitomir High School apparently ended on this dispute, and with it the name of the poet Varshavsky passed into oblivion.

PART TWO

Rovno

5
Autocratic Russia

ONE DAY DURING OUR FIRST AUTUMN IN ROVNO[1] CAME the news that the Governor was coming on a tour of inspection. In Zhitomir we somehow hadn't heard much about the Governor. Here, however, he seemed a sort of comet moving on a frightened world. The local policemen began bustling about, the streets were better cleaned, the long-broken street lamps were repaired, the floors in the court-house was washed, and work was tidied up and finished in a hurry. My father was tense. His work was in exemplary order, but he felt he had two defects: his wife was Polish, and he had been struck with partial paralysis. The new Governor's words had already gone round the province: 'I am a healthy manager and I need healthy men.' In Dubno he had already discharged a sick judge from office.

He arrived and stayed with the Inspector of Police. He had been in the police-station and in the local Treasury. My father set out for the court wearing a new uniform with the Vladimir decoration in his button-hole. My mother blessed him on his way, making the seditious sign of the Polish cross, and sent us to watch what happened. Our observation point was in the tall weeds of the kitchen-garden opposite the windows of the magistrate's room. 'He' had not yet arrived, but two or three dandified officials were already digging into files, which the court secretary was respectfully handing them. The evening drew on. Candles were lit in the room—an unusual number of candles. The

---

[1] The family moved to Rovno in the middle of June, 1866.

prism,[2] cleaned with chalk, was gleaming. There was a stern and solemn atmosphere. The rumbling of a carriage was heard at the gates. My father and his subordinates got up from their seats. The Assistant Inspector of Police himself opened wide the door of the room, and in the doorway appeared the gallant figure of the general, polished up, as it were, and gleaming like the prism itself. Behind him were the sleek faces of Special Commission officials, and behind them through the doorway we could see the chancellery—unrecognizable, all lit up, and in trepidation. We ran as fast as we could to mother.

'Well, what happened?' she asked anxiously.

'He went in and gave father his hand. Asked him to be seated.' There was a sigh of relief.

'Thank God,' and my mother made the sign of the cross.

'Thank God,' repeated women behind her, who'd gathered anxiously in our house. 'Will anything happen to our husbands?'

I do not remember any clear, critical questions stirring in my mind after witnessing this, my first inspection—questions like: what was the nature of this menace? Why did the young, dandified officials belonging to the Governor's suite behave with such familiarity, while my father, so worthy and universally respected a man, stood before them like a pupil at an examination? Why could that important general destroy without cause the living of a whole family without anyone asking him to give account whether it had been done rightly? Such questions did not exist for me, or for those around me. The Tsar could do anything, the general had his power from the Tsar, and the fops had theirs from the general. So, they too could do anything. Thank God they hadn't destroyed everything, hadn't dismissed everyone, but had left some in peace. When the comet had moved away into space and the results of its passage were calculated, it turned out that the dismissals, transfers, and displacements had, for the most part, struck unexpectedly, senselessly, fortuitously, like a whirlwind, which rips out one tree and leaves another untouched. The power of Authority was illustrated very clearly every time, but it was a purely elemental power, from which, because of its very nature, nobody expected rationality or appropriateness. In some families there were thanksgiving services, while other families wept and tried to guess who had denounced, slandered, whispered. It was the slander-mongers who were guilty. They had brought on the storm. The storm itself was not to blame. It was supposed to be like that by the laws of nature. Society, meek and

[2] The prism (called the *zertsalo* or mirror) stood on a table in the court-room. On its three sides were glued printed copies of statutes of Peter the Great.

without rights, merely bent, as under the onslaught of a whirlwind.

The holidays were coming to an end. I was faced with an examination for entrance to the Rovno Modern High School.[3] This was an institution of a special transitional type, which soon disappeared. The reform of D. A. Tolstoy,[4] dividing secondary educational establishments into 'classical' and 'modern', had not yet been completed. In Zhitomir I had started studying Latin only in the third class, but after me it was started in the very first year. The Rovno High School, on the other hand, was being transformed into a Modern High School. Latin was disappearing class by class, and the third form, into which I was to go, was already following the 'modern curriculum', without Latin and with a preponderance of maths. Only when I was actually in Rovno did I gather from the conversations of adults that I would have no access to a university, and that henceforth mathematics would be my main subject of study.

In the examination I passed brilliantly in all subjects, except maths: I appalled the algebra teacher with my stunning ignorance. The senior master, shaking his head perplexedly, said to my father, who had been waiting for me, 'We don't mind taking him, but it would be better if you had him do the Classical curriculum.'

[3] Modern High Schools (*real'nye gimnazii*) had been created by a statute of 1864. Latin and Greek were not taught in them, and they were intended to prepare pupils chiefly for higher technical institutions, while the Classical High Schools prepared their pupils chiefly for the universities. Korolenko is mistaken in saying it was Tolstoy who divided secondary educational establishments into 'classical' and 'modern'. In fact, Tolstoy looked with disfavour on the Modern High Schools (see note 4 below). However, Korolenko is quite right in ascribing to Tolstoy policies aimed at restricting the numbers eligible for university education.

[4] D. A. Tolstoy, appointed Minister of Education in 1866, shortly after Karakozov's attempt on the life of Alexander II, was a convinced and uncompromising reactionary. In his activity as Minister of Education he found support in the writings of the prominent publicist M. N. Katkov. Tolstoy (supported by Katkov) was of the opinion that a science-based education was 'one of the chief reasons for the materialism, nihilism and baneful self-conceit, which have taken so strong a hold of our student youth'. The only effective means of combating this evil was, in Tolstoy's view, the setting up of a very strict classical system of education in the high schools.

In his work Tolstoy was opposed by a number of men in the Council of State, and it was, in fact, only in the field of secondary education that he succeeded more or less fully in implementing his plans. His triumph came in May 1871, when, despite the opposition of a majority of the Council of State, Alexander II gave final approval to Tolstoy's projects and they became law. By the Statute of 1871 governing secondary education, the Modern High Schools were reduced to 'modern schools' (*real'nye uchilischcha*) with an extremely narrow technical course lasting for six years only. The Statute marks an attempt to preserve the social ascendancy of the nobility. It was in direct contradiction to the spirit of the Statute of 1864 which had created the Modern High Schools alongside the Classical, and had broadened the curriculum of the Classical High Schools.

This was absolutely true, of course, but it had no practical meaning whatsoever. My father, like other civil servants, had to educate his children in the place he worked. This meant, in effect, that the choice of further education was predetermined not by the intellectual bent of the children, but by the chance transfers of the fathers.

At this time there was as yet no talk of school politics, nor were there any 'evilly disposed agitators' stirring up young people. A drowsy quiet surrounded the school. Now and again newspapers brought echoes from a far-off world, but they were alien to the little town and its interests, which were centred around the old castle and the lively, white school-building.

Only once did an opportunity arise on our horizon for something like disturbances with a political colouring. This was in 1867 or 1868. The town was awaiting the Governor-General Bezak.[5] He was to stay with the Inspector of Police, on High-School Street, and so the Inspector's apartment became the focus of everyone's attention. From behind fences, from the lane, and from various other covers the inquisitive townspeople looked out timidly. Directly opposite the Inspector's house was the house of the widow Savitskaya, who took in boarders from the school, and as classes were now over, a little group of boys had come out into the small garden to view the scene. The street had a solemn and subdued appearance, as befitting the occasion. Policemen were standing upright as posts by the front steps. Everything had been swept, tidied, cleaned up, and there was a throb of anticipation. It must have been around five o'clock when a fireman came galloping up from the direction of the prison on a sweating horse, and soon a carriage drawn by three horses in the Russian manner came into view. The driver skilfully reined in the horses, the little bell tinkled, the Assistant Inspector and the policemen rushed to unfasten the door, but . . .

Something unexpected and awful happened. The carriage suddenly opened on the other side and from it emerged a stout, shortish figure in a military uniform, and amid general alarm and bewilderment His Excellency the Commander of the forces of the Kiev Military District and Governor-General of the South-Western Region ran across the street with short little steps away from the Inspector's house. After a few seconds the reason became clear: the Regional Commander's sharp eyes had spotted from inside the carriage that the schoolboys, standing in the small garden, had not taken off their caps. They naturally corrected this oversight immediately, except for one, the land-

[5] He was Governor-General of the South-Western Region from 1865 to 1868. A fanatical Russifier. (Korolenko's note.)

lady's brother—a little fellow in the second year, I should think—who
gazed with wide-open eyes and gaping mouth at the strange general,
who for some unknown reason was tripping heavily across the street.
Bezak ran into the garden, seized the boy by the ear and handed him
over to the policemen who had run up:

'Put him under arrest!'

The police-station was close by, and the frightened boy was
quickly locked up in a cell where drunks were usually detained until
they sobered up. Only then did the stern Commander proceed to the
Inspector. The news of this incident spread through the whole town in
a matter of minutes.

That particular day I had been kept behind after class for something
or other, and was returning home later than usual, carrying a pile of
books that were constantly edging out of my grasp. The street was
empty, except for some blue-uniformed figures ahead of me, whom a
policeman was ushering away from the Inspector's house. Here and
there a solitary figure would flit across the street like an arrow, and disappear. . . . When I had come up to the Town Treasury and turned
the corner, I came across a group of schoolboys, about ten in all.
Among them I noticed the Peretyatkevichs and the Domaratskys,
representatives of two interrelated Polish families. They were for the
most part a bit old for school and well-off, and adopted a fairly inde-
pendent position with regard to the school régime. Not long previously
one of them had been obliged to leave the school. On seeing me, they
blocked my road and plied me with questions:

'They let you through? Well, what's happened? Is it true that
Savitsky has had a fit? Have you seen his sister?'

'What are you talking about?' I answered in bewilderment, looking
at their flushed faces.

'A fine friend!' jeered the elder Peretyatkevich. 'Where have you
been all this time, then?'

'In detention.'

'Ah! That's different. So, you don't know that Bezak caught
Savitsky by the ear and flung him in jail. Go home and call your friends
into the street.'

The story had an electrifying effect on me. In my mind I pictured
vividly the simple-hearted figure of Savitsky, with his peaked cap and
naïve eyes. The memory evoked a keen feeling of pity and something
else besides—dark, vague, confused and fierce. A fellow pupil not in
the punishment-room, but in a cell, ill, helpless, alone. And put there
not by the senior master. Another power, enormous and elemental,

was now awakening the feeling of comradeship, and the heart involuntarily quivered from its summons. What was to be done? I ran home, threw down my books, failed to find my brothers and rushed headlong into the street again. There was no sign of the Peretyatkevich and Domaratsky boys. They must have gone off somewhere to deliberate. But groups of boys were wandering about the square, stunned by what had happened and not knowing what to do. The police weren't even succeeding in driving them off High-School Street. They were talking, questioning each other and recounting in various forms what had taken place. They were coming together and dispersing in an anguished state of mind. Some of the most enterprising had reached the window of the cell through the hedge of the neighbouring garden and had seen Savitsky lying on a bench. The policeman on duty had covered his face with a dark rag.

It is hard to say what might have ensued had the Peretyatkevich boys managed to formulate and present some definite plan, such as going in a crowd to the Governor-General or throwing stones at the windows of the Inspector's house. Perhaps nothing would have happened, and we would have dispersed and gone home, bearing within our hearts a bitter awareness of our powerlessness and hatred. And only, perhaps, in the night the windows of the Governor-General's room would have shattered, giving occasion for repressions against the seditious school.

But before this could be determined, something else happened. From his house on that same street the headmaster Dolgonogov came out, formally dressed, imposing, and straight as a rod. He was wearing a cocked hat and a sword. He had been appointed only a short time before, and we did not know him very well. In fact, we didn't get to know him any better later on. He was a Great Russian, and for that reason there was no russifying fanaticism in him; he was just—at times he admitted the school authorities were wrong in their clashes with the boys—and he was strict. But for us he was still an official of the Pedagogical Department, a precise, conscientious formalist, exacting towards himself, the teachers, and the boys. As it proved, he had, besides, a consciousness of his own dignity and of the dignity of the profession he was serving. That is the way this man appears to me now, as I remember him on that significant day.

At that moment there was something resolute and sternly calm about his whole figure. He clearly knew what he had to do, and walked among the agitated groups of boys like a big ship among little dinghies. Replying to their bows, he only said, 'Go home, children, go home.'

And there was that in his air which made the boys feel that they really were children, and could rely on that calm, serious man.

He thus went into the house where the Governor-General was staying. Three minutes later he came out, accompanied by the Assistant Inspector, who respectfully ran in front and side-on to him, holding his hat in his hand, and they both proceeded to the jail. The Assistant Inspector opened the door, and the headmaster went in to his pupil. Then the school doctor arrived, accompanied by Didyatkevich, while another supervisor escorted Savitsky's frightened sister, whose face was red from crying. There was something reassuring and impressive about the sight of the police-yard full of men in the uniform of the Ministry of Education, and even the lame Didonus, who was fussily running in and out of the police-station, seemed near and dear to us at the time. And when another supervisor, the big, red-haired Butovich, a very good-natured man, though always rather under the influence, came out to the gates and said, 'The headmaster asks all the boys to return home!'—in a moment there wasn't a single school-uniform to be seen around the police-station or the Inspector's house.

The details of the scene between the headmaster and the Governor-General were recounted in local official circles. When the headmaster went in, Bezak, glowing red-hot like a field-gun that has been firing for a long time at enemy positions, went for him straight away:

'What's this you've got! Disorders! Disrespect! Polish boys don't take their caps off in front of authority!'

'Your Excellency,' said Dolgonogov coldly and firmly, 'at another time I should be ready to listen to anything you might wish to say, but now before all else I require the prompt release of my pupil, who was unlawfully arrested near the police-station. I have already sent a telegram to my superiors about the occurrence.'

Bezak looked distractedly at the headmaster and ordered the immediate release of Savitsky.

At one of the card evenings at our house the local officials began talking about the episode. Everyone sympathized with and was rather surprised at Dolgonogov. Some thought he would come off badly for it, while others surmised that this Dolgonogov must have a strong pull in Petersburg. My father said in his usual quiet yet categorical manner:

'Guess on! The man simply acted on the basis of law, that's all!'

'But—Bezak! Appointed by the Tsar himself!'

'We are all appointed by the Tsar,' my father rejoined.[6]

[6] In *Russian Wealth* (1908, No. 3) there were the following additional lines at this point: 'Apparently, this episode had no adverse consequences for Dolgonogov.

Dostoyevsky, in one of his *Diaries of a Writer*, tells of the impression a meeting with a courier on a postal route made on him as a young man. The courier was standing in the open carriage and thumping the driver on the neck without stopping, and the driver was furiously whipping the horses, which sped with mortal terror in their eyes along the straight road past the striped distance-posts. To the young Dostoyevsky the spectacle seemed to symbolize Autocratic Russia as a whole, and, possibly, contributed to his having to stand by the scaffold awaiting execution.[7] In my mind the figure of Governor-General Bezak became symbolical in the same way. A great fissure immediately appeared in my integrated picture of the elemental nature of authority. On the one hand was a powerful satrap seizing a frightened schoolboy by the ear; on the other there was the law, separate from power, but arming a humble headmaster for battle and victory.

6

The Yellow-Red Parrot

EVEN NOW, WHOLE DECADES LATER, I STILL OCCASION-ally dream of myself as a pupil in Rovno High School. . . . The familiar, quick ring of the school-bell echoes in my ears, and I know the

---

He remained about another eighteen months in Rovno, and was then transferred to Moscow—that is to say, he got a big promotion. They were dark times, but "the bases of law" had far greater importance then than later. The Ministry of the Interior had not yet managed to swallow up all the other Ministries, as at present.'

[7] In 1847, as a young man, Dostoyevsky had joined the Petrashevsky Circle—a group of men who met regularly at the house of M. V. Butashevich-Petrashevsky to read and discuss proscribed literature. In April 1849 the members of the circle were arrested, and twenty-six of them, including Dostoyevsky, were sentenced to death. On 22 December 1849 the condemned were bound to posts and blindfolded. The death-sentence was then read to them, and the soldiers were given the order to take aim. Only at this point were the condemned informed that their sentences had been commuted. This had all been done on the order of Nicholas.

old caretaker has gone to the corner of the school building, where the swaying bell is fixed on two tall posts, and is pulling on the long rope. The insistent, hurried, almost breathless sound of the bell soars over the smooth surface of the ponds and enters the pupils' lodgings. There is a rapid clatter of feet on the planked footways, and the gate, its pulley weighted with stones, squeaks and bangs. . . . The noise swells, like a tide, and then becomes intermittent. The colossal senior master, Stepan Yakovlevich Rushchevich, walks by, the yard becomes silent, and only I am still running across it or entering the empty corridors with the unpleasant awareness that I am late and that the towering Stepan Yakovlevich is looking sternly down upon me.

I also sometimes dream that I am sitting at a desk and waiting for a test or to be called out to the blackboard to give an answer—and then I am weighed down by the usual awareness of being in some way un-prepared and at risk. Such impressions are so durable. And it is no wonder. I spent five years in the Rovno High School and two years in the Zhitomir one. Counting 250 days a year spent either in class or in Church, and four to five school hours a day, that makes a total of about 8,000 hours during which I and hundreds of other young hearts and minds were in the direct power of a few dozen teachers. The hushed school-building during those hours seems to me now a kind of enor-mous resonator, in which a chorus of teachers tuned in a certain way the hearts and minds of hundreds of future men. And I should like, at least in outline, to describe the basic, prevailing music in that chorus.

When I was in Zhitomir in the second class we had an art master, the elderly Pole Sobkevich. He always spoke Polish or Ukrainian, and had a fanatical love for his subject, considering it the fundamental basis of education. One day, when he was angry with the whole class for something or other, he seized his brief-case from the desk, raised it high above his head and flung it on the floor as hard as he could. With his blazing eyes and mane of grey hair, he was like Moses breaking the tablets. 'Blockheads! Sheep! Donkeys!' he shouted in Polish. 'What's the point of all your grammatics and arithmetics, if you don't under-stand the beauty of the human eye!' Perhaps it was primitive and funny, but we didn't laugh. From the powerful figure of the old artist there passed, like a whirlwind, over the class of uninformed youngsters the breath of fanatical belief in his subject, in the higher meaning of art. . . . When he went up to a boy who was drawing and moved his thumb over the paper, saying: 'Aha! This is the way . . . can you feel it, son? It gets round just here. That's it—now stronger, thicker! Aha! You see: it's come to life, it's looking!' it seemed that under his gestures living forms were beginning to swarm on the paper and one had only to catch them.

Another figure, again while I was in Zhitomir: the priest Ovsyankin. He was as white as milk, with superb dark-blue eyes, in which an expression of kind uneasiness shone. And when I had to answer his questions and he looked into my eyes in this way, it seemed to me that he was searching in me for something with tender concern, something necessary and important not only for me but for him too.

Finally, in Rovno, I heard stories about a certain teacher of physics. He too must have been a forceful personality in his way, since stories about him passed from generation to generation. He was 'a natural philosopher' and materialist. In his opinion, physical laws did or could explain everything. He carried out experiments with the enthusiasm of one who looked upon each of them as a revelation, raising the curtain of universal mystery, and in the staff-room he had carried on a passionate dispute with the priest, opposing geological periods to the six days of the creation.

The art master Sobkevich was taken away from us at the end of my first year in the Zhitomir High School: 'russification' had started, and he could not get used to speaking only Russian in class. However hard the poor old fellow tried, he couldn't get anything 'to become round' or 'come to life' in Russian. And, anyway, his whole original personality fitted badly into the frame of a state institution. Ovsyankin was also soon replaced by the scripture teacher[1] Solsky, who was dry and strict. Finally the Rovno natural philosopher was removed following a report by his protagonist, the priest, who thus restored the authority of the Book of Life.

However different these figures may be, they all seem to me now to possess one feature in common—belief in what they were doing. The dogmas were different. Sobkevich probably rejected physics along with grammar before the beauty of the human eye. Ovsyankin was just as indifferent to the beauty of human forms as to the beauty of exact knowledge, and the physicist, no doubt, would have been quite ready to argue with Ovsyankin about the creation of the world. The content of belief was different, but the psychology was the same.

Now—a striking figure of a different kind: he was a teacher of German, a distant relation of mine, Ignaty Frantsevich Lototsky. He came to Zhitomir from Galicia before I had even entered the boarding-

---

[1] *Zakonouchitel'*, the master in charge of religious instruction, was always a priest. The catechism (*zakon bozhiy*) was a compulsory subject, except for non-Orthodox pupils.

school. He had a degree from a foreign university, giving the right at
that time to teach in our high schools. At the Rykhlinskys' somebody
laughed in his presence at foreign degrees. Lototsky got up, went out
of the room, came back with his degree and tore it to pieces. Then he
went to Kiev and passed a new exam in the university there. After that
he got a post in Zhitomir High School and married one of my aunts.
She was thought very fortunate. After a time, however, we children
began to notice that our cheery aunt often came to the house with eyes
red from crying. She would shut herself up in a room with my mother,
tell her something and start crying again. If on occasions, visiting her,
we happened to get a bit high-spirited, the study door would open
slightly and in the gap would appear a clean-shaven face with brilliant,
bulging eyes. That was enough: we quietened down immediately and
sat down in corners, while our aunt went pale and trembled. If I am not
mistaken, it was then that I first recall hearing the word 'tyrant'.

Everyone, however, recognized him as a model teacher and forecast a brilliant career for him. He was a typical *bratushka*,[2] such as in a
few years under Tolstoy filled our Department of Education, but with
the advantage that he spoke Russian superbly. Always immaculately
dressed, well-shaven, and without so much as a speck of dust on his
shining uniform, he appeared in class on the dot and walked to his desk
with measured steps. There he would stop and look round the class with
his brilliant, bulging, alert eyes. Under his gaze everything became
hushed. It would be hard to imagine a teacher with greater authority
over a class. This was the ideal of discipline in the usual sense of the
word. The boys were afraid of him, and prepared their work more
thoroughly for him than for the other teachers. His voice had great
weight in the Council. The gaze of every Inspector rested with pleasure on this figure who, with his strictly precise and authoritative ways,
seemed the very model of a civil servant.

However, the boys had not taken long to notice the model teacher's
weaker sides, and caricatured him more frequently and more successfully than any other teacher. It was well known that he had not missed
a single lesson in six or seven years' service. He always walked down
the corridors with the same goose-stepping stride, holding his body
unusually erect. He always took a fixed number of steps from the
classroom door to his desk. For some time now the boys had noticed
that if he happened to arrive at the door on the wrong foot, he would

[2] A 'brother-Slav' (ironical). Under Tolstoy emphasis was laid on Latin and
Greek in the high schools. Because of a shortage of Russian teachers of Classics, it
became necessary to bring in teachers from abroad. The majority were Czechs.

take a step back and correct himself, like a soldier who has broken step. At his desk he always adopted the same initial pose.

If at this time someone made a sudden movement or started talking with his neighbour, Lototsky would stretch out his hand and, curiously bringing together the index finger and the little finger, would point to the corner, pronouncing the offender's name quickly, shouting the last syllable, and missing out almost all the vowels: 'Kr-ch-nkó . . . Vrshv-sky . . . Abrm-vich . . .' This meant that Abramovich, Kirichenko and Varshavsky were to go to the corner. Silence, total, oppressive, grim, reigned in the classroom, broken only by the sharp, quick questions of the teacher and the hurried answers of the pupils. In a word, it was rather like the penal servitude of a model pedagogic order!

But even in penal servitude men dig tunnels and make breaches. It turned out that there were significant chinks in this ideal and apparently tight-sealed authority of my stern uncle over the class. One day, soon after I had entered the school, the register was being called out, and the pupil Kirichenko happened not to be present. When Lototsky called out his name, the boy sharing Kirichenko's desk got up, stood strangely taut and still, and rapped out, obviously mimicking the teacher's manner: 'Kr-ch-nkó . . . not pres-e-ént.' This aping was so obvious and so insolent that I looked with dread and astonishment at Lototsky. He hadn't noticed anything and continued rapping out name after name. His metallic voice resounded amid the silence, along with the short replies: 'Here . . . here . . . here . . .' There was an ironic twinkle in the boys' eyes.

On another occasion Lototsky set about explaining the declension of adjectives, and immediately a barely noticeable ripple of anticipation ran through the class. The boy next to me nudged me with his elbow. 'Here comes "the parrot",' he whispered. Lototsky's brilliant eyes ranged over the class, but once more there was not a sound or a movement from the desks.

'Der gelb-rothe Pap-gaj,' he said slowly. 'Right! Nomi-native! Der gelb-rothe Pa-pa-gaj. Genitive! Des gelb-rothen Pà-pa-gà-a-aj-én . . .' Peculiar jumping notes started appearing in Lotosky's voice. He had begun to scan, obviously enjoying the rhythm. With the dative case the teacher's voice was reinforced quietly, stealthily, encouragingly by the chanting voices of the whole class.

'Dem . . . gelb-ro . . . then . . . Pà-pa-gà-a-aj-én . . .'

On Lototsky's face there appeared an expression reminiscent of a cat, when it's being tickled behind the ear. His head was falling back, his big nose pointing at the ceiling, and his thin, wide mouth was open like a sweetly croaking frog's. The plural was got through amid a thunder of noise. It was a veritable orgy of scansion. Several dozen voices were hacking the yellow-red parrot to pieces, throwing it into the air, stretching it out, rocking it, raising it to the very highest notes, then lowering it to the lowest. Lototsky's voice had long been drowned, his head was resting on the back of his easy-chair, and his white hand with a dazzling white cuff was beating out the rhythm in the air with a pencil, which he was holding in two fingers. The class was as if possessed, the boys were mimicking their teacher, throwing their heads back, like him, rocking back and forth, pulling faces, and leering. Two or three desperadoes even jumped up on the desks.

Then suddenly—no sooner had the last syllable of the last case ended, as if cut off, when the class was again transformed, seemingly by magic. The teacher was once more sitting at his desk, erect, strict, alert, and his brilliant eyes were darting over the desks like lightning. The boys were sitting stone-still. Only I, caught unawares, was looking at everything with mouth agape. Kryshtanovich gave me a nudge, but it was too late. Lototsky called my name sharply and distinctly, and pointed to the corner with two fingers. And once again several lessons passed amid benumbed order, until Lototsky hit on the yellow-red parrot or some other hypnotic word. The boys had evolved by some instinct a whole system whereby they imperceptibly drove their teacher to such words. It was like a struggle between two hypnoses, and victory in this struggle inclined to the side of the mass. Lototsky, it seems, sometimes felt that something was not right, and before the scansion and after it his eyes would range over the desks with suspicious alarm. But the tense silence allayed his suspicions, and, besides, the chorus began and grew so stealthily, so gradually, so imperceptibly. Sometimes, attracted by the strange shoutings of the yellow-red parrot, the astonished faces of the supervisors or the senior master could be glimpsed in the corridor through the glass door. But when Lototsky went from the classroom to the staff-room—reserved, cold, unapproachable, and aware of his exemplariness—no one could bring himself to mention to him the fact that his class at times resembled a mad-house.

One day his wife came to see my mother urgently. She was alarmed and said that 'Ignatiy has had trouble in school'. This probably meant that the senior master had finally made up his mind 'to bring to my colleague's attention the fact that . . .'. Lototsky had flared up, as on the occasion when his degree had been laughed at, and shortly afterwards he moved to Chernigov. It transpired, however, that the yellow-red parrot had followed him. By the same instinct the boys there too had sensed traits of fatal automatism in him. To the hypnosis of discipline they replied with counter-suggestions. The pattern took firmer and firmer possession of my uncle. His walk became more and more wooden, his explanations assumed set forms, in which the boys knew in advance not only the sentences and words, but even the stresses. They mimicked him with an insolently-respectful air, and the parrot thundered out more and more loudly and more and more often. In the end the fatal bird destroyed a career that had begun brilliantly. Lototsky moved from school to school and gave up four years before his pension.

Of course Lototsky obviously had certain congenital peculiarities, which were fostered by the stultifying influence of school routine. On other people the effect was not so complete or so dramatic, but nevertheless when I recall the endless succession of hours spent within the school walls, it seems to me that the tense stillness of those hours is shattered every so often by the maniacal shouting of the yellow-red parrot.

Now the class of the French master, Lumpi. A Swiss by birth, he had somehow or other landed in Rovno and had been teaching there for forty years. He had no family. His whole world was the classroom, the staff-room and his apartment a few yards away from the school. For forty years at fixed times he had taken automatic steps along those few yards to the school and back. To see Monsieur Lumpi outside this area was very rare indeed. He spoke Russian badly. His explanations amounted to a few stereotyped formulas, which were remembered for their curiosity-value. He still retained a sufficient degree of attention and persistence, and thus his grammar class, which he separated from translation, was a real torment. However, through his robot-like shell there sometimes burst something from another life. He loved to talk about his past. In every class there was a particular expert who could wind Lumpi up, as a clockmaker winds up a clock. He had only to touch a certain spring and Lumpi would put his dull book aside, his small eyes would burn with an oily light, and endless stories would start.

There was something vaguely legendary, fantastic about them. He had been born in Switzerland. He had gone to school under the great Pestalozzi. Pestalozzi was a teacher of great genius. . . . Lumpi had been a gunner in the school corps. . . . He would relate all this in a childishly moved voice, lisping, screwing up his eyes, and raising up the palms of his hands with their unbending fingers. The boys, who knew the whole story (sometimes from their fathers), devoted themselves to other activities, swotting up the next lessons or playing various games. The poor Swiss went on talking and talking. He had known the great Napoleon. At a difficult moment of his life he had done him a service by acting as a guide through the Alps. They had climbed across perpendicular cliffs, greasing their hands with resin. The great Napoleon had tapped him on the shoulder and said, 'Mon brave petit Lumpi', which meant: 'Lumpi, my man, you are a fine fellow'. If the theme was beginning to dry up, the winder-up would mention the African desert. Lumpi would obediently set off into the African desert and travel over the burning sands, where he had seen a boa-constrictor swallow a young ox. The horns of the hapless quadruped had stuck out through the skin of that monster, enfolded like fingers in a glove. In this way they had moved before the spectator's eyes from the snake's neck to its stomach. The welcome sound of the bell cut short this endless journey, and the questions on grammar remained unasked. But sometimes the winder-up would not manage to give the cue and Lumpi's fantasy would fade away. He would give a deep sigh, his hand would move to his mark-book, and in the remaining five or ten minutes he would manage to put down a few twos.[3] The first to suffer would be the winder-up.

Of all the teachers, the geography master Samarevich was most like Lototsky, only he had nothing of Lototsky's imposing and assured manner. Thin, tall, yellow, dried-up, he invariably spoke in a ringing, half-plaintive, half-threatening drawl. Like Lototsky, he walked along the corridors with big steps, as if he were stepping over puddles. He wouldn't grasp the metal handles of the doors until he'd pulled down his sleeve and covered the palm of his hand with cloth. On arriving at his desk, he always stopped, like Lototsky, in one pose, holding a clump of hair which nature had caused to stick out on his throat (he had no beard or moustache whatsoever). The class fell silent. The atmosphere would get oppressive. Samarevich's thin neck, with its large Adam's apple, would move like a snake in his wide collar, and his dry, splenic eyes ran over the boys from left to right. In the expression of his eyes and face one sensed an objectless malice and suffering. In this unpleasant minute, following Samarevich's prickly gaze, a kind of numb rigidity came over the class. One had only to move, turn round, shift one's foot, and an ominously singing voice would ring out: 'Prefect! Take him to the dark punishment-room.' There was no 'dark'

[3] The Russian scale of marks was from nought to five; a two was thus a poor mark.

punishment-room, nobody took us there, and we would simply spend our time in some empty classroom. This was very handy, especially for those who hadn't done their work, but we seldom availed ourselves of it: the experience of that minute was too unpleasant. Still, we could achieve the same result in another way: we had only to open a pocket-knife and start cleaning our nails. Samarevich would begin waving his arms about, like a gaunt scarecrow in a gusty wind, call the boy a waster and send him out.

The boys learned his lessons. Not because they were interesting, but because it was too painful not to be able to answer his questions. Hence, as a teacher, he was in good repute. No one, of course, bothered to think what he, in fact, substituted for a knowledge of the wide world. Once, before a geography exam, I had a strange, what they would now call symbolical, dream. On an enormous floor lay an endless geographical map with coloured squares, the winding lines of rivers, the black circles of towns. I was looking at it and couldn't remember either the names or which of those circles was famous as a timber centre, and which traded in wool and tallow. And in the middle of the map—in a whirl of mist—there was a head on a thin, twisting neck and prickly eyes were looking sharply at me waiting for an answer. The boundless oceans with their storms, the vast expanse and beauty of the world, the tireless and varied activity of men—was all replaced by the idea of a sheet of paper with spots, lines, and circles.

There was something sinister and tragic about this dried-up figure. He met a terrible end. He was transferred from our school to another town, and there his wife—a kindly woman, whom fate had tied to a maniac—obtained permission to take in boys as lodgers. It was assumed that this would be her special department, but Samarevich soon extended his authority over this too and made it like a nightmare. It was related that every evening before going to bed he would go round the whole place at the head of his retainers, looking into every corner, under tables and settees. Then he locked the rooms and slept with the key under his pillow. One night—it was in the eighties—there was a knocking at the doors of the locked fortress. Arming his retainers with brooms and pokers, Samarevich went down to investigate. The banging from outside continued and was, as it turned out, 'in the name of the law'. When the door was opened, gendarmes and policemen came in. A search was made of the belongings of one pupil and he was arrested. This completely stunned Samarevich. For several days he went about with a look of stupefied alarm, and one morning he was found dead. He had cut his throat. The gendarmes had seemed more terrible than the razor.

The Rovno teacher of German, Kranz: a short, spry man, with a face completely devoid of hair, he had the dried-up appearance of a fabulous lemur, consisting only of bones and sinews. This man, it seemed, had sought to make his subject completely unintelligible, and yet still get his pupils to master it. He had contrived to turn the whole of grammar into the learning of endings. 'Leóntovich,' he called out, purposely distorting the name and transferring the stress. 'Decline, der Mensch.' Leontóvich would get up and decline it, not saying words, but only endings: nominative—s, c, h; genitive—e, n; dative—e, n; accusative—e, n. Plural—e, n; and so on.

If a boy made a mistake, Kranz began mimicking him, grimacing and distorting the words in all imaginable ways. He asked prepositions through gestures: if he poked his finger down and stretched his lips into a sort of little trunk, you had to answer '*unten*'; if he raised his finger and made a face as if his eyes with their yellowish whites were following the flight of a bird— '*oben*'. If he ran quickly to the wall and slapped his hand on it—'*an*'. 'You. Is it "*at*" or "*jat*"? And should it be "*ali*" or "*eli*"?' The boy had to answer as fast as he could with the same gibberish. He turned the language of Schiller and Goethe into a senseless mixture of sounds and grimaces. This buffoonery was really humourless and malicious. One felt as if a lively, nasty, dangerous monkey was performing in front of a few dozen children. Perhaps to a bystander its movements and jumps would have seemed funny. But the boys felt that this jumping, squealing, gesticulating creature had very sharp claws, and power; until the bell. The bell was a real cock-crow dispelling a nightmarish vision.

In every class Kranz had particular boys whom he was especially eager to torment. In the first class Kolubovsky, a little fellow with a big head and fat cheeks, was the martyr. Coming into the classroom, Kranz would usually pull a face and begin sniffing with distaste. Everyone knew what this meant, and Kolubovsky went pale. In the course of the lesson he pulled these faces more and more often and, finally, addressed the class:

'What's smelling here, eh? Who knows the German for "smelling"? Kolubovsky! Do you know the German for "smelling"? And what's the German for "to foul the air"? And how do you say: "the lazy pupil"? And how do you say: "the lazy pupil has fouled the air in the class"? And what's the German for "a cork"? And how do you say: "We shall put a cork in the lazy pupil"? Kolubovsky, have you understood? Kolubovsky, come here, *komm hier, mein lieber Kolubowski*. No-ow!'

With comic gestures he proceeded to take a cork out of his pocket.

The poor boy blanched, not knowing whether to go out to the front as he was told, or run away from this evil clown. The first time Kranz gave this performance the boys couldn't help roaring with laughter. But when it was repeated there was sullen silence. Finally, one day Kolubovsky rushed out of the class in an almost hysterical state and ran to the staff-room. But there, instead of a coherent explanation, he could only shout words of abuse: 'Kranz is a rotter, a fool, a dirty skunk.' The senior master and the teachers were astonished at this outburst from the little fellow. When the matter had been cleared up by the reports of older boys, the Council drew Kranz's attention to the inappropriateness of his music-hall sketches.

For a time after this Kranz came to the first class yellow with rage and tried not to look at Kolubovsky. He did not talk to him or ask him any questions. But he couldn't keep it up for long: his clowning mania came out, and, though he didn't dare to repeat the performance in full, he would still sniff the air, grimace, call Kolubovsky out, and show him the cork from behind his desk.

It is with some hesitation that I have decided to add Mitrofan Aleksandrovich Andriyevsky, the teacher of Russian language and literature, to this collection. In outlook he was really closer to the type described at the beginning of this chapter. In his heart there burned enthusiasm, and belief. He devoted all his free time, all this thought and feeling to his never-ending thesis on *The Tale of the Host of Igor*.[4] Perpetually concerned about the obscure expressions in *The Tale*, he would walk along the streets of the sleepy town, without noticing anything around him and sometimes even forgetting why he had left the house. If one of his galoshes got stuck in the mud, he would walk on without it. On one occasion before my eyes the wind blew out the ends of his hood and one of them got stuck on the fence. The poor teacher, unexpectedly arrested in his thoughtful progress, calmly unwound the hood from around his neck, leaving it on the fence, and walked on unimpeded.

The boys felt a sort of condescending affection for him, but didn't learn his subject at all. He would explain things in a loose, confused way, and only livened up when he could draw an example from *The Tale*. His thesis got bigger and bigger, but he couldn't bring himself to have it printed as long as certain parts of *The Tale* remained unclear to

[4] The greatest work of Old Russian literature. It describes a campaign undertaken in 1185 by Prince Igor of Novgorod-Seversk against the Polovtsians. *The Tale* survived in a sixteenth-century manuscript, discovered in 1795, but it was destroyed in the Moscow fire of 1812. An edition of it had been published in 1800, and a second copy prepared, but both were faulty. As it stands, the work contains a number of obscure passages.

him. At times he really was very interesting, but this didn't happen often
in class. Under his absent-minded smile shone a child-like soul and,
possibly, an outstanding mind, which from loneliness and the emptiness
of life around him had departed into the impenetrable forests of *The
Tale.* He passed before us with his harmless eccentricity, without
leaving any deep mark, but also without ever provoking a single bad or
hostile impulse in anyone. In his thoughtful smile there was a gentle
humour, in class he occasionally came out with an apt judgement or
word, but even in the best pupils he did not manage to instil any idea
of 'the theory of literature'.

Of course, as well as maniacs like Lototsky or Samarevich, the
chorus of teachers that tuned our hearts and minds also contained voices
of a middle register, singing their parts more or less passably. And it was
they who did the main work, conscientiously and stubbornly pumping
factual knowledge from textbooks into our heads. This was, of course,
useful in its way, only this intellectual nourishment was carried out in
much the same way as with geese in cages: forcing down repellent food
which the poor bird refuses to take in sufficient quantities of its own
volition.

And that tender, delicate, living filament, which links the process
of learning with the eternal desire for knowledge and illuminates it,
bringing it to life, lay still or was touched only rarely, by mere chance.
Men with some originality, some individual substance, were out of
place in an official system which demanded dogmatic conformity. The
strong left, the weak conformed, and life in the sleepy town built around
the derelict castle took its toll. First, dreams of a thesis, of a transfer to
another place, then marriage, the sweetness of drowsy lassitude, cards
in the club, out-of-town walks, gossip, visits to the wine-cellar, from
which teachers emerged with arms round each others' shoulders and
unsteady steps, or to the little house past the hornbeam-tree where
teachers sometimes met their pupils from the senior forms.

One of the best teachers I ever knew, Avdiyev (whom I shall speak
of further on), put the following playful proposition to his class at the
beginning of his second year: 'Do any of you gentlemen have notes of
my first lesson last year? You have? Excellent. Test me, please: I shall
speak, and you must point out the sentences I repeat the same as last
year.' He started walking around the classroom, making up an introduction to literature, while we followed our notes. We had to stop him
every now and then, as he was departing from our synopsis and con-
structing his talk differently. Apparently, only once did someone spot a
repeated expression.

'Well, so far so good,' he said cheerfully. Then, sighing, he added: 'In ten years' time I'll be saying it word for word. Oh yes! You laugh at us and don't realize what a tragedy this really is. At first it's all so alive! You're still learning yourself, and looking for new ideas and vivid expressions. But, as the years go by, you grow stale and become set in a mould.'

A teacher grows stale and turns at best into a phonograph, transmitting information in a middle-register voice and with middling success from textbooks into heads. But in the chorus as a whole it is the squeaking falsettos and the mental dissonances of the maniacs, who have been pecked once and for all by the yellow-red parrot, which stand out most vividly. Who will assess the influence of that deadly automatic bird on the life and fate of the generations passing line after line through our secondary schools?

Our headmasters changed fairly often. For a long time the senior master was Stepan Yakovlevich Rushchevich, who was subsequently appointed headmaster. He too was a characteristic, one might almost say a symbolical figure. Towering, heavily-built, in a broad tunic and wide-legged trousers, he was a sort of bureaucratic mountain with a face that looked as if it had been hewn out of oak, and framed by a pair of greyish, official-style side-whiskers. His voice too was heavy and very loud, and it was on all these quantitative advantages that his authority in the school rested.

He usually summoned an offender to his room. You had to cover the whole distance between the door and the desk under his heavy, hypnotic gaze, which, as it were, enveloped the victim in something stifling, thick and viscous. Your feet stuck to the floor. It seemed an offence to walk towards him freely, and an even greater offence to stop. You would involuntarily lower your eyes, and yet you would feel close above you his huge, almost expressionless face, his big dull-grey eyes and two greyish side-whiskers. It was a sensation of something physically crushing, insensible, but imperious. There followed a minute of painful silence. . . . Then a question in a deep bass voice. . . . A timid negative answer. . . . Then suddenly the giant would get up to his full height and a hurricane of shouting would break out high above. Mostly Rushchevich would shout two or three sentences of no real importance; their whole effect was in his crushing height and the thunderous claps of his voice. This first moment was worst of all: you felt as if you were standing under a falling rock. You wanted to shield your head with your hands, efface yourself completely, fall through the floor. After this you would go to the punishment-room eagerly, as to a refuge.

Later on, in the senior classes, when the physical disparity between the pupil and the headmaster was less striking, Rushchevich lost some of his terrifying fascination. As I later became convinced, he was at heart a good, rather than a vicious man. In any case he was better than the average headmaster of later years, if only because internal politics[5] with secret recommendations and base political spying had not at that time entered the school to such a degree. Only he wasn't a teacher at all, and his overpowering size was his sole resource in the struggle for order and discipline. Small-scale, continuous partisan warfare constituted the basic tone of school life.

Early on winter mornings, when lights twinkle diffuse and sleepy in the misty gloom, a lame figure would emerge from the long, two-storey school building and, casting glances all around, would dart into the half-light. Dityatkevich' was an indefatigable hunter. . . . By seven o'clock pupils living in hostels were supposed to be sitting at tables preparing their lessons. This was not done very often, and the chief delight of illegal morning sleep consisted in the knowledge that somewhere in the mist the spy Didonus was stealing along the planked footways and falling with his galoshes in the mud, and was perhaps at that very moment looking through the window from the street. Mud, mire, rain, snow-storm, blizzard—nothing could stop the tireless detective. On the contrary, in bad weather the boys were especially susceptible to sleep and could be caught more easily. If, on looking in from outside, he saw a room in apple-pie order, he would go away disappointed, like a hunter who has made a mistake. Otherwise—he would appear suddenly in the doorway, cheerful, with eyes beaming, and demand the 'room-book' in a kindly, satisfied tone of voice. If in the darkness he noticed the huge figure of Rushchevich fairly near at hand, he would eagerly 'point' for him, putting him on to offending rooms. Stepan Yakovlevich would enter with grim solemnity and stand like a dark obelisk over the bed of the sleepyhead. I still remember the unpleasant moments of waking up under his fixed, heavy gaze.

When the boys had gone off to school, Didyatkevich went into the empty rooms, rummaged in trunks, confiscated cigar-cases, and wrote down everything he found in his book. Smoking, forbidden books (Pisarev, Dobrolyubov, Nekrasov—we had not heard of illegal litera-ture at that time), bathing in forbidden places, boating and walking

---

[5] As a result of the Statute of 1871 the Staff Councils lost all authority, and power was concentrated in the hands of the headmasters. Very strict discipline was intro-duced, students were subjected to a rigorous system of inspection, and encouraged to report on their schoolfellows.

[6] Dityatkevich, also familiarly called Didonus, was a supervisor.

after 7 p.m.—all came under the code of school offences. In their classi-
fication that same maniacal automatism could partly be felt: it was a
question not of the seriousness of the offence, but of the difficulty of
detection. In and around the town there were many ponds and little
rivers, but boating was forbidden, and a pool where flax was retted was
assigned for bathing. Naturally, the boys went boating and bathed in
the rivers or under watermill-locks with their spray and noise. Often, in
the middle of bathing, as we were diving happily into the river by the
Police Inspector's bath-house, a dark blue peak-cap suddenly appeared
out of the tall rye over the edge of the hill, and the hobbling figure of
Didonus came quickly down the path. We snatched up our clothes and
rushed into the reeds, like fugitives during the Tartar invasions. The
lame supervisor began running along the bank, like a brood-hen, calling
out names at random, telling us he knew us all and demanding surren-
der. We stood in the rushes, blue with cold, but didn't often give in. If
he managed to get hold of the swimmers' clothes, then we had to dress
and follow him to the senior master, and then to the punishment-room.
And the punishment corresponded always not to the seriousness of the
crime, which was obviously not great, but to the amount of effort wasted
in catching the offender.

After seven in the evening it was also forbidden to leave our rooms,
and when sunset came the little town with its streets and lanes was
transformed for the boys into a series of ambushes, traps, sudden attacks,
and more or less skilful withdrawals. The narrow lane linking the parallel High-School and Poplar Streets was particularly dangerous. On dark
autumn evenings it was very easy suddenly to bump into Didonus; and
sometimes, worse still, the senior master himself, hearing stealthy steps,
would flatten his back against the fence and suddenly at close range
flash a concealed lamp. These were frightening moments which were
related the next morning in class. Yet, I remember these strange con-
tests with gratitude. The high school failed to make the teaching interesting, it didn't try and didn't know how to use the surplus of nervous
energy and youthful spirit not swallowed up by cramming and the
mechanical attendance of uninteresting classes. We could have gone
completely stale from boredom or—as happened to many boys—been
turned into apparatus for automatic cramming, if this original sport had
not enlivened the monotony of life.

But I remember with special gratitude the wide ponds, smooth and
overgrown, and the little rivers that trickled quietly from one pond to
another. In summer, like pirates, we used to sail on them, trying to get
quickly across the open spaces, darting into the rushes, hiding under the

bridges, over which would pass the senior master's heavy tread or Dityatkevich's hobbling step. When autumn came and a thin film of ice started to cover the ponds, we would wait impatiently for them to freeze hard. I can still hear the modulating, glassy ringing of stones thrown from the bank across the thin ice. The ice became thicker. The swans, which would soon be taken away for the winter, are already standing on it. Then my brother and I put on our skates and try the ice, braving the danger of falling through or of ending up in the punishment-room. A week after our attempts Stepan Yakovlevich solemnly climbs down the bank on to the pond, the caretaker Savely tests the ice with a pick-axe, and finally skating is officially allowed. Every day after dinner hundreds of boys twist and turn on the pond, running together and running apart, and falling down amid laughter and shouts. Among the small-fry, like sturgeons in a shoal of little fish, the teachers sway awkwardly on their skates. There's the huge Petrov, like a falling tower, and even Lumpi, without skates and red with the frost, telling of how they used to skate in Pestalozzi's school. The German Glück, who replaced Kranz, couldn't learn for a long time even to stand on skates, and ordered himelf a pair with double runners. It was easy to stand on them, but hard to turn. The strong wind catches his small figure in a wide fur-coat and speeds him over the mirror-smooth ice straight to the river. We shout that the river is dangerous; the poor German waves his arms, his coat flies open, like a sail. In a minute he's on black, unsound ice, which cracks and gives way. Glück splashes into the water, fortunately in a fairly shallow spot. The boys tie their hoods together, line up, the lightest runs to the river and throws him the line. Then on command the whole chain, singing and shouting 'hurrah', pulls the drenched Glück to safety.

It's getting dark. Two caretakers, a supervisor, and the senior master circle the pond, driving off the lingerers. The ice is becoming deserted. The moon rises from behind the wide rushes, touching the edges of the old castle with its cold light; the whole surface of the pond glistens, occasionally cracking and groaning. Five or six dark figures are still twisting about on it. On the bank, or the steps of his house beside the school, a tall, dark shadow appears. It's Stepan Yakovlevich, watching the offending skaters. Several dark silhouettes come down from the school: there'll be a round-up. Dityatkevich, perhaps, is already coming up from the other side, from the island. But the moonlight is deceptive— they can't make out who it is skating. We give our pursuers time to get near and almost surround us, then quickly run to the dangerous spots. The ice rings thinner and thinner, we splash through yielding, water-covered ice, unfrozen water looms black nearby. Zh-zh-zhi . . . one after another, but keeping some distance apart, the fugitives run down the dangerous river on to another pond. The pursuers stop, deliberate, and more often than not go back. Their figures grow diffuse in the frosty gloom; and once more the squeal of steel against ice is heard on the smooth pond, as the silent circling in the moonlight continues.

From one of the best in the class I have long gone down to the middle and find it suits me better: ambition does not torment me, nor do average marks grieve me. Instead, on the pond on these moonlit nights you breathe so freely, and the imagination works so well as you move effortlessly along. The moon rises and looks into the empty windows of the deserted castle, catching a golden cornice, and bringing vague shadows into cautious movement. Something is stirring, breathing, coming to life. And then you sleep so soundly, although your homework isn't done.

Now, when I recall my first two or three years in Rovno High School and ask myself what was brightest and healthiest there at that time I have only one answer: a crowd of comrades, the interesting war with the school authorities, and—the ponds, the ponds. . . .

7

My Father's Death

WE WERE SPENDING OUR SUMMER HOLIDAYS IN GARNIY LUG,[1] when my mother, who had stayed in town, sent for us all to come home. Father was ill.

[1] *Garniy Lug*—the estate belonging to Korolenko's uncle, Captain Kazimir Tutsevich, who had married the eldest sister of Korolenko's mother. By a family arrangement one of the captain's sons, Aleksandr, lived with the Korolenkos during the school year, when he attended Rovno High School, and the Korolenkos spent the summer holidays in the country at Garniy Lug. In 1877 Aleksandr began working as a compositor in Petersburg, and in 1879 lived with the Korolenkos. On 4 March 1879 he was arrested with all the male members of the family (see Part Five, chapter 26).

The last few years he had become progressively weaker. He had long abandoned all his crazes, the study of languages, philosophy, veterinary medicine, and similar surprise-pursuits through which the lingering restlessness of his youth had previously been expressed. Yet even in the very last years of his life he conducted one more experiment. He had always shaved himself, and, as this became increasingly difficult for him, he thought of a more radical method: he bought small tweezers and plucked out hair after hair. 'I am rendering a great service to all officials,'[2] he said with a touching flicker of his old quiet humour: 'it's torture to have to shave three times a week. But this way—once they're plucked, it's over and done with.' At that time bald patches could be seen on his cheeks, but they soon grew hair again. He used the tweezers a second time, thinking that he could thus exhaust the growth of hair, but the results were the same. He had to admit that the project of becoming a benefactor of members of officialdom was not going to be successful.

He did not have long to go to his pension. With the dissatisfaction of youth he had twice given up work, and now lacked those two or three years to qualify. This caused him a great deal of anxiety: to hang on at whatever cost and leave a pension for his family was now his final aim in life. All his remaining strength, it seemed, was concentrated on this. He no longer looked to the sides of life's road—he didn't even arrange harmless card-evenings, or interest himself in the running of the household, or ask us how we were getting on at school. On getting up in the morning, he made the servant sponge him down with cold water, drank his tea in silence, put on his uniform and set off through our little yard for the court-house. There he always held himself in such a way that no one could notice his weakness. When my mother once sent me to him on some urgent errand during those working hours, I was surprised at his appearance. He was seated at his place imposing and brisk, receiving reports and giving out clear, precise orders. It was obvious that in his weakening hands he had firm hold of all the threads governing the functioning of the court. At this time, it was true, he had a good assistant, a man called Popov, who'd been sent fairly recently and who shared my father's view of his work. He was a good, efficient, honest man, whom my father regarded with respect and trust.

When he came home, my father weakened straight away and, as soon as he'd had dinner, went to bed. In the evening he again worked, and then, following the doctor's advice, walked around the room for half an hour, moving his legs with difficulty and tapping his stick. He

[2] Government officials were not allowed to grow beards.

had to qualify—qualify at whatever cost by serving out the remaining few months. All the reserves of energy and will, which this not altogether ordinary man possessed, were now directed at that task.

When the Jewish messenger brought us mother's letter, we were in a high-spirited mood, which evaporated immediately. That same day we rode off on village horses to the nearest posthouse. While the stage horses were being harnessed, my younger brother and I walked over to a copse of trees by the roadside. It was an unusually light autumn evening, when the twilight fades almost unnoticed and a full moon is suddenly shining overhead, almost in the middle of the sky. This again was one of those moments in my life which has remained in my memory in its every detail. Everything around me seemed filled with a peculiar, gentle, sad awareness. The leaves of the nut and alder trees were whispering quietly, the breeze caressed my face, from the posthouse yard came the tinkling of the bell being tied to the shaft—and all these restrained sounds, the murmuring of the trees, the fields, the posthouse, seemed to be speaking in their own way about the same thing: about the end of life, the awesome significance of death.

My cousin,[3] who had just finished military school as an officer, came up to us quietly and put his arms around us: 'He may get better,' he said. But I was aware that there was no hope, that it was all over. I felt it in the deep sadness all around, and was surprised that the previous day I had been capable of not feeling it, and even that very morning had been so happy and carefree. And for the first time the question rose in my mind: what would happen now to our frail, ailing mother, and to us?

The bell started tinkling louder, the wheels began grinding, and a minute later we were driving along the white ribbon of road, stretching into the night gloom, towards the dark shapes of distant coppices, which were just as indistinct and obscure as our future, but bathed in a glow, like youth.

We found our father still alive. When we greeted him, he could not speak and only looked at us with eyes full of suffering and tenderness. I wanted to show him in some way how deeply I loved him for his whole life and how I felt his grief. Therefore, when they had all gone out, I went up to his bed, took his hand and pressed it to my lips, looking into his face. His lips moved, he was trying to say something. I leaned over him and heard two words: 'Don't worry . . .'

---

[3] Vladimir Kazimirovich Tutsevich (1849–1921), elder brother of Aleksandr, and an artillery officer. In his youth he served in Kronstadt, and Korolenko's mother and sisters lived with him there for a time. When Korolenko was in Kronstadt (1876–7, see Part Five, chapter 21), he became very close to his cousin, but in later life they met only rarely.

The next morning he was dead. A great crowd of people walked behind his coffin, including a lot of poor people, small tradesmen, and Jews. The military commander sent a band, and to the accompaniment of a funeral march, the flapping of the banners in the wind, the restrained tramping of the crowd the coffin was borne to the cemetery. The old soldier raised the turnpike beam high, and from the windows of the prison the pale faces of the prisoners looked out; they had known this man well, who was now lying in his coffin with a pale face, dressed in his uniform. 'May his memory live for ever.'[4] The thud of earth on the lid of the coffin, my mother's stifled sobs, and in the Rovno cemetery under the wall of the humble wooden church rose a fresh mound.

The burden of the family fell straight away on my mother's shoulders. My father had still been a few months short of the full term of service, and so a great deal of trouble was involved in obtaining even a small pension. For more than thirty years' service the widow of a magistrate who had been known for his exceptional honesty in those dark times received a widow's pension of somewhere around twelve roubles. Together with the children this made about seventeen roubles a month, and that thanks only to the strenuous efforts of two or three good people, who respected father's memory and helped mother with their advice. In order that we might somehow finish our schooling, my mother asked immediately after the funeral for permission to take in boarders from the school, and from that time on, sick, frail, and alone as she was, she tried to ensure our future with the true heroism of a woman. Our father could rest in peace in his humble grave in the churchyard: his wife, as far as she was able and even more than that, fulfilled the task which had so tormented his suffering soul at death.

Her life changed sharply and suddenly. From being 'the Judge's wife', one of the foremost people in the town, she became a poor widow with a crowd of children and no means (she only managed to obtain her pension a year later). She had to ask favours of people who only a short time before had thought it an honour to know her, and as a school landlady she depended on the school authorities. True, with very few exceptions, I cannot recall cases where the townspeople made my mother feel this change; there were, indeed, touching examples of kindness and help.

My father's grave was enclosed with a railing and was soon overgrown with grass. Over it stood a wooden cross, and a brief inscription gave the meagrest details of his life: born, had been a Judge, died. . . . His orphaned family had no money for a stone. As long as we were in Rovno, my mother and sisters took garlands of flowers to the grave

---

4 Words from the Prayer for the Dead.

every spring. Then we all dispersed to various places. The grave stood alone, and probably no trace of it now remains.

What remained of a life, its mistakes and sufferings? At that time I still shared my father's beliefs and thought that his accounts had been satisfactorily squared: he had been a religious man, all his life he had prayed, done his duty, defended the weak against the strong as far as he was able, and had honestly served the law. God would recognize this—and now, of course, he would be happy. Later on, this simple faith evaporated, and I would picture his humble grave: he had lived, hoped, striven, suffered, and died tortured by anxiety for his family. What significance did his life, his aspirations and his premature integrity have now?

'He was an eccentric,' complacent townspeople concluded more than once, 'and what happened? He died and left paupers behind him.' People of simple faith in God and in His laws also said such things. But not so much as a shadow of such doubts ever troubled my mother or indeed any of our family.

8

The New Men

I MUST HAVE BEEN IN THE FIFTH CLASS WHEN A NUMBER OF young teachers came to our school at more or less the same time. They had gone through high school under Pirogov and had just come out of university.

One of the first to appear was Vladimir Vasilyevich Ignatovich—a teacher of chemistry. He was a short young man, fresh from university, with a barely noticeable little moustache, chubby red cheeks, and gold-rimmed spectacles. There were boys who looked older than their teacher. He spoke in a thin, reedy voice, in which there still seemed to be boyish notes. In class he was somewhat diffident, and frequently

blushed from shyness. He treated us politely, was diligent in his teaching, seldom asked questions on work he had set, evinced little regard for
marks, and gave his lessons like a professor reading a lecture. His voice
was tender, not firm. We wished he would speak at least one note
lower in pitch and more strongly. The first result of his system was that
the class almost stopped working, and the second that the boys occasionally became slightly cheeky to him. The poor young man had come to us
with idealistic expectations and was paying for the overall system,
which induced rudeness and cynicism. Still, this did not last long. One
day, when the class was making a noise and Ignatovich was straining
his soft voice to no avail, one of us thought he heard him call us a flock
of sheep. Other teachers often called us a flock of sheep, and sometimes
worse things than that. But that was other teachers. They were habitually
rude, and we habitually submissive. Ignatovich himself had given us a
taste for different treatment. One of the boys, Zarutsky, a very nice lad
really, but easily swayed by the mood of those around him, stood up
amid the noise.

'Sir,' he said loudly, flushed and insolent. 'Apparently, you said that
we were a flock of sheep. May I reply that—in that case. . . .' The class
suddenly became so hushed that you could hear a pin drop. 'That in that
case—you are a sheep yourself. . .'

The glass vessel Ignatovich was holding in his hand rang against the
retort. He blushed to the roots of his hair, and his face trembled somehow helplessly with anger and injury. For a moment he didn't know
what to do, but then replied quite firmly, 'I did not say that. You were
mistaken. . .'

This simple reply took us aback. A murmur ran through the class, the
meaning of which was hard to determine straight away, and coincided
with the bell. The teacher went out, and the boys surrounded Zarutsky.
He stood in the middle of them, looking stubbornly down, aware that
the sympathy of the class was not behind him. To be openly insolent to
a master was usually considered little short of heroic, and if he had
openly called one of the old ones—Kranz, Samarevich, Yegorov—a
sheep, the Council would have expelled him and the boy would have
been given a rousing send-off. As it was, however, the atmosphere was
heavy, bewildered, unpleasant.

'That was dirty, friend,' someone said.

'Let him complain in the Council,' Zarutsky replied morosely.

The complaint was a sort of moral escape for him: it would immediately put the new teacher on a level with the old ones and justify his
piece of insolence.

'He will complain, too,' somebody said.

'Of course he will. Do you think he'd let him off?'

'No, he won't complain.'

'He will.'

This question now became the centre of the drama. Two days passed and nothing about a complaint was heard. If there had been a complaint, Zarutsky would first of all have been summoned by the senior master Rushchevich for one of his thunderous reprimands, or would perhaps even have been ordered to go straight home pending the Council's decision. We waited. The day the Council met had passed. There was no sign of a complaint having been made.

The chemistry lesson came along. Ignatovich came in somewhat uneasy, looked down at his feet more than usual, and his voice kept breaking. It was obvious that he was trying to get on top of the situation and was not really sure that he would succeed. Through the teacher's seriousness one glimpsed a youth's sense of injury, and the lesson got under way in an oppressive, tense atmosphere. After ten minutes or so Zarutsky stood up with paling face. It seemed that in getting up he was raising a weight upon his shoulders, the strain of which could be felt by the whole class.

'Sir,' he said with some effort amid complete silence. The young teacher's eyelids quivered under his spectacles and his face flushed. The tension in the class reached a peak. 'I . . . last time . . .' Zarutsky began in a hollow voice, and then, with sudden abruptness, ended: 'I apologize.'

He sat down, looking as if he'd given another piece of cheek. Ignatovich's face lit up, though he was still scarlet to the roots of his hair. He said simply and unselfconsciously, 'I have already told you, gentlemen, that I did not call anyone a sheep.'

The incident was closed. It was the first time such a clash had ended in such a way. The new teacher had passed the test. We were pleased both with him, and—almost unconsciously—with ourselves, because we had not taken advantage of the young man's weakness, as we would have of the weakness of one of the old ones. The episode itself soon faded from our minds, but a thread of special sympathy, formed between the new teacher and the class, remained.

There were two or three other teachers, whom I didn't know. One felt that a group of new men had appeared in the school, and the general tone was raised. One or two of the better teachers, who had been there some time but had felt isolated, now revived, so to speak, and we heard echoes of arguments and differences of opinion in the Council. In that mass chorus, where up till now the shrill falsettos of the automatons and maniacs had dominated the voices of the middle register, a new note made itself heard.

And then another man appeared, on my recollections of whom I should like to dwell a little longer.

Our former teacher of Russian literature, Mitrofan Aleksandrovich Andriyevsky, had somehow found time to get married and had moved for family reasons to another school. We saw him go with regret, as we liked his good nature, his gentle smile, occasional apt remarks, and touching devotion to *The Tale of the Host of Igor*. For a while the literature post remained vacant, and lessons were taken by Stepan Yakovlevich Rushchevich, who conceived the idea of teaching us to read expressively. He himself read somehow ponderously, in a stentorian voice; he read with a concern for the meaning of what he was reading, but with completely groundless pretensions to expressiveness. He required us to imitate his intonations exactly, and this we felt ashamed to do: it seemed like hypocrisy. At the same time, literature was always traditionally considered the most interesting and intellectual subject. We thus waited for the new teacher all the more impatiently. One day we heard a rumour that he'd already arrived. His name was Avdiyev and he was young. Someone had seen him in the town and was talking about it just before the beginning of a lesson which we thought Rushchevich would again be taking. But almost at the same time as the bell rang, the classroom door opened and on the threshold appeared the new teacher. He stopped for a moment, calmly watching as we, caught completely unawares, scrambled into our proper seats; then he walked to his desk, giving us a nod on the way. As this was the first lesson of the day, he waited in silence for the boy on duty to read the usual prayer; then he sat down and opened the register. His face was slightly morose, and he called out the names in a displeased tone of voice, occasionally stopping at a name and peering at its bearer. When he'd finished this, he stepped down from his seat and walked unhurriedly up and down the lines of desks, thinking about something apparently unrelated to the present moment and to the fact that fifty attentive, inquisitive eyes were fixed on him, studying his every movement.

He was a young man, possibly only about three years older than Ignatovich, but more mature and solid. His face was not an altogether ordinary one: even features with a Greek profile, large, expressive eyes, full lips, a thin moustache and a small, light-coloured beard. All this made him rather handsome, but for some reason made an unfavourable initial impression on the class. Besides, he was wearing narrow trousers and low-heeled boots, while we considered wide, Cossack-style trousers and high-heeled boots to be the height of elegance. Among us, narrow trousers were worn only by notorious slaves of fashion and dandies in the sixth and seventh forms. We managed to take stock of all this, right down to the last button and too wide lapels of his dark blue dress-coat, while he was walking around the room. It seemed strange and rather impudent that he was behaving in so off-hand a manner, as if we, the class, were not there at all.

When he'd walked up and down a few times, he stopped, as if driving away the irrelevant thoughts that had been occupying him, and once more looked closely at the class.

'What have you been working on lately?' he asked. We looked at one another.

'Stepan Yakovlevich has been reading us . . .'

'What?'

'*Krylov's Fables.*'

The new teacher raised his eyebrows ever so slightly. 'Why?' he asked. The question seemed odd. He ought to ask the senior master himself. But somebody guessed.

'To fill up the lessons.'

'Ah! And did he make you read as well?'

'Yes.'

'I see. Who can read well?'

The class was silent. We could all read loudly, some of us very rapidly, but had never heard good reading; and Stepan Yakovlevich's expressive reading seemed artificial to us.

'Come on!' he said impatiently, moving his shoulders, 'Why don't you answer?'

'We all read the same,' I blurted out with annoyance, but said it too quietly.

The teacher turned to me and asked point-blank, 'Do you read well?'

'No,' I replied, blushing. 'I didn't say that.'

'But that's what I was asking about. You read!' he said to a boy who had the book of fables in front of him.

The boy got up, opened the book at random, and began to read. The teacher frowned with displeasure. 'Poor,' he said. 'And you all read like that? Isn't there anyone who can read? Well, what did you do before that?'

'The theory of literature—Minin's book,' several voices replied.

'And what is *slovesnost*?'[1]

---

[1] A subject taught in high schools, which aimed at giving a systematic knowledge of Russian literature. The teacher of this subject was often simply called the *slovesnik*. However, the word has rather a wider meaning than the English 'literature'

Silence.

'It comes from *slovo* ['word'],' somebody ventured.

'Let's suppose it does—but what is a word?'

'The expression of a thought.'

'Not always. You can say a lot of words and still talk nonsense.... And what is thought?'

Silence.

He looked at us with a comical grimace and said, 'Each of you think to himself and say whether he's ever really thought in his life.'

This was an insult. A low murmur ran through the class.

'We all do,' someone said.

'You all do what?'

'We all think', several voices answered irritably. The teacher was beginning to get on our nerves.

'You "think",' he mimicked, hunching his shoulders. 'You're thinking how long it is to the bell. And you *think* that that's what *thought* is. You are mistaken. "Thought"—you understand: not mere wondering, but thinking in the true sense—is something quite different. Get out your books and take this down.'

Walking slowly around the class, he began with the simplest definitions. At first, in his eyes and the furrow between his brows, that same morose displeasure could be seen. But as he developed his theme, he plainly became carried away by it. His dark face became flushed. The lesson had obviously not been memorized: the words were forged spontaneously and reached us still warm. Occasionally he would pause awhile, searching for the right word, the right expression, and would then continue, getting more pleased all the time. It was rather hard for us to take it all down. He spoke slowly, but didn't wait for us to catch up. And we really wanted to take it down. The remaining part of the lesson passed in this way, and when the bell rang I was surprised the lesson had ended so quickly. Avdiyev finished off, took the register and walked out with a nod. An animated buzz of conversation filled the class. The general impression was unfavourable.

'So that's the animal!' one said.

'Better watch out with that one . . .'

'Where did they dig that devil up?'

'He insulted us, you know . . .'

We were talking like this when the bell for the second lesson rang. I remember the history master Andrussky came in. He too was a new man and had come a few months before Avdiyev. He was a short young man with an intelligent, energetic face. In class he behaved formally,

rather stiffly, but not unsympathetically. The hour's lesson he carefully
divided into two unequal parts. In the first part he asked questions and
put down marks. When he dipped his pen in the ink-well to put a mark
down, his face became serious and thoughtful. It was clear that he was
carefully weighing up all the pros and cons and when he subsequently
entered a figure in the mark-book in his firm hand, we felt that it had
been put down after due consideration, with complete fairness. Twenty
minutes before the end of the lesson he reached for the textbook and,
opening it, invariably began his exposition by saying:

'Now then. We ended up last time on such-and-such. Now we'll go on.'

And, keeping to the book, he laid out the material of the next lesson
conscientiously, thoroughly, drily. We knew that he put forward his
opinion just as circumstantially in the Council. It was always condescending and unshakeable. We respected him as a man and conscientiously prepared the work he set us, but history seemed an extraordinarily boring subject. Some time later he weighed up his work as a
teacher just as honestly and fairly, gave himself an unfavourable mark
and changed his occupation.

Now, as always, I looked at his square, energetic face with pleasure,
but behind his monotonous voice I heard the deep voice of the new
literature teacher with his caustic observations. 'Mere wondering' and
'thought' . . . yes, it was true. The difference was clear now. Yet, there
was something irritating about him. How would things develop?
I quietly took out my notebook and began reading the lesson I'd taken
down, risking a reprimand from Andrussky. The lesson was well-
constructed and interesting.

Three days later news reached the school from the town that the new
teacher had been seen drunk. Something stabbed at my heart. He missed
the next lesson. Some said caustically 'because of a hangover'; others,
that he was settling into his flat. Whatever the reason, everyone felt a
pang of disappointment when Stepan Yakovlevich again appeared at
the door, with his register in his hands, for 'expressive' reading.

Two days after that another sensational piece of news hit the class,
like a firework. Among us was a boy called Domanevich: he was older
than us, for he had been kept back at school, and seemed completely
grown-up among the small-fry surrounding him. He was a decent enough
fellow, but held himself aloof, like a professor who accidentally happens
to be sharing a desk with youngsters. This particular day he appeared in
class with an especially grand and arrogant air. He let drop casually
(though one sensed his satisfaction in the matter) that he and the new
teacher were already 'friends'. They had become acquainted in rather

special circumstances. The evening before, Domanevich had been returning home in the moonlight from friends of his. At the corner of Poplar Street and the high road he had noticed a gentleman, who was sitting on a stack of logs, rocking from side to side, exchanging wise-cracks with surprised passers-by and singing Ukrainian songs.

'His voice, I tell you, is magnificent!' the narrator added with a certain pride for his new-found friend.

Domanevich, who hadn't recognized the new teacher in the merry gentleman, was passing by, when he was called: 'Mr. schoolboy! Come over here!' He went over and, recognizing who it was, bowed. 'What's your name?' Domanevich had to 'admit I was a bit scared'. It was late, it was forbidden to leave rooms in the evening, and this new fellow seemed strict. He might be drunk but he could still report to the Head. Nevertheless, summoning up courage, Domanevich gave his name.

'Very pleased to meet you,' the teacher said politely, offering his hand. 'I'm Avdiyev, Veniamin Vasilyevich, the teacher of literature. At pre-sent, as you see, slightly drunk.' As he said that, he burst out laughing ('he's got an amazingly infectious laugh') and, leaning heavily on the pupil's arm, he got up on his feet and asked to be taken home, as he had not got to know the town yet.

'Hell's bells,' he said, laughing, 'you've got queer streets here, and the wine is strong. . . . Before I knew what was happening, I was out of the town . . . I went back . . . and logs or something started rolling under my feet. . . . Ha-ha-ha. . . . My head is always clear, but my legs, damn them, get drunk . . .'

Domanevich escorted the teacher to his flat overlooking the pond, supporting him by the arm all the way. At home Avdiyev was very nice, offered him a smoke and a small glass of red wine, urging him at the same time never to get drunk or fall in love. The first was harmful, the second—not worth it.

The story created a sensation in the class. 'What kind of behaviour is this?' I thought with an aching heart, which was all the more strange in that Avdiyev seemed even less likable to me now.

'Well, old son,' someone drew the practical conclusion, 'you needn't bother with Russian the whole year.'

'Why do I need to bother with it anyway?' Domanevich replied casually. 'I know everything he dictated from last year. I've been "thinking" since Form One.' And, giving us his usual, slightly scornful glance, he proceeded slowly to his seat. Now he had outmatched us in one more respect: the teacher could hardly have approached one of the small-fry for that sort of service. . . .

The bell rang. The door opened. Avdiyev came in and walked to his desk with easy, carefree steps. Everyone's eyes were fixed on the teacher, who, as we all knew, had been drunk the previous evening and had been taken home by Domanevich. Not the slightest trace of embarrassment was to be seen on his face. He looked fresh, his eyes were sparkling, and a slight smile was playing on his lips. Looking at his face intently, I suddenly felt that it was not at all unsympathetic, but on the contrary—intelligent and handsome. Yet—yesterday he had been drunk. Avdiyev opened the register and started calling the names.

'Vardensky. . . Zabotin . . . Domanevich.'

'Here,' replied Domanevich with a lazy movement which scarcely raised him from his seat. Avdiyev stopped for a moment, screwed up his eyes to look at him as if remembering something, and then went on. When he'd finished, he leaned both elbows on the desk and asked, 'Did you manage to get down everything I dictated last time?'

'We did.'

'And of course, you've learned it? Yes? Well now—Mr. Domanevich.'

Domanevich's name had an electrifying effect on the class. All heads turned towards him. The poor fellow looked round, bewildered and helpless, as if not realizing what was going on. An involuntary ripple of laughter passed along the class. The teacher's face was serious.

'Mr. Domanevich is going to tell us what the first lesson was about. How did we approach the definition of our subject? We are listening.'

Domanevich got up, stood for about half a minute with lowered head, and then said confusedly, 'Sir, I . . .'

'Yes?'

'I didn't manage to prepare today.'

'Today? And what about yesterday? And the day before?'

'Well, I . . . er . . . haven't prepared at all.'

'At all? That's a mistake, Mr. Domanevich, a mistake. Work is given to be done. You had three days to do it. Was there good reason why you didn't?'

Domanevich did not answer.

'It's a pity, but'—he took out his pen and opened the mark-book—'with great regret I am forced to give you nought.'

As he entered the mark, he glanced at poor Domanevich. Our veteran had such a bewildered and hurt look on his face that Avdiyev suddenly started to laugh, throwing his head back a little. He did, indeed, have an unusual laugh—melodious, infectious, ringing—and when he laughed, even, white teeth, glistened beneath his small moustache. We never liked to laugh at a schoolfellow's misfortune, but on this occasion Domanevich himself started to laugh. With a gesture of resignation, he sat down.

The complication had been cleared up straight away. We realized that what had happened the day before had no bearing on his teaching and that his authority had been firmly established once and for all. By the end of this second lesson we were entirely under his authority. When, as in the first lesson, he had freely dictated further explanations, he sat on his chair and opened a thick book in an elegant new binding, which he'd brought in with him.

'Now we'll relax. I've already told you what thinking with concepts means. Now you'll hear how some men think and explain the most complex things through images. You already know Turgenev?'

To our shame, many of us knew Turgenev only by name. We got books either from a Jewish booklover, who, at a moderate price provided us with tattered copies of the novels of Dumas, Montepin, and Gaboriau,[2] or from the school library. One evening a week we would tumble out into the dark, resonant corridors, which seemed strange and mysterious in the doubtful light of the tallow candle-end which Andriyevsky used to carry in front, and go up the stairs, exchanging jokes and wisecracks with the good-natured teacher. Each time he would fumble with the key in the lock of the library door, until it finally gave a loud click and opened on to a large room, the walls of which were lined with enormous cupboards. The contents of the cupboards were extraordinarily meagre: they contained mostly devotional books, *Sunday Leisure*, and for some reason *Soldiers' Reading* and *The World-wide Traveller*.[3] We would grumble, and Andriyevsky would try to laugh it off, sometimes very wittily, provoking general mirth. We would end up by asking to read Livingstone's *Journey*, then Cook's *Voyages*. Arago's[4] *Journey*, *The Journey of Baker-Pasha*.[5]

Anyway even I who, comparatively speaking, had read a good deal, though quite haphazardly, and already knew *The Three Musketeers*, *The Count of Monte Cristo*, and even Eugene Sue's *Wandering Jew*—even I knew Gogol, Turgenev, Dostoyevsky, Goncharov and Pisemsky only through a few stories that had happened to come my way. At that time

---

[2] Emile Gaboriau (1835–73), a writer of popular French detective novels.

[3] *Sunday Leisure* (*Voskresniy dosug*), an illustrated weekly, which first appeared in 1863. *Soldiers' Reading*, probably *Soldatskaya beseda* (1858–67), a bi-monthly. *The World-wide Traveller* (*Vsemirniy puteshestvennik*), an illustrated weekly (1867–78).

[4] Jacques Arago (1790–1855), a French explorer.

[5] Sir Samuel White Baker (1821–93), British explorer, discoverer of the Albert Nyanza.

my reading was simply entertainment and had taught me to regard
fiction as interesting descriptions of things that didn't really happen.
Sometimes I tried to fit the actions and conversations of the heroes of
books into the conditions of life as I knew it, and found that no one ever
spoke or acted as they did. What I remembered of works by Polish
writers, which I'd read earlier, stood out by comparison. They were
closer to life. Somewhere, perhaps not far away and not very long ago,
people *could have* spoken and acted like that, but all the same they didn't
speak and act like it any more.

Avdiyev began reading in an ordinary tone of voice, as though he
were continuing a normal, everyday talk:

Mardary Apollonovich Stegunov is a short, plump and bald little old man
with a double chin, soft hands and a fair-sized paunch. He is a great host and
a great jester. Winter and summer alike he goes about in a striped and wadded
dressing-gown. His house is of old-fashioned construction: in the hall, as is
proper, there is a smell of *kvas*, tallow candles and leather.

This was 'Two Landowners' from *A Sportsman's Sketches*. The narrator, still a young man, and influenced by new ideas, is staying with
Mardary Apollonovich. They have had dinner and are sitting on the
veranda, drinking tea. The evening air is still. 'Only occasionally was
there the stirring of a breeze which now, dying away around the house,
brought to our ears the sound of rhythmically repeated blows from the
direction of the stable.' Mardary Apollonovich, who has just raised a
saucer of tea to his mouth, stops, motions with his head and with a
kindly smile starts to echo the blows: 'Chooki-chooki-chook! Chooki-
chook! Chooki-chook!'

It turns out that the 'scamp of a butler', a man with large side-
whiskers, who, not long before, had served at table in a long-tailed
frock-coat, was being whipped in the stable. Mardary Apollonovich
has a kind face. 'The most fierce indignation would not withstand his
clear and kindly gaze.' On leaving the village, the narrator meets the
scamp himself: he is walking along the street, husking sun-flower seeds,
and when asked why he has been punished, he simply replies: 'Served
me right, sir, served me right! We aren't punished for nothing here.
Our master—you won't find his like in the whole province . . .'

Amid absolute silence Avdiyev read the last sentence: 'That's Old
Russia!' Then he said a few, very simple words about serfdom and the
horror of a system in which this two-sided indifference is possible. For
the first time the sound of the bell was unexpected and unpleasant.

From that day on, literature ceased to be merely an entertainment in my eyes, and became a fascinating and serious business. Avdiyev possessed the instinctive sensitivity of youth and—talent. Everything he read, said, and did assumed a special significance for us. The history of literature stood out from its misty distance as an important, significant subject, organically paving the way for future revelations. The short time towards the end of the lesson, when Avdiyev would open a book he'd brought with him and read out an excerpt, a scene or a poem, became a necessity for us. In his reading there was never any trace of artificiality. It always began simply, and we didn't notice how or where Avdiyev had passed to pathos, which hit us like a series of electric shocks, or to humour, which produced a whirlwind of laughter in the class. He read a passage from *Dead Souls*, and we rushed to Gogol. He loved Nekrasov especially,[6] and I never heard Nekrasov read in quite the same way thereafter.

One day Avdiyev appeared in class serious and displeased. 'We are required to send quarterly essays to the District Office for inspection,' he said with special significance. 'They will be used to judge not only your writing, but also your way of thinking. I want to remind you that our syllabus ends with Pushkin. Everything that I've read to you by Lermontov, Turgenev, especially Nekrasov, to say nothing of Shevchenko, is not in the syllabus.'

He didn't say anything else, and we didn't ask. The reading of works by new writers went on, but we understood that someone wanted to take from us everything that was awakening so many new emotions and thoughts; someone felt he had to close the window through which so much light and fresh air was pouring, clearing the stuffy atmosphere of the school.

'It seems I'll be leaving you soon,' Avdiyev said with some sadness a little later, when I called on him.

'Why?' I asked in a disappointed voice.

'It's a long story and perhaps not worth the telling,' he answered. 'I'm just not suited here.'

A new headmaster, Dolgonogov, of whom I spoke earlier, had come. Everyone, beginning with the colossal senior master and ending with Didyatkevich, had immediately felt the hand of authority over them. Dolgonogov was feared and respected, especially after the incident with Bezak, but nobody really knew him. Somehow he was

---

[6] Nikolay Alekseyevich Nekrasov (1821–78), one of the greatest Russian poets. His poetry, expressing love and idealization of the peasantry, was directed at the Russian intellectual and had great influence on the young generation of the 1860s and 1870s.

remote from us by his position. One could easily have guessed that it would be hard for Avdiyev to get on with this inflexible man. Moreover, Avdiyev did not change his behaviour in any way. He continued to read us in class the most modern writers; we continued to visit him at home in groups; the town continued to talk about his occasional antics.

I sensed what the matter was, without any explanations from Avdiyev; and I began to find Dolgonogov's stiff figure unpleasant. On one occasion, when I met him on the planked footway, I gave way to him but was backward and casual in bowing. He turned but, seeing that I had, in fact, bowed, he immediately went on with firm, measured steps. He was not small-minded and did not pay attention to nuances.

Shortly after this, the Kiev Director Antonovich visited us. He was an unassuming old gentleman in the uniform of a retired soldier, with very simple and sympathetic manners. He arrived unobtrusively, without any fuss at all, and came to school on foot, when the bell rang, together with the teachers. He also came to lessons at the very beginning, stayed right through to the end, and his presence was almost forgotten. He was very pleased with Avdiyev's lessons. He stayed in town a few days, and during that time the news spread that he was being transferred to the Caucasus as Director of an educational district there.

One day, as I was going home with an armful of books, I was overtaken on High-School Street by Avdiyev. 'What sort of walk is that,' he asked with a laugh, 'ambling along? You ought to straighten yourself up a bit. And why aren't you working at your maths?'

'I'm no good at it, Veniamin Vasilyevich . . .'

'Nonsense! Nobody's asking you for mathematical discoveries, and anybody can do school maths. You can't be an educated man without the discipline of mathematics.'

At this point Antonovich came out of the headmaster's house on the opposite side of the street. After saying good-bye to the headmaster, who had seen him to the door, he crossed the street and walked on a little in front of us.

'Here we are,' Avdiyev said quietly; 'my fate will now be decided.' Giving me a friendly nod, he quickly caught up with the Director and, raising his hat slightly, said in his open, pleasant voice: 'I have a big favour to ask of you, sir. I'm the teacher Avdiyev. I teach literature.'

'I know,' the old general said in a tone of voice the significance of which was unclear. 'What favour?'

'They say you're being transferred to the Caucasus. If that is so . . . take me with you.'

'Why so?'

Avdiyev smiled and said, "Since you remembered me, permit me to assume that you also know the reason why it . . . doesn't suit me to stay here.'

The old general stopped a moment and looked into the face of the young teacher who had approached him so freely. Then he strode on, and I heard him say quietly, 'All right. If you like.'

I felt awkward overhearing them, so I fell back. At the end of the street Antonovich said good-bye and turned right. I again caught up with Avdiyev, who was happily whistling.

'Well, the matter is settled. I knew you could talk to him as a human being. In Tiflis, so they say, the boys go to school with daggers, so there's all the less reason to carp at trifles. Well, think kindly of me.'

'Surely it won't be . . . so soon?' I asked.

'Yes, in three weeks' time.'

Three weeks later he left. At first it seemed to me that the school had suddenly darkened. Recalling our conversation on the street, I brushed up my maths, as best I could, and tried to straighten my walk.

Sergey Timofeyevich Balmashevsky was appointed in Avdiyev's place. He was a tall, thin young man, with a somewhat sunken chest and a slight stoop. He had a pleasant face, with a kindly smile on his thin lips, but his appearance was spoiled by his eyes, which were short-sighted with inflamed, swollen eyelids. It was said that he had worked terribly hard, which was why he had a stoop, a sunken chest, and permanent styes on his eyelids.

He had no sparkle, and there were now no new, unexpected and fascinating ideas, such as would come up from time to time in Avdiyev's lessons. Balmashevsky would conscientiously explain: such and such a work is divided into so many parts. In the first part or the introduction such and such a subject is treated; and in dealing with it, the author has recourse to this or that apt comparison. 'Literature' once again became only another subject, the rays of light, which it had so recently been radiating, disappeared. Once again there was no focus in the Rovno Modern High School for our thoughts and feelings. And again the screeching of the yellow-red parrot stood out sharply above the voices of the middle register.

Soon, however, an episode occurred which raised the new teacher in our eyes. One day, two or three boys from poor families were expelled for non-payment of fees. I was going unconcernedly to school with a boy called Gavrilo Zhdanov, when we met one of these boys who had been sent home. When we asked him why he was coming from school, he turned away sullenly. He had tears in his eyes.

That same day after school Gavrilo came to see me and together we worked out a plan: we decided to impose a tax on the daily consumption of buns during the main break. On making an approximate calculation, we found that by applying a certain amount of fiscal energy we could collect the necessary sum of money fairly quickly. I composed a kind of short appeal, which Gavrilo and I copied out and distributed around the classes. The appeal met with success, and the very next day during the main break Gavrilo sat down very seriously on the steps, alongside the Jewess Sura and other sellers of pies, sausages, and apples, and stated his requirements:

'Two pies: give a kopeck. What have you got? A three-kopeck sausage? That's a kopeck too.'

It had got off to a good start. Some boys paid several days in advance and we were already thinking of keeping registers and records, as our financial operations had been noticed by the supervisor Dityatkevich.

'What's all this? What are you doing?'

Feeling that our cause was a righteous one, we candidly laid out our plan and its aims. Didonus was somewhat bewildered and limped off to the headmaster straight away. Dolgonogov had already gone by now. He had been transferred shortly after Avdiyev, and Stepan Yakovlevich had been appointed in his place. After a few minutes Didonus returned, excited, triumphant, gloating. Learning from the headmaster that we were doing something highly reprehensible, he gleefully took us off to the staff-room, pushing aside a noisy crowd of boys.

Leaning back on his chair, Stepan Yakovlevich looked us up and down, and when he'd held us under the threat of an explosion of anger for half a minute or so, he said in a low, rather hoarse voice, 'What's this you've been starting? Proclamations? Secret and illegal collections?'

'Stepan Yakovlevich, we . . .' began the surprised Gavrilo, but the headmaster glared at him fiercely and said,

'Silence! I say: secret collections, because you said nothing about them to me, your headmaster. I say: illegal, because,' he straightened up in his chair and continued solemnly, '*tax-es* are laid down only by the Council of State. Do you know that if I took an official stand on this matter, you would not only be expelled from the school, but prosecuted too.'

Gavrilo's fine eyes froze in an expression of tremendous, almost supernatural amazement. I too was surprised at such an unexpected interpretation of our enterprise, though I felt that the legislative rights of the Council of State had nothing to do with the matter.

At this point I chanced to look at Balmashevsky. He had come up at the very beginning of the conversation and was now standing by the table, leafing through a register. A slight smile was playing on his thin lips. His eyes, as always, were curtained by heavy, swollen eyelids, but in the expression on his face I read quite clearly sympathetic support and approval. Stepan Yakovlevich lowered his voice and said 'Meantime—go to your class.'

That same day Balmashevsky called me as I was coming out of school and said with a smile, 'So you copped it, then? Well, never mind! Naturally, there won't be any further developments. But you gentlemen really went about it the wrong way. You and Zhdanov come to see me today.'

That evening, Gavrilo and I went to see Balmashevsky. He gave us a cordial welcome and put forward his plan simply: we would collect facts and instances of extreme hardship among our schoolfellows and set them out in the form of a report to the Pedagogic Council. He would deliver it himself, and the teachers would work out regulations for 'a society to assist students of the town of Rovno'. We left him, moved and grateful.

'He's not Avdiyev, but he's a fine chap all the same', my friend said on the street. 'You know, he doesn't sing badly either. I heard him at Tyss's nameday party.'

We composed the report. This first official-style piece of work didn't come easily to me, and Balmashevsky had to correct it. The young teachers backed the report, and the proposed regulations were sent to the Ministry; in the meantime they made a single collection by way of exception and paid for the boys who'd been expelled. As a result of the usual red-tape, the proposal was only ratified three years later, when neither I nor Gavrilo nor Balmashevsky were any longer in Rovno. Nevertheless, when I'd finished school, I retained a warm affection for this far from brilliant young teacher, with the sunken chest and eyelids swollen from overwork.

Ten years passed. 'The system' in the high schools had finally taken shape. In 1888 or 1889 appeared the memorable circular about 'the children of cooks', for whom a high-school education was pointless. Headmasters were required to furnish special statistics of the exact status of the parents of their students, the number of rooms they occupied, and the number of servants they possessed. Even at that dead and passive time this circular of the dotard Delyanov[7] provoked general indignation: not all headmasters even responded to the demand for the statistics, and the public at large would accost men in the dark blue uniforms of 'public instruction', expressing the general feeling of indignation even on the streets.

At that time I happened to be in one of the towns in the south, and there I heard a familiar name. A Balmashevsky was headmaster of the high school in the town. My memories of Gavrilo and our attempt to usurp the rights of the Council of State and Balmashevsky's sympathetic interference came back to me at once, and I felt a strong desire to see him. But friends, to whom I'd related the episode, expressed doubt: 'No, it can't be! It must be someone else!'

It turned out that it was the same Balmashevsky, but the circular, which had aroused everyone's indignation, he had set about implementing not so much from fear as from conviction. He had summoned children, interrogated them, and written down the 'number of rooms and servants'. The children had gone away frightened, with tears and grim forebodings, and then the executive headmaster had started summoning the poorest parents, and on the basis of the circular had tried to convince them that it was hard for them to educate their children in high schools and quite unsuitable too. His expressive words on the subject had gone right round the town:

'Why do you keep badgering me? I am a civil servant. If they ask me to hang every tenth boy, come to the school: they'll be hanging in a row, like crows on a fence. Address yourself to the higher authorities.'

Once again I recalled Turgenev's Mardary.

The Balmashevskys of this world are not, of course, villains. They started out on their roads with good instincts, and had those instincts been demanded, encouraged, or even tolerated, they would have cultivated them carefully. But the harsh, lustreless school régime demanded other things instead, and in the course of decades carried out a systematic process of selection. The diligent Balmashevsky made a career for himself, while Avdiyev died an inconspicuous teacher of literature in a remote part of the country.

[7] An erstwhile liberal who became Minister of Education in 1882. As Minister he showed himself obsequiously obedient to the arch-reactionaries Pobedonostsev and Tolstoy (now Minister of the Interior).

9
My Elder Brother becomes a Writer

MY ELDER BROTHER WAS TWO YEARS OLDER THAN I. HE had, it seemed, inherited certain traits of my father's character. Like my father, he was hot-tempered but quickly cooled down, and was a person of short-lived enthusiasms. Once he started sticking together houses, then ships out of paper, and achieved a remarkable degree of skill in this useless pastime: his miniature frigates were duly equipped with masts, rigging, and even little cannons peeping out from the gun-ports. Then he suddenly gave this up and started on something else.

He acquired a special passion for reading. He could often be seen on the sofa or his bed in the most inelegant pose: on all fours, propped up on his elbows, with his eyes riveted to a book. Beside him on a chair stood a glass of water and a piece of bread, thickly sprinkled with salt. He would spend whole days like this, forgetting about dinner and tea, to say nothing of his lessons. At first there was no system at all in this reading: *The Wandering Jew, The Three Musketeers, Twenty Years Later, Queen Margot, The Count of Monte Cristo, Secrets of the Madrid Court, Rocambole*, and so on. He got the books from the little Jewish book-stalls and sometimes sent me to change them. I would open a book on the way and avidly devour page after page. But my brother never let me finish them, saying that I was 'still too young for novels'. Much of this literature has thus remained to this day in my memory in the form of vivid but disconnected episodes. . . .

Once—when my brother was in the fifth form at the Rovno High School—whimsical old Lumpi proposed that those who felt inclined should translate into Russian verse the French poem:

> De la tige détachée
> Pauvre feuille desséchée,
> Où vas-tu ? Je ne sais rien.

The whole class declined, except for two—a boy called Pachkovsky and my brother. The latter gave himself to the poem with just as much enthusiasm as he had recently shown in the construction of paper fri-gates, and finally managed to convey in elegant verse the melancholic reflections about the leaf carried away by the torrent into unknown regions. The boys and the teachers talked of the poem. My brother now passed for 'a poet' and began spending whole days choosing rhymes. We smiled as we saw him tapping out the number of feet and syllables on the chair with his left hand, while with his right he scribbled something down, altered it, and wrote it again. When he heard us laughing he would stop his inspired labours, threaten us with his fist and bury himself in his poem again.

As Pachkovsky had also translated the poem, the class at first said: 'We've got two poets.' Pachkovsky was the son of a poor widow who took in boarders from the school. He was rather old for his class; he had a pimply face, and was big-boned, bear-like, and clumsy. His translation had not been very good, but nevertheless earned a certain amount of encouragement. After this Pachkovsky started walking around quite differently, held his head drawn in between raised shoulders and thrown slightly back, and spoke through his teeth. My brother's success greatly disturbed him, and so he decided to eclipse his rival by bringing out an original poem and satire simultaneously. The satire was in the form of 'An Epistle to a Fellow-poet', in which venom was concealed behind the apparent recognition of another's superiority. The poem depicted the sufferings of a young Greek girl, who proposed to throw herself into the sea from a cliff because of hopeless love for a young Italian. The poet appealed in vain to her reason, trying to persuade her not to end her young life. The Greek girl carried out her dread intention and threw herself into the sea. But the cruel-hearted Italian did not evade his fate either; 'the waves cast up the maiden's body on the steep shore' at the very spot where the young Italian lived. The poem ended with the convincing couplet:

> And this he was unable to bear
> And had to take his own life there.

My brother circulated a kind of verse fable about 'Pachkoon,[1] the poet from the people'. This nickname stuck to Pachkovsky.

This tiny polemical episode stirred literary interests within the high school, and from it there might well have developed a general and serious enthusiasm for literature, as had once been the case in the lycée of Tsarskoye Selo or in the Nezhin High School in Gogol's time. However, Andriyevsky, the teacher of Russian literature, was wholly engrossed in *The Tale of the Host of Igor*, and soon after circulars appeared prohibiting all out-of-school meetings and essays. D. A. Tolstoy was concerned that intellectual interests in the high schools

[1] A word meaning 'scribbler', 'dauber'.

should not gush and bubble noisily, but should murmur gently and anaemically within the channels of bureaucratic programmes.

Pachkovsky adopted the manner of an unrecognized genius: with the stamp of rejection on his brow, he continued to scribble long, dull poems. When Andriyevsky once asked him something on the theory of language he got up from his seat half-mockingly and half-pompously and said:

'For a man with the Castalian spring in his soul tedious theories are superfluous.'

Andriyevsky replied with his usual prolonged 'a-a-ah!' of surprise— and gave the poet a low mark.

Towards the end of the year Pachkovsky gave up school and went into the telegraph. My brother continued climbing Parnassus alone, without a guide, by dark and difficult paths: for hours on end he would drum out feet with his fingers, translate, compose, search for rhymes, and even undertook a dictionary of rhymes. His school work went from bad to worse. To my mother's dismay he continually skipped lessons.

Once he read the prospectus of some ephemeral little magazine, and decided to send a poem to it. It was accepted and, seemingly, even published, but the magazine disappeared without the poet receiving a small payment or even a printed copy of his verse. Encouraged, none the less, by this doubtful success, my brother selected a number of his works, made me copy them out in my best writing and then sent them away to the great Nekrasov of *Fatherland Notes*.[2]

Two or three weeks later a reply from Nekrasov himself arrived in our small provincial town. True, it was not a particularly comforting reply: he found my brother's poems smooth, quite good, and literary; they would probably be printed from time to time, but it was still only versification, not real poetry. The author should study, read a lot, and then, perhaps, try using his literary abilities in other branches of literature.

At first my brother was dismayed, but then stopped tapping out feet and got down to serious reading: Sechenov, Moleschott, Schlosser, Lewis, Dobrolyubov, Buckle, and Darwin. Again, he read with great enthusiasm, writing out long extracts and sometimes, as my father used to do, he would throw me, by the way, some thought that had impressed him, a characteristic aphorism or apt couplet that was still, so

[2] Nekrasov acquired *Fatherland Notes* (*Otechestvennye zapiski*) in 1868, and edited it with the satirist Saltykov-Shchedrin and G. Z. Yeliseyev. It was finally closed down by the government in 1884.

to speak, warm, freshly taken from a new book. He now got his reading matter from the battalion library, where all progressive literature was to be found.

'Ha! Remember my words: that boy will end up a scholar or a writer', forecast our uncle, the captain, with a wise air.

In the town too my brother had the firm reputation of a future writer on credit, as it were. People had got to know in some mysterious way of Nekrasov's letter and this gave my brother a special importance in their eyes.

He had to leave school. It was assumed he would still sit the final exams, but instead of preparing for them he devoured book after book, writing down quotations and pondering over plans for some writings of his own. Sometimes, for lack of a better audience, he would read me passages from his compilations, and I was very impressed by the elegant exactness of the way he set things out. But then a new enthusiasm came along. The cause of it this time was the then well-known publisher Trubnikov. He had just founded the paper *The Exchange Gazette*, which he was promising to make an organ of the provinces, and his bright, attractive, appetising advertisements made a strong impression on the provincial reader. 'I've ordered Trubnikov's paper' or 'You ought to write to Trubnikov about that'—people would say to one another, and *The Exchange Gazette* made its appearance in the town, edging out the traditional *Son of the Fatherland* and competing successfully with *The Voice*.

One day an envelope with the stamp of the editorial office was delivered to my brother. On opening it, joy and amazement appeared on his face. The envelope contained a letter from Trubnikov himself. True, it was a typed letter, but at the beginning stood my brother's Christian name and patronymic. How the keen publisher had got to know of his existence and literary inclinations is hard to say. The letter spoke of the important tasks of the press in our time, and invited my brother to contribute to the awakening of civic awareness in the province by sending dispatches, notes, and articles relating to local issues.

For a while my brother even gave up his reading. He got hold of some back numbers of Trubnikov's paper, read them through from cover to cover, got in a stock of notepaper, pondered, wrote things down, revised them, counting letters and lines so as to squeeze what he had written into the frame of a dispatch, and after several days of dedicated labour made me write out his new work. It began with the words:

ROVNO (*from our correspondent*).

This was followed by a vividly sketched characterization of a small town with its drowsiness, gossip, scandal, and low-brow interests. Provincial types were drawn in general outline, and here and there literary turns of phrase and quotations stood out elegantly, bearing witness to the author's erudition. The only thing was that he seemed to me to be writing about some small town in general, and not about ours in particular, and that the types were taken from books rather than from life around us. My remark to this effect did not dismay the author in the least. It was supposed to be like that. After all, this was 'literature', always a little different from life.

The dispatch was sent off. About ten days later the old postman, accompanied by the barking of dogs which he kept at bay with his short little sabre, brought my brother a copy of the paper and another letter with the editorial office's stamp. My brother grabbed the paper straight away and beamed. On the third page, in bold type and italics, stood the familiar phrase:

ROVNO (*from our correspondent*)

This seemed almost like a miracle to me. It was only a short while ago that I had written out these same words in longhand on uninteresting notepaper, and now they had come back from the mysterious, unknown editorial office printed on news-sheet and had entered simultaneously various houses where they were being read and discussed, with people snatching the paper one from another. I re-read the dispatch and it seemed to me that on the enormous grey page it stood out almost in letters of fire. My criticism respectfully ceased before the printed text. This was 'literature', something far more interesting than the dull town with its weed-choked ponds and drowsy shanties. The paper with the column of vivid lines written by my brother had the effect of a stone thrown into stagnant water. It was as if a mysterious and awe-inspiring phantom had suddenly leaned over the sleepy town: from his magnificent far-off abode Mr. Trubnikov himself was peeping into it with amused, intelligent eyes. And the town started to swarm, like an ant's nest, suddenly uncovered.

The town really did begin to swarm. The paper was passed from hand to hand, guesses were made as to the identity of the mysterious correspondent, in whose general characterizations people thought they recognized real figures and real allusions. And as the correspondent in conclusion had promised to reveal against this background 'various episodes typifying the narrow vegetable life of the town', Trubnikov's paper acquired some more subscribers.

This episode definitely weakened the beneficial effect of Nekrasov's letter. My brother felt that he was a sort of Atlas, who was holding the Rovno sky on his shoulders. While the town was trying to guess the author, the author was seated at the table, rocking dangerously on his chair, and gazing at the ceiling, thinking up new themes. He was entirely absorbed in this activity. One dispatch followed rapidly after another, and although not all of them were published, some were, and once the postman delivered an order for 18 roubles 70 kopecks. At a time when a permanent court-official got between three and five roubles a month, this sum seemed a fortune. True, the sluggish town did not offer many themes, but my brother was inventive in that respect. The biggest sensation was produced by the letter in which he described the dance in the local club to which senior boys from the high school had been admitted. The correspondent portrayed their success in rather exaggerated colours. 'Minerva's charges (the schoolboys) decisively repulsed the sons of Mars (the garrison and infantry officers), and the lovely goddess of love, hitherto favouring moustaches and epaulettes, held out her hand with a modest smile of encouragement to the moustache-less young gentlemen in dark blue uniforms.' The officers took offence and talked of 'an insult to military honour'. The colonel drove off to see the headmaster. The town couldn't settle down for a long time. The practical result of it all was that the boys were forbidden to attend dances.

And so my brother didn't try the exams after all. He grew a little moustache and beard, began wearing a pince-nez, and the instincts of a dandy suddenly awoke within him. Instead of the former scruff, who would sit reading books for days on end, he now represented a sort of elegant dandy in ruffed shirts and polished boots. 'I have to appear in society,' he would say; 'it is essential for my work.' He went to clubs, became a superb dancer and won social success. Everyone had now known for a long time that he was 'Trubnikov's contributor', 'a writer'.

On one occasion he touched on a more serious topic. Some citizen or other had been robbed in the town, and my brother picturesquely depicted the helpless town on dark autumn nights, without street lights and with night-watchmen sleeping safely in their corners. The Assistant District Inspector of Police, who, because of the final decrepitude of the Inspector Gots, represented the highest police authority in the town, invited my brother for a confidential conversation. When he had courteously offered him a cigarette, the highest representative of police authority embarked on a diplomatic explanation: he had known our father well and had greatly respected him. Besides this, he had respect for literature. He had found the descriptions of the dance very witty, very nice. But of late Trubnikov's paper had started touching in a way on the activity of the government. My brother expressed surprise: there had not been anything about the government, as far as he could see. No, not directly. But there had been something about night-watchmen and the inactivity, so to speak, of the authorities. Robberies had increased. 'And who, may I ask, is obliged to keep an eye on this?' The police! The police is a government organ. And if in future the dispatches were to touch on the activity of a governmental authority, then he, the Assistant District Inspector of Police, would be forced, in spite of his respect for our father and for literature, to institute a secret investigation into the harmful activity of the correspondent and even—he found it unpleasant to speak of this—to solicit the Governor for the expulsion of the writer from the town. Then he politely said good-bye with the assurance that he respected the press, was impressed by the witty pen of the unknown correspondent, and had nothing against the exposing of abuses, so long as it didn't undermine authority.

My brother returned home rather worried, but at the same time flattered. He was a force the government had to reckon with. That evening walking in the moonlight around our little garden, he told me in detail his conversation with the Assistant Inspector and added, 'Yes, that's the unpleasant side of fame. Tell me: did you think your brother would become a guide of public opinion so soon?'

'Well—er . . .' I said sceptically, 'that's going a bit far.'

He stopped on the path, speckled with spots of moonlight, and said with some irritation (my doubt had struck a discordant note in his mood), 'You're still stupid. I'll prove to you by all the rules of logic that I'm right. Premise: the press guides public opinion! Answer: yes or no?'

'Well, all right, yes!'

'And I'm a writer now?'

'Y-yes,' I answered less firmly.

'Of course I am, since a man who publishes his articles is a writer. Hence, the conclusion: I too am a guide of public opinion. I advise you to read Mill's logic, then you won't raise foolish objections.'

I didn't raise any further objections, and he relented, continuing his walk along the path and unfolding his plans.

The reader will regard my brother's little exaggerations with indulgence, if he bears in mind that he was then only seventeen or eighteen years old, that he had only just left dreary school discipline behind, and that all the signs of so-called literary renown were, in fact, at hand.

What, indeed, is literary fame? Zola, in his memoirs, draws an amusing picture when discussing this subject: on one occasion one of his admirers asked him, when he was already 'a universally famous writer', to do him the honour of acting as a witness for the bride at the marriage of his daughter in a small village commune near Paris. Writing down the names of the witnesses the mayor, a well-known tradesman, looked up from his book on hearing Zola's name and asked with great interest, 'Monsieur Zola? The hat-shop on such-and-such street?'

'No, the writer.'

'Ah!' said the mayor indifferently and wrote the name down. A certain Monsieur Michel came next.

'Monsieur Michel. The linen shop on such-and-such street?'

'Yes.'

The mayor started fussing about:

'A chair for Monsieur Michel. Please sit down. Most flattered.'

This little episode, which I relate from memory, draws pretty accurately the limits of the greatest 'universal fame'. Fame means that a man's name is spread through the world along certain paths. At the very best he is known to people who read. And in this world there is not a lot of reading done. Reading humanity is approximately equivalent to the surface-area of rivers in relation to the whole expanse of the continents. A captain who sails on a given stretch of river is very well known in that region, but he has only to go a few miles away from the bank and he encounters another world: broad valleys, forests with villages scattered about them. Over all this the winds blow and storms rage, it has its own life, and the name of our captain or universally famous writer has never once been added to the usual sounds of that life.

Yet in his own circle, on his own stretch of river my brother really was quite well known. 'The government' took him into account, 'educated society' knew him, officials, Jewish tradesmen—people who had great respect for the intellect.

On fine evenings the whole town walked along the main street, its inhabitants flowing in gay waves between the prison at one end and the post office at the other. People walked along sedately in the dust, meeting and greeting one another and exchanging occasional pieces of news. Sometimes among the familiar faces appeared a visiting magnate, Count Plyater, Prince Vishnevsky or an official from the capital on his way to a mysterious inspection. Everyone's eyes followed him, and the crowd around him would thicken. Sometimes the headmaster of the high school would appear, the judge, the Assistant Inspector of Police, or the town treasurer—who represented in their way a sort of aristocracy. But there were also unofficial celebrities. The official Mikhalovsky, recently arrived from the capital, wore multi-coloured jackets and ties and unusually narrow trousers. It was said that he jumped into them in the morning from the table, like Prince d'Artois in Carlisle's story, and in the evening a sturdy valet shook him out of them on to the bed. All this was funny, but his initials coincided with the name and patronymic of a well-known poet and translator of the time, and so, when his lively colourful figure appeared in the golden haze of dust raised by the feet of the throng, people would look round at him and whisper.

'Mr. Mikhalovsky. The poet. You know? In *The Cause*.'[3]

'Of course, of course. I've read him.'

And not until the misunderstanding was cleared up did the newcomer's prestige fall. There remained only multi-coloured trousers and funny stories.

One evening a young man appeared among the promenaders, foppishly dressed, thin, lively, and cheerful. He was shaking hands right and left, exchanging wisecracks. As he passed along people said, 'Arepa, Arepa. Contributor to *The Spark*. He unseated the Governor Besse.'

Arepa had gone to our school and worked in Zhitomir, apparently as an attorney's clerk. Once, a piece appeared in *The Spark* entitled 'The conversation between Chemodan Ivanovich and Samovar Nikiforovich'. In Chemodan Ivanovich people saw the Governor, and in Samovar Nikiforovich the merchant Zhuravlev. The conversation related to a bribe on the awarding of the postal contract. People started talking and the Governor's position was dangerously weakened. One day in the club he caught sight of Arepa in the billiard-room and probably wanting to force a repentant confession from him, went up to him straight away and said, 'You, young man . . . I've heard. . . . You've been spreading a dirty piece of slander.'

Arepa straightened up, and pretending to be frightened, said, trembling and stuttering, 'I beg leave to ask, Your Ex'lency, what was th-that?'

The general took heart from this. There were witnesses to the conversation, officials, and even the dark blue uniform of a gendarme could be seen.

[3] *The Cause* (*Delo*) a monthly scientific and literary magazine published in Petersburg from 1866 to 1888.

'Well, you inferred,' the Governor continued with majestic disdain, 'what was it, five thousand roubles—from Zhuravlev.'

'It's a lie, sir, Your Ex'lency,' said Arepa, his whole person expressing the most pitiful servility. 'My enemies, Your Ex'lency, want—want to ruin me in your eyes.'

Then, suddenly straightening up, he added, 'ten thousand, Your Ex'lency; I said ten thousand.'

The Governor almost had a seizure, and soon afterwards he tendered his resignation 'for domestic reasons'.

That was the way the townspeople told the story. The fact was that the Governor had given up his post after the correspondence, and his accuser remained safe and sound, and now, visiting his father, was enjoying his fame in his home town.

Arepa passed by like a meteor and disappeared, leaving behind him great respect for the job of a correspondent. To unseat a governor was no mean feat. My brother was also a correspondent. And though he had not as yet unseated a single governor, everyone knew that it was in fact his pen that shook our little world from time to time, alarming the officials, or the night-watchmen, or the officer-ranks. People paid attention to him. He was invited to parties, where respected citizens took him by the arm to one side, showering praises upon his talent and asking him to have a go at such and such a person.

Is it surprising that for a time my brother floated along in the atmosphere of this 'fame' without noticing that he was revolving in empty space and that his stunning dispatches were creating sterile agitation, that they were not really moving anything in any direction at all?

My brother's 'literary success' left a special trace in me. It threw a living bridge, as it were, between literature and life around me: I had witnessed words being written on paper and then returning from the capital in print. Even before, when I read a book, I sometimes compared what I had read with the impressions made by life itself, and had been much occupied by the question: why is everything in a book always somehow different. With my brother it was also different. After my initial reverence before the printed word had passed, I once again felt this as a deficiency, and became interested in trying to find words which came as near as possible to the phenomena of life. Everything that struck me I tried to put into words that would capture the essential nature of what I had experienced. On our main street stood a little hut, the lower supports of which had rotted and subsided. Its walls had sunk lower than a man's height. Passing it, I said to myself: it is frowning . . . squashed . . . squinting . . . injured . . . sad. . . . And when the drunk official, Krasusky came out of it, stooping, I tried to find words for him.

This became a habit with me, and when after Turgenev and other Russian writers I read Dickens and Shchedrin's *History of a Town*, it seemed to me that the humorous manner should embrace the external forms of life and their essential, inner character. I started trying to sense the town officials, my teachers, Stepan Yakovlevich, Didonus in Dickens's and Shchedrin's characters. It still turned out 'not right'. And it was strange: at times, when I made no conscious efforts, lines of poetry and rhymes would run through my head, and smooth, graceful sentences flit by. But they passed beyond the reach of my will and did not capture anything from life. The form seemed to be born quite distinct from any concrete meaning and would fly away when I tried to make it embrace something definite.

I sometimes dreamed I was reading my own poems and stories. They were printed and contained everything I required: our town, the turnpike, the streets, shops, officials, teachers, tradespeople, the evening promenades. Everything was alive, and over it all there was something else, which was not part of this reality, but which illuminated prosaic scenes with a magic kind of light. I read page after page in delight. But when I woke up, it all flew away like a flock of birds frightened at the approach of a hunter. And the bits that I occasionally managed to hold in my memory proved to be worthless: the poems had no metre, the prose often lacked even grammatical sense, and the words had other than their real meanings. This again was just excitement in a void. The stimulus had been provided by Avdiyev and partly by my brother's dispatches. Avdiyev had gone away. The dispatches were losing their flavour.

Their sole practical result, it seems, was that the schoolboys were forbidden to visit the club. Still, one day, in the very centre of the town by the bridge, they repaired a street lamp. For a while on dark evenings the lamp burned in honour of publicity. This was after all a triumph. Everyone who passed the lamp late at night thought: 'Ah! Trubnikov's correspondent shook them up.' But soon this solitary light went out, too.

10

My Last Year in School—Freedom

I SPENT THAT LAST YEAR IN SCHOOL IN A SPECIFIC FRAME OF mind. The holidays were coming to an end when those that had finished school went away—some to Kiev, others to Petersburg. Among them was Suchkov. In Zhitomir we had been in the same class. Then he had got a year in front of me, and the thought that I too might now have been free emerged with especial and irritating clarity.

I had seen him off. In his civilian clothes, with a suitcase at his feet and a travelling-bag slung over his shoulder, he was sitting in the coach which was carrying him into the mysterious distance. We had said good-bye on the high road beyond the prison, and I stood gazing for a long time at the cloud of dust that was moving along the road. I yearned to be free myself. Oh to be travelling on and on like him to somewhere there was room to breathe, to a new life!

The cloud of dust disappeared. I turned back to the town. It was lying in its basin, quiet, sleepy and repugnant. Above it wafted the same light shroud of dust, smoke and mist, in places one caught the gleam of patches of an overgrown pond, and the old soldier was dozing in his usual pose when I passed through the turnpike. Then, by the pond, on a narrow wooden footway, there suddenly loomed in front of me the huge figure of Stepan Yakovlevich, who was now headmaster. He looked at me from his full height and said sternly,

'Do you want the punishment-room again?'

I looked at him in surprise. What did the man want? I had lost my dread of him a long time ago. I was aware that there was nothing dreadful or nasty about him, that he may even have been kind-hearted in his way. What was he on to me for?

A thick finger moved to my chest. The two middle buttons of my tunic were undone.

'Is that all?' I thought and, as I did up the buttons, I couldn't help shrugging my shoulders. He peered into my face sternly.

'Where are you coming from?'

'I have been seeing Suchkov off.'

'Well—what then?' he asked, not altogether to the point, perplexed, I suppose, by the expression on my face.

'Nothing, Stepan Yakovlevich,' I replied woodenly.

The headmaster looked at me, as if seeking an excuse to flare up and shake my lack of susceptibility to authority, but he didn't think of anything and went his way.

I looked around me with a feeling of anguish. Suchkov was already far away. He was driving up to the station, and would be signing the book: 'student of the Technological Institute'! He would be giving the driver a tip, then he'd take his seat again, and the little bell would start its enigmatic chatter. And before me was the same old pond, overgrown with green duckweed. Clear patches of water, sultry and motionless, reflect the sky and the sunlight. The duckweed stirs here and there—its tadpoles and frogs swimming beneath it. A deeply bored swan swims out of the rushes. A woman is beating her wet washing. Stepan Yakovlevich had just threatened me with the punishment-room. And there was all this for another whole year! What a prospect!

The year dragged awfully for me, and I could well understand my brother who, once out of the rut, could not and did not want to get back into it. For me the end was near now. Of course, I must finish at all costs. The headmaster continued to scrutinize me with suspicious but more or less uncomprehending eyes. One day he stopped me as I came out of church.

'Why don't you pray?' he asked. 'You used to pray. Now you just stand like a post.'

I looked up at him, and in my eyes there must again have been an expression that perplexed him. What could I say in reply? Start praying to order under the head's stare?

'I don't know,' I replied briefly.

Now that my mother took in boarders from the school, I was senior among them. That year a boy by the name of Podgursky, the son of a wealthy landowner, took a room with us. He was preparing to enter one of the top classes. One day the headmaster, who was visiting our rooms, went into Podgursky's room in his absence and began sniffing.

'Does he smoke?' he asked me.

'I don't know,' I replied.

'You are senior?'

'Yes, but he hasn't started at school yet.'

'That doesn't matter. You *must* find out. Understand?'

'Very well, Stepan Yakovlevich, I'll ask him,' I said innocently.

Anger flared on the headmaster's monumental face. He considered that I, as senior here, was obliged to collaborate secretly with him in his surveillance of his future pupil: I should watch, and if I found tobacco, I should report it. In my reply he saw a sneer; but, it seems, it wasn't even a case of a sneer. I had simply not bothered to think what effect my words would have on him, and *could now actually be absent-minded* in the headmaster's dread presence. It was, if you like, an instinctive disrespect, which they would now qualify as 'a harmful way of thinking'. But at that time 'mind-reading' was not yet in vogue even in the high schools, the Councils demanded offences, and my frame of mind was elusive.

Even today I think many people who have gone right through school experience to a greater or lesser extent that final-year mood. Education must have its cult, which raises separate pieces of knowledge to a level of overall meaningfulness. Our system drums assiduously on separate keys. There is a boring surfeit of isolated sounds, and no overall melody. Fear, which supports discipline, evaporates with the years and with habit. There is no inner discipline or respect for the school system, and life is already looking in and beckoning from near at hand.

At five o'clock on a lovely summer morning at the end of June 1870 I walked to the witch-elm grove outside the town with Filaret's[1] *Catechism* and a book on Church history. That day there was a divinity examination, and it was the last exam.

I was in a grim, cheerless mood. I was tired with examinations. The day before I had gone to bed late and had got up today before sunrise. I could hardly keep my eyes open, my head felt heavy, and I had come to this place in the hope that the clear morning air on the hill would drive away the cobwebs. Reaching the hilltop, I admired the wide view. The town was spread out below me. In the mornings it was often covered with mists from the ponds, and now the misty shroud was coming apart, revealing a rooftop, a patch of ground, a white wall. The statue of the Madonna seemed to be floating in the air and in the distance fields, villages, and strips of forest were just visible. For several minutes I could not tear myself away from the spectacle, to which the imperceptible movement of the mist gave a sort of life. It seemed to me that I was really seeing nature for the very first time and beginning to catch its inner essence, but there was no time to gaze. I had to memorize an arid list of dogmas, synods, and heresies, which had not even a remote connection with the beauty of this amazing world. This made me unhappy. At that moment I saw happiness as being able to stand on that hill, free to look at the wonderful beauty of the world and to catch that strange expression which flits, part of nature's enticing mystery, in the gentle movement of its light and shadows. I promised myself that, as soon as I

---

[1] Filaret (1783–1867), Metropolitan of Moscow. His *Catechism* first appeared in 1823 and was used in all high schools.

got through the exam, I would come straight back here, to this same spot, gaze at the landscape and finally capture its expression. And then fall fast asleep beneath the rustling, dark green foliage of the tree standing nearby.

I was still swotting Divinity when the modulating sound of the bell reached me, summoning me to school for the last time. Well, come what may! I closed the book and in a quarter of an hour I was entering the school yard.

And an hour after that I ran out of it, filled with a new feeling of relief, freedom, and happiness! How it happened that I passed and passed 'with distinction' in a subject which, basically, I failed to understand, I no longer remember. I only know that when I'd passed I ran home like a madman, kissed my mother happily and, flinging aside books no longer needed, ran out of the town.

The early morning was over, its freshness vanished, there was no mist, only over the ponds barely perceptible grey wisps still lingered. Turgenev says that he was actually abroad, somewhere near Berlin, when he first took conscious delight in nature and the song of the lark. It is strange, but true. It doesn't mean that he had no feeling for nature before then. But there comes a moment when a man observes this feeling within himself as a particular spiritual phenomenon. And this happens late, and with some people perhaps it never happens at all. At that moment I too, perhaps, was looking at nature for the first time in this way, with a full awareness of what I was experiencing. And for the first time the symphony of morning that was ending seemed finely proportioned, inspired, perfect. Something was coming to a close, as vespers come to a close with the singing of 'Quiet light'. I did, indeed, feel in nature a religious rite, full of harmony and meaning.

I didn't feel like sleeping under the tree at all. I again rushed like a madman from the hill and sped to the school, from which my friends were coming out one by one after their examination. It wasn't done to plough people in Divinity, and at their very last exam too. Everyone had passed, and the sorry little town seem filled with our intoxicating joy. Freedom! Freedom! The feeling was so strong and so unfamiliar that we simply didn't know what to do with it or where to put it. We finally decided, the whole group of us, to take it to 'the Czechs', that is, to the newly opened beer-house. The strong Czech beer seemed bitter and revolting to us all; but only yesterday we had not had the right to come here, and so had come today. We sat at the tables, soberly drinking from our tankards and trying to suppress involuntary grimaces.

A few days later, when we'd received our certificates, we decided to celebrate our freedom all together. And the occasion was rather like the bitter beer. We gathered in the wine-merchant Weintraub's large room, access to which was forbidden to schoolboys on pain of expulsion, and invited our teachers. The teachers drank with us, brewed punch, became tipsy and embraced us like friends. The punch tasted disgustingly strong, but we drank it with our teachers and slapped them on the shoulders. It was all new and unusual, and seemed called-for and pleasant. It was late into the night when someone demanded music. The nimble Jewish agent got the musicians up, and at dawn we were walking through the sleeping and still dark town, accompanied by a clarinet, a flute, two or three violins, and a Turkish drum. The music disturbed the quiet of the sleeping streets. We were shouting 'Hurrah', rocking the teachers, and feeling that it was all somehow forced, false, unnatural. Yet, what were we to do with this new feeling of freedom that excited us so ?

The next day, with a heavy head and a nasty taste in my mouth from the memory of the night before, I went off for a swim. On the path across the fields which led to the river the history teacher Andrussky caught up with me. I have already spoken about him: his teaching was dry and rather boring, but he enjoyed general respect as an intelligent, firm, and fair-minded man. The previous day he had merely put in an appearance at the beginning of the evening, had not drunk anything, and had left early. Now he was walking with a towel slung over his shoulder, brisk and fresh. I stopped and like a pupil I took off my cap before a teacher; but he came up to me and stretched out his hand. Again, I felt in this one more feature of my new position.

'Are you going for a swim ?' he asked.

'Yes.'

'Let's go together.'

We went to the very spot where Dityatkevich would lie in ambush for the boys. There was a new sort of pleasure in this too. After the swim Andrussky shook hands with me outside his flat and said:

'I've a samovar and a newspaper with an account of a very interesting case. Want to come in ?'

I went in readily. On the table stood a samovar. Andrussky made some tea, put a clean serviette over the teapot and handed me a copy of *The Voice*.

'Read it aloud, please, Just here.'

It was an account of the Nechayev trial.[2] I did not know anything

[2] Nechayev (1847–82), a young primary teacher who, influenced by the writings of such theorists of revolution as Pisarev, Bakunin, and Tkachev, set about

about it at the time and started reading without much interest. Gradually, however, a curious sense of excitement came over me. The paper
mentioned the printing-press run by Tkachev[3] and Dementyeva, and
Nechayev's proclamation to students was quoted. 'Having developed
our intellects on the money of the Russian people, and having been fed
on the corn harvested from its fields, shall we be counted among its
oppressors ?' In the proclamation it was argued that the interests of the
students and the people were the same. 'We have comrades who are
without rights, whose position is the worst in Europe, and whose
exasperation is all the greater in that it has no outlet.'

When I finished reading, Andrussky's intelligent eyes were watching me across the table. Observing the almost intoxicating impression
produced on me by what I'd read, he explained simply and very
objectively the essentials of the case, Nechayev's ideas, the murder of
Ivanov in the park of the Petrovsky Academy. Then he said that in the
student world, in which I would soon find myself, I would encounter
this same ferment, and must examine everything carefully. All this was

organizing a vast conspiracy to overthrow the government. His organization consisted of cells of five members. Only one member of a cell would know the leader of
the next cell, and so on. At the head of the organization was the mysterious committee,
consisting only of Nechayev. Since the cells were thus insulated one from another,
only Nechayev could be aware of the scale of the organization, and if a cell were
uncovered by the police, it could not, he thought, bring down the whole organization. Nechayev visualized his cells as spreading throughout Russia. When the time
was ripe, he would give his order, and revolution would spread in a chain-reaction,
as cell after cell was put into action.

One of the members of his initial cell, the student Ivanov, became suspicious of
Nechayev's claims and methods. Nechayev therefore instructed the other members
of the cell to kill Ivanov as a spy, calculating that the murder must make them
totally subservient to him. Ivanov was murdered, but the affair was disclosed,
and led to the sensational trial of the Nechayev group from the beginning of July to
the end of August 1871. Eighty-seven people were put on trial, including Tkachev.
Nechayev escaped abroad before he could be arrested, but in 1872 he was handed
over to the Russian government. He was sentenced to twenty years' hard labour. He
died in the Peter-Paul Fortress in 1882.

The public at large was horrified by the disclosures made at the trial. In radical
circles the very idea of a centralized, authoritarian revolutionary organization,
such as had been advocated by Tkachev, was wholly discredited. In 1872 Dostoyevsky wrote *The Devils*, the basis for which was the Nechayev trial.

In 1874 Korolenko became a student at the Petrovsky Academy, where the
murder of Ivanov had taken place (see p. 174 below).

[3] Pyotr Nikitich Tkachev (1844–85), theorist of revolution. In the 1860s and
1870s Tkachev continually stressed what he saw as the futility of moderation and
gradualism. The work of revolution was a task for an *élite*. There could be no question of the active participation of the people either before, during, or after. In 1871
he was sentenced to sixteen months' imprisonment. In 1873 he fled to Switzerland,
from where, in collaboration with his wife A. D. Dementyeva, he issued his paper
The Tocsin (*Nabat*) from 1875 to 1880.

again falling on a virgin soul, like snowflakes on a naked body. The murder of Ivanov seemed to strike a sharply discordant note. 'Perhaps it's not true?' But one thought dominated everything else: so, we too have now got *this*—what exactly? A student-body, intelligent, serious, 'with angered faces', thinking grim thoughts about the lack of rights of the whole Russian people. And with the mention of 'generals Timashev[4] and Trepov',[5] I remembered Bezak.

On one of my last evenings I was taking a walk, like other townspeople, along the high road, aware all the time of my new feeling of freedom, when two figures emerged in front of me out of the dusty twilight gloom. One of my friends, Leontovich, was walking with a tall young man in dark glasses and a soft wide-brimmed hat on his long hair. He obviously wasn't a Rovno man.

'The Kiev student Piotrovsky,' my friend said, introducing the stranger. 'And this is the future student Korolenko.'[6]

Piotrovsky shook my hand firmly and invited us both to his hotel room. In a corner of this room stood two bundles of papers, bound with string and wrapped in sheets of newspaper. Leontovich looked respectfully at the bundles and said, lowering his voice:

'Is that—them?'

'Yes,' the student nodded importantly.

'You know, those things in the corner were forbidden books', Leontovich said to me when we were on the street again. 'They sent Piotrovsky. You understand. A very dangerous mission.'

This was the first 'agitator' I had ever seen in my life. He stayed in town a few days, going for walks along the high road in the evenings, attracting attention by his student appearance, glasses, panama hat, long hair, and plaid. I went with him once or twice, expecting revelations. But the student said nothing or talked only pretentious trivia. After he left, there remained in the town some secretly distributed, rather harmless Ukrainian pamphlets, and in my heart—a dual sensation. It seemed to me that Piotrovsky was an empty fellow, puffed up with unwarranted self-importance. But this was hidden somewhere in the very depths of my consciousness and was afraid to come forward, where a naïve sense of awe reigned: such an important person, in spectacles, and with such a dangerous mission.

[4] Minister of the Interior, 1868–78.
[5] Prefect of Petersburg. Seriously wounded by Vera Zasulich in 1878 (see p. 223 below).
[6] Korolenko does not often refer to himself by name. Here he uses the word '*takoy-to*' (so-and-so). He is not altogether consistent in this, however, and it seems best to disregard the device.

Finally the happy moment came when I too was leaving the quiet little town, which remained behind in its hollow. And in front of me stretched the distant ribbon of the road, and on the horizon there was a whirl of vague outlines: strips of forest, new roads, distant towns, a new unknown life.

PART THREE
Student Years—Petersburg

I I
Rose-Coloured Spectacles

THIS MOOD OF EUPHORIA BEGAN WHEN I WAS STILL IN ROVNO, the morning the postman handed me a letter with the stamp of the Technological Institute. My heart beating wildly, I opened it and took out a printed sheet of paper with my name written at the top. Yermakov, the Director of the Institute, was notifying me that I had been accepted for the First Year Course and was to present myself by 15 August.

When I looked around after reading it, it seemed to me that a whole day and night had passed during those few minutes: before the postman had come it had been yesterday, and now there was a new today. It was as if I'd slept through a night and woken up not only a different man, but also to some extent in a different world. This sensation was produced by the thick grey paper with its printed text and Yermakov's signature at the bottom. And when I then sped through the streets, it seemed that the houses, and the fences, and the townspeople who crossed my path were also looking at me differently. After all they too were in fact seeing for the first time since the creation of the world—*the student Korolenko*.[1]

For several days I was not parted from my notification. Every now and then I would take it out in private and read it through with fresh pleasure, as if it weren't a dry, official letter but a poem. And it really was a poem: a break with the old world, a summons to something new, longed for, and radiant. Director Yermakov was calling me. His name was linked in my imagination with something very firm, almost granite-

[1] Again, Korolenko does not refer to himself by name (see p. 111, note 6).

like (probably because of the Siberian Yermak),[2] and at the same time unattainably lofty and clever. And this Yermakov was expecting me by 15 August. He needed me in order to fulfil his high purpose.

The mood was foolish and, of course, I was aware that it was foolish: Yermakov's very signature was printed. He didn't sign such notifications himself, they were sent out in their hundreds by the office. I knew this, but the knowledge didn't alter the way I felt. I knew in my mind, but my reaction remained foolish. Even while I impressed these sober truths upon myself, I would grin from ear to ear and would have to turn my head so that people wouldn't see that idiotic smile and guess that I had been called by Yermakov, who needed me personally by 15 August.

In my youthful egoism I took no part in my mother's cares about my outfitting. She mortgaged her pension book somewhere, sold some articles, borrowed where she could, and finally scraped up something around 200 roubles. Then followed long consultations with the tailor Shimko. He was a short, stocky Jew with a broad face, to which his thin lips and pointed nose gave an almost comically morose expression. When my father had been alive we had always laughed at Shimko, sharpening our wit at his appearance and presumed swindles. When father died and mother was left without any means, he came to see her and, critically examining the condition of our clothes, said seriously,

'Well, it's time to make a coat and two tunics.'

'Shimko, you know I don't have the money now, and I can't tell what else I shall need,' my mother answered sadly.

'So,' Shimko countered, 'you haven't got money, but you've got children. Isn't that money?'

And once again he worked for us, never so much as mentioning terms of payment or bargaining as he had before. Now he displayed his activity in our home. Inquiring whether I wanted clothes made in the latest fashion and learning that I despised them he uttered a hum of pleasure and gave free rein to his creative fantasy. He soaked and steamed materials, measured, cut, tried for size, and I finally emerged from his hands equipped not particularly stylishly, but cheaply. He had made me a summer suit from very hard-wearing and stiff material with

[2] A Cossack who in 1581 led a small force of Cossacks against the Siberian prince Kuchum, whom he defeated. He handed over his conquests to the Tsar (Ivan the Terrible) in return for a pardon (he had been under sentence of death for rebellion) and some gifts. His victory marked the beginning of Russian expansion into Siberia. The Russians encountered little resistance and by 1643 they were established on the Pacific.

miniature yellow bouquets on a brown background. He had also made me a coat. I vaguely sensed that the hard-wearing material with the bouquets suggested furniture upholstery rather than a Petersburg suit, while the coat ressembled a Spanish cloak or almaviva. But on that score I was undemanding and unconcerned. Leaving aside the question of fashion, I felt immaculately dressed, rather simply, but tastefully. Alas! Shimko's flight of creative fantasy was to bring me quite a few bitter, unpleasant moments.

Suchkov, who'd already spent a year in the capital, had come home for the holidays and I naturally bombarded him with questions. For some reason he was chary of words, but I nevertheless discovered that the Institute was quite different from school, the professors were not at all like teachers, and the students were not schoolboys. There was complete freedom. . . . No one kept an eye on attendance of lectures. And among the students there were truly remarkable individuals. You'd take some for professors. And what arguments! On what subjects! You've got to read and study a lot just to understand what they're talking about. He informed me casually and by the way, so to speak, that for various reasons he would be repeating the first year and so we'd be together again.

In the middle of those holidays I became eighteen, but it seemed to me that I had far outgrown the little world surrounding me. Here it all was, as in a shallow saucer, surging within the twin boundaries of the post-office and the prison—familiar, prosaic, repugnant. On one of my last evenings I was taking a farewell look at the crowd of people walking along the main street, when suddenly out of the dusk emerged the face of the official Mikhalovsky, whom I'd formerly considered a well-known poet. In his teeth he had a large cigar, which, glowing suddenly, lit up a surprisingly uninteresting, flat face with bulging eyes completely lacking in expression. Only a short time ago this man had seemed to have a poetic halo. And how many other people had seemed higher beings only because they were adults and I was a boy. I had grown up now, and this close-knit little world had narrowed and shrunk. The clever people of a short time ago seemed either stupid or too ordinary. Whom was I now to put on a pedestal, before whom or what was I to bow? Where were there people here who knew and could point to the higher things in life for which a young heart yearns? Who even thought about these higher things, sought them, longed for them, dreamed about them. No one, no one!

I developed the arrogant conviction that I was just about the cleverest person in the town. My yardstick was this: I could understand all the people who appeared before me in this stream, which rolled, like water in a saucer, from the turnpike to the post-office and back. I knew everything they knew of what each needed to know, while they did not even suspect the thoughts about them and the dreams that were in my head. I was foolish. Later, when I'd got more sense, I never had any difficulty in finding people superior to myself in the most remote backwaters of life. But at that moment I apparently measured everything with the one yardstick of literary development.

Still, I must say I was not arrogant with regard to the other world that awaited me beyond 15 August. On the contrary. I was getting ready for it with the sincere conviction that I was tiny, colourless, and insignificant in relation to it. True, I nourished the hope that there too, in that fuller life awaiting me, I would also go forward, drawing level with some and overtaking others. But if someone had wanted to convince me that between the world I was leaving and the attractive world to which I was hastening there was no qualitative difference, that the great student-body was only a simple sum-total of units, for the most part just as colourless and of just as little interest as myself at the given moment, I would not have believed him and would probably even have felt offended for my dream.

12
A Truly Remarkable Man

MY MOTHER AND ONE OF HER BROTHERS, WHO LIVED FAIRLY near, saw me off, coming as far as Berdichev where the railroad began. It went via Kiev, Kursk, Oryol, Tula and Moscow. The third bell rang. I hugged my mother, who then hid her tear-stained face against my uncle's chest, and I got into the carriage. There was a sharp whistle, which frightened those not used to it, and then a jerk that made several people in the carriage lose their balance. The jerk was followed by a clang, then a rumbling (trains were not as smooth then as they are now), and the station and platform fell behind. The figures of my mother and uncle disappeared. I sat down and tried to hide from those sitting near me the tears that came welling into my eyes.

There were no through services at that time, each railway acted independently. The train to Kursk had left Kiev before ours arrived, and so I had to spend the night in the Sofia Hotel. The following morning I went out and stopped in the square, stunned and bewildered by the noise and movement of the city. It was then that two Rovno school-ma'ams, Zavileyskaya and Komarova, chanced upon me. They greeted me warmly and invited me to go with them to see round the cathedral. Then they asked me back to their room in the same hotel for a glass of tea. I very much wanted to accept this kind invitation, but declined out of shyness, regretting it at the same time. Before leaving me, these young ladies looked me over critically, and one of them said, 'Listen. When you get to Petersburg, order another suit. That one isn't right for the capital.'

'Yes,' the other agreed. 'Have a proper suit made. And a coat as well. You've got a sort of mantle. They're wearing narrow coats now, close-fitting, and much shorter.'

'You can keep the hat. It suits your curly hair.'

They went away, talking happily together and giving me affectionate nods. And I remained with an ache of loneliness in my heart and the unpleasant awareness that my unfashionable, but simple and elegant suit was attracting ironic attention.

The next morning found me in the train between Kiev and Kursk. The previous evening I had gradually fallen asleep, and now the first thing to meet my eyes was an eloquent notice on the wall of the carriage: 'Beware of thieves'. My mother and my uncle had impressed this same thing upon me, and I grabbed my bag. Yes, it was still there, but I immediately felt surrounded by probable conspirators, who were trying to gain access to my money. I sat down on the bench-seat and gave a keen and searching look around: of course, I'd guess straight away from which people to expect danger.

The train was standing at a little station and was filled with bright sunlight. There weren't a great many people, most of them were still sleeping, sprawled out on the seats and upper bunks, and some were even on the floor under the seats. From one end of the carriage came a lively, nervous murmur of conversation, carried on in Jewish jargon. Nearer, by the window, the other side of the next seat, sat two young men who were talking quietly, their heads almost touching. One of them was wearing a faded, reddish-brown coat. When I shifted on my seat, he turned his face in my direction—it was broad, rather pimply, with small, greenish eyes—and then began speaking to his friend even more quietly. 'I'll have to watch that one,' I decided, and only then did I glance at my immediate neighbour.

This was a gentleman in a grey coat and oilskin cap, such as were very popular at that time. He had, I think, got in at this station, and had apparently been looking at me while I was waking up. It was hard to tell his age. At first sight he seemed scarcely more than a boy, but then I realized this was a mistaken impression: the wrinkles around his eyes, the yellowness and puffiness of his face seemed to indicate a fair number of years, or possibly premature wasting away. His small hazel eyes were looking me over with an expression of ingratiating affection, as if he were on the very point of speaking to me and expressing his instinctive sympathy. I daresay I would have been ready to declare the feeling mutual, but at this point my eyes fell on a new and more interesting figure.

He was a young officer in gold-rimmed spectacles and a grey great-coat of plain soldiers' broadcloth. Such greatcoats with officer's epaulettes were popular at the time among young, liberal-minded officers of the Milyutin[1] school. There were quite a few such figures with a democratic stamp, and among officers as a whole there was more of an 'intelligentsia' than later. In remoter places they frequently ran superbly planned battalion libraries, and even guided the reading of local young people. The officer had a serious and likeable face. A sword was hanging from a hook beside him, and a bundle of newspapers lay on a small suitcase. He had just laid one aside and lit a cigarette, blowing the smoke through the open window. There was an empty place beside him, and I thought how nice it would be to go and sit next to this pleasant officer. But shyness was stopping me: a sudden change of place might seem strange, possibly even suspicious.

While I was hesitating, the carriage door opened and in came a new passenger. He was a middle-aged gentlemen, dressed with stylish simplicity, and wearing gold-rimmed spectacles and brown gloves. Alert hazel eyes looked cheerfully and somewhat mockingly from behind the

---

[1] D. A. Milyutin, Minister of War (1861–81). A Liberal who enjoyed the confidence of Alexander II. His reforms, which began as soon as he took office, culminated in the Army Reform of 1874, which stands as the most successful and in many ways the most enlightened of all the Great Reforms. A subsequent reform (1875) made literacy one of the objectives of military training, so that army service helped to compensate to some extent for the absence of an adequate system of elementary education in Russia.

gold rims. Beneath a soft, fair moustache his lips had, like one of Omulevsky's heroes, a distinctive intellectual set. I awfully wanted him to sit next to me, but his eyes merely strayed across my uninteresting figure, and he immediately indicated to the porter the corner by the officer.

'Kindred spirits,' I thought to myself.

The porter put the case on an empty seat. The gentleman opened his purse, took a small silver coin in his gloved fingers and handed it behind him to the porter. The porter took it, looked at it disappointedly and seemed as if he was going to say something. However, he thought better of it and went out. The gentleman turned to the officer.

'I shan't be disturbing you? I say! What a fortunate coincidence! You don't recognize me?'

The officer looked intently at him and said, 'If I'm not mistaken—it's Mr. Negri?'

'Indeed it is, sir. Teodor Mikhaylovich Negri, Professional Reciter. We met in N—. Please don't worry, there's enough room. What have you there, what pile of newspapers is that? Ah, *The Voice*—a full account of the Nechayev trial?[2] Yes, an interesting little affair. Very interesting indeed,' he added, sitting down. 'After the Decembrists[3] I suppose you could call it the very first.'

'There were the Petrashevtsy[4] too.'

'Yes, but that was exaggerated by the government, you know. A harmless group. Do you mind?'

'Of course not.'

The gentleman took a newspaper and opened it. A minute later he said, 'Did you notice the phrase Spasovich[5] coined to christen our brethren—the in-tell-ectual prole-tariat. Very apt, don't you think?'

The officer nodded and said something with a smile. I pricked up my ears, waiting for more conversation between these two likeable people, who had found each other so immediately in the indifferent crowd. 'Just like members of the same Order'—again I found a literary formula. The corner where they were sitting seemed a bright island in a dismal, uninteresting, and perhaps even hostile world. How I should like to get to that island myself. But that, of course, was a hopeless dream. Perhaps

[2] For Nechayev and the trial of the Nechayev group see page 109, note.

[3] A group of Russian nobles, mostly army officers, who on 26 December 1825, the day Nicholas I proclaimed his accession, staged a hopeless revolt in St. Petersburg. They acted in the name of constitutional ideals, and the revolt was the first in Russian history to have a truly *political* basis.

[4] For the Petrashevtsy, see p. 57, note 7.

[5] Counsel for the defence in the trial of the Nechayev group.

some day, with time, when I'd become cleverer and more interesting, I would be able to approach such people openly and simply, and give them to understand from my very first words: 'I too am one of you.'

The carriage had been speeding along for some time, rattling over the points, its couplings clanging. Mr. Negri and the officer were reading newspapers, occasionally exchanging brief comments in low voices. The Jews continued talking quickly and nervously in their own jargon, while my neighbour in the oilskin cap had long ago made my acquaintance and was talking and talking—smoothly, affectionately, and boringly. I listened with half an ear, afraid of losing something of the exchange of opinions in the corner, as my neighbour expressed his friendly goodwill towards me. I was obviously a fresher, wasn't I? I was travelling from a remote little town to the capital? He advised me to be very careful: the trains were full of pickpockets, and I had money with me, hadn't I? He wasn't afraid of anything himself. In the first place, he was very experienced, and secondly, apart from his ticket, he only had one rouble thirty. Right here, in his purse.

He opened his purse, laughing, and turned it inside out. I looked with some surprise at this manoeuvre, which for some reason he repeated several times, and I felt guilty that I somehow couldn't pay sufficient attention to his stories. He seemed kind and likeable, but extraordinarily uninteresting. My eyelids grew heavy. His eyes were again looking into my face with kindly sympathy, but my eyes were closing in spite of myself. I blinked less and less often, and found it harder and harder to keep awake. I leaned my back against the side of the carriage and began falling asleep, feeling my benevolent neighbour leaning his head on my shoulder and trustingly falling asleep too on my chest. In a few minutes I was sleeping contentedly, with a sensation of tight-crowded warmth and someone's wearying benevolence. A few minutes later I woke with the feeling that something had changed.

To begin with I couldn't grasp what, in fact, was going on. My neighbour was indeed lying with his head on my chest in a strange and obviously uncomfortable position, and on the seat directly opposite me (I could hardly believe it) sat Mr. Negri, his elbows on his knees, looking at the two of us with his alert, intelligent and twinkling eyes. Several other passengers were standing around us and also smiling. I blushed and shifted in my seat, but Mr. Negri signalled me not to move and, pointing to my friendly neighbour, recited:

> At dawn do not wake her!
> At dawn she sleeps so sweetly.[6]

[6] The opening lines of a poem by Fet.

There was laughter from the passengers surrounding us and I felt the warm weight resting on me shift immediately. Although my friendly neighbour was even snoring fairly naturally at this moment, I was now quite aware that he was not asleep, but was only pretending not to hear the impolite sneers. I felt sorry for him. . . . Then came a whistle, deadened by the rumbling of the train, which began slowing down, obviously approaching a station. The man in the oilskin cap woke up with a jolt, rubbed his eyes and stood up.

'Station ?' he asked anxiously.

'Ye-es, a station. I don't know which one yet,' Mr. Negri answered innocently. 'But you, of co-ourse, will be getting off here, won't you ?'

'Yes, that's right,' the friendly man muttered and reached for his little bag.

There was a nasty banging of buffers as the train crept up to the platform. Mr. Negri placed his hand on the stranger's sleeve: 'Just a moment, please. Young man,' he said, turning to me, 'are all your things in order ?'

It all became clear to me, and I grabbed my bag so violently that people started laughing. My bag was there all right, and the purse was in the bottom. I breathed a sigh of relief. The man in the oilskin cap got out hurriedly, accompanied by partly scoffing, partly hostile remarks. When the train moved on he was standing at the edge of the platform and, as we passed him, he brandished his fist at the window. For some time after this the passengers exchanged stories about various cases of robbery. Then they went back to their seats, but Mr. Negri stayed with me.

'Well, I congratulate you, young man,' he said wryly. 'You got off pretty lightly. You were undoubtedly dealing with a professional thief. Did you notice that he showed you his own purse several times ? That's a favourite trick. Pardon the expression, but gulls like you—I mean novices, travelling by rail for the first time from the depths of the country, immediately grasp the bag or pocket where they have their money every time a purse is mentioned. You, I observed, went for your bag; and so he stuck to you. And had I not woken you. . . . Come, come, it's nothing. What's there to thank me for ?'

I had blushed deeply, and was vexed that my damned shyness prevented me expressing my feelings properly. In such cases I only thought of the right words after I'd already said others—confused, colourless, and inappropriate. At all events I was extraordinarily pleased to feel obliged to such a remarkable man.

My dream had come true. The train was speeding on, I was sitting next to Mr. Negri, and we were talking quietly together. He had guessed straight away that I had finished school that year. Where was I going? To the Technological Institute? He approved of that: the future of the country depended on the progress of technical knowledge. Besides, the labour question was next in turn. When I admitted that I was entering the Technological Institute temporarily and against my will, as a 'modernist', but hoped later to transfer to a university, his eyes expressed derision.

'In other words, straight on to a beaten track? You want to become a civil servant? No? What then? The bar? Mm . . . that's better still. You want to rake in the money, eh? Quite right, young man, quite right. Barristers do very well indeed.'

I tried to justify myself. Take Spasovich and others. . . . In the Nechayev trial. . . . They didn't take a fee.

'Ah, so that's it! Well, forgive me, if that's the way it is. If that side attracts you, it's another matter. Only you'd best drop the idea anyway. You won't make an orator, because you've an appalling accent. Not Russian, and not Ukrainian, but some sort of local accent. With such pronunciation it's hard to deliver speeches and move people.'

'But there again . . . Spasovich,' I timidly defended myself.

'Come, my dear fellow, come! Spasovich is one thing. Not everyone can be a Spasovich. Still, never mind, good luck to you.'

The train was speeding on, swallowing up the miles, and it seemed to me that it was swallowing up the time just as quickly too. In a little while the wonderful fairy-tale would end. I should have to part forever from this man who had already won my heart. Negri rose.

'Well, young man, we'll have a chat again. It's still quite a way to Kursk.'

'I'm only going as far as Vorozhba,' I answered despondently.

'How so?' he asked.

'I've an uncle in Sumy whom I have to visit on my way. I'll hire horses in Vorozhba.'

A gleam of animation appeared on Mr. Negri's face. He sat down again, looked at me thoughtfully and said, 'You know, this is a happy coincidence. Actually I need to go to Sumy too. I'll give a performance there. Is your uncle a man of standing? Has he been in Sumy long?'

'He's Investigating Magistrate. He's been there five years.'

After a moment's consideration he said, 'Yes, it's positively on my way. Let's go together. By the way, the horses will cost you less too. But, please permit me. You've told me all about yourself, and I still haven't introduced myself. Teodor Mikhaylovich Negri, Professional

Reciter, and, I may add, quite well-known in the provinces. What? You're disappointed? Speak the truth. You're thinking: a clown, a buffoon, who contorts himself on the stage to amuse the public.'

He placed his hand affectionately on my arm and said in a quietly moved tone of voice, 'No, dear boy. You are mistaken. I am not a buffoon, but an artist—and a man with an idea! For me the stage is a pulpit, and declaiming poetry is like preaching. I bring Nikitin, Lermontov, Koltsov, Nekrasov, Petoefi,[7] Hugo to the ignorant masses. I awaken in the crowd feelings which would otherwise have gone on sleeping deep below the surface. And when from the height of the stage the sound of my voice, like a tocsin, makes them quiver, touches those simple, untouched hearts like an electric spark . . .'

He was speaking quietly, from the heart, just for me. Even so, my neighbour in the reddish-brown coat turned his face towards us in curiosity. Negri immediately broke off, was silent for a while and then, stretching out his hand, said, 'Right then, we'll go together?'

I gave him a look in which he probably read appreciative delight. When I recall that moment now, it seems to me that our carriage was speeding through radiant, sunlit fields, and all around me there was a golden haze in which floated the splendid figure of Teodor Negri, Professional Reciter, preacher, new man . . .

'Vorozhba, ten minutes.'

I grabbed my case. Negri said good-bye to the officer. The passenger in the reddish-brown coat with a duck-like nose wanted to say something to me, but, caught up in a whirlwind of excitement, I did not pay any attention to him and jumped down from the carriage. Negri followed me out, accompanied by a porter, and gave a nod in the direction of my case; he then took me by the arm, and led me to the first class waiting room. I felt awkward, but he sat me at a table so gently and authoritatively that I didn't dare resist.

'The menu,' he said to the waiter.

I felt in an awkward situation when the waiter in a tail-coat and cotton gloves handed us the menu. It seemed an unforgivable piece of extravagance to be paying for dinner in the first class. Still, my eyes hit upon 'borshch—30 kopecks'. That was bearable. Negri ordered himself a glass of vodka, a glass of cognac, and a third empty glass. Then caviar and sturgeon. In the empty glass he mixed vodka and cognac, and drank with relish.

The noise around the buffet subsided as the people poured out again. The train whistled, rumbled, and pulled away. There remained an

---

[7] Sandor Petoefi (1823–49), Hungarian lyric poet.

empty room with a modest buffet and just the two of us. Through the open door I could see an unpaved yard, plain railway buildings, and the fresh, alluring emptiness of fields. There was a ringing of little bells, and some bony horses, harnessed in the Russian fashion, came into view.

Negri wiped his moustache with a serviette and beckoned to the waiter. Afraid he'd pay my thirty kopecks too, I hurriedly grasped my purse. Negri smiled at me and said, 'You want to pay? Well, fair enough. We'll settle up in Sumy. When travelling, it's best for one person to do the paying. Get into the way of things, young man, get into the way of them. I owe one rouble, fifty, yours was thirty. A ten-kopeck tip. Call a coachman, waiter.'

Twenty minutes later the roof of the station and the top of the water-tower could just be seen over the undulating steppe, and somewhere very far away over the horizon a little ball of white steam was speeding. Negri took a long, deep breath of fresh air and said, 'Thank you, my country, for your healing vistas! You, of course, don't understand that yet, do you? You don't need healing vistas. Do you like Nekrasov?'

'Very much.'

'And do you know any?'

'I know a lot of Nekrasov.'

'Recite something.'

I looked around. The harvest had almost been gathered in, but here and there sheaves of corn still lay in crosses on the fields, patches of buckwheat showed up rose-coloured in the dusk, and loaded carts crawled along the road. The straw roofs of a little village stood out from behind a hillock. I began to recite:

> Our humble village lies lost
> Amid tall fields of corn . . .

Negri frowned slightly at first, but then began listening attentively. He suddenly took the last stanza from me and finished it himself. It seemed to me that he had caught the quiet poetry of those fields—the whispering of the wind in the stubble, and the ring of a sharpened scythe in some dell—and translated it all into the moving harmony of Nekrasov's verse. Tears came into my eyes from an ache of happiness and sadness.

He gave me a sidelong glance and said, 'You've got feeling. Let's say you don't recite too well as yet. Still, with some training I think you could be quite good. What about Shevchenko?'

'Even worse,' I replied.

'Have a try.'

I recited something uncertainly and confusedly, as I couldn't pronounce it properly. He frowned again and said, 'Mm-yes. . . . That *is* poor. But you have a feeling for Nekrasov. Yes. It would be all right with Nekrasov,' he added to himself.

Night was coming on. The fields were silent in the deepening dusk. Bright stars were imperceptibly appearing one after another. A light band lay for a long time on the horizon, then it too melted away. We travelled on without talking. We would soon reach our destination and part company. I was loathe to waste the time in silence.

'Tell me, please,' I said timidly.

'What is it, young man?'

'You were talking with that young officer about the Nechayev trial.'

'Yes. I was. You were listening?'

'I heard one or two things. And I'd like to ask why they killed Ivanov.'

'It had to be that way,' Negri said stiffly.

'But Ivanov was a man of principle; everyone says he wasn't an informer.'

'Yes, he *was* a good man; but it had to be that way,' Negri rapped out categorically and said no more.

He probably knows more than is in the papers. Perhaps he has also taken part in these things. Both he, and that young officer.

The night became full of vague, mysterious figures. Although I still did not understand why it had been necessary, and could not agree that it could have been necessary, I didn't dare to ask any further questions.

Somewhere far in front dim lights appeared. It must be the town. Another half-hour and the journey would be over. I found this just as unpleasant as if I were travelling with a girl I loved. As if guessing my thoughts, Negri turned to me and said, 'Listen, young man! You couldn't stay a few days in Sumy?' And, without waiting for an answer, he added briskly, 'You know, you and I should give a concert together.'

I was amazed, almost alarmed. I? Giving a performance on stage, before an audience? It was impossible! But Negri held that there was nothing to it. He had thought it all over. In my delivery there *was* feeling. In the two days, while the posters were being printed, he would prepare me. I could get a dress-coat on hire. My uncle would try to get people interested, and distribute tickets among his colleagues. Why, it would be marvellous!

I don't know what would have come of this and whether in other circumstances I would have been able to refuse this remarkable man who had so strong an influence on me, but I didn't have much time:

15 August was near, and I still had to stop off in Moscow to see my sister, and I had to find a room in Petersburg.

'It's a pity,' Negri said disappointedly. 'Well, you certainly won't refuse what I'm going to ask of you now, will you?'

'Anything I can do,' I answered eagerly.

'This you can do: we shall spend tonight together in an hotel, and you'll look out your uncle tomorrow morning. Quite candidly: it simply grieves me to say good-bye to you.'

'Yes, of course,' I blurted out in confusion. 'I also. . . . You don't know . . . I . . . my er . . .'

I became utterly confused and shut up.

We arrived in Sumy late and booked into rather a seedy hotel. I managed to settle myself on chairs, which moved from under me several times. Still, the sleep I got, and even the frequent waking up from my restless couch, were pleasant. I thought out a letter to my mother: she need not feel any anxiety on my account. I would be able to find what I wanted. I was lucky: I had already got to know a remarkable, exceptional man!

When I woke up next morning Negri, already washed and fresh looking, was sitting at the table writing something.

'Ah, you've woken up! Get up and we'll have some tea. Meanwhile I'll just finish a little piece of business.'

I had a quick wash and was ready in five minutes. Negri rang the bell. A man came in and stopped by the door.

'Here, take this, my man, and tell them to send the proof quickly. Got it?'

'Yes, sir. They told me to demand a deposit.'

'Be off with you!' Negri said peremptorily, and turned to me. 'Now then. I've found out where your uncle lives. It's not far. How long will you spend with him?'

'Not more than two days.'

'I see. Of course, we'll see each other again. Today you will spend in the arms of your family, but tomorrow morning come here. Without fail! Then we'll settle our little accounts too. Are you still here?' He turned to the messenger from the printing-office, who was standing motionless in the doorway.

'Yes, sir. They told me to demand a deposit,' he repeated like a robot.

Rather a fine nervous grimace ran across Negri's face.

'How do you like that!' he said disgustedly. 'The inevitable prelude to any performance. The other side of a wandering artist's life. You know what? I'd like to take a little token from you, so as to be sure you will visit me again: you paid in the buffet, and for the horses. Let's continue our common expenses until tomorrow. Give that robber there two roubles.'

I hurriedly handed over the money.

'Thank you. Now go and see your uncle, while I attend to business. I need a hall, police permission, and so on. You really won't stay, not even to hear your friend, the artist Teodor Negri? You can't? Well, never mind, never mind. Till tomorrow then!'

My uncle had been expecting me the previous day from my mother's letter, and was rather anxious. When he'd heard the story of my lucky meeting, he comically raised his brows and said, 'He asked you for a loan?'

I blushed, feeling insulted for my new friend.

'Uncle!' I said reproachfully. 'You don't know what kind of man this is. An artist, preacher. It's the only sort of social persuasion in our country that . . .'

'How much did he borrow?' he asked again, but, seeing that I was hurt, said, 'All right, all right. Let's hear your artist.'

This uncle of mine had been a jovial, witty man. Now he was suffering from consumption; but at times his eyes still twinkled with humour. I was very fond of him, but, still, he was only my uncle, while Teodor Negri, professional reciter and preacher, stood far above his judgement and sneers.

The following morning I ran off to the hotel as if I were going to see a girl. A boy-waiter was walking along the corridor in front of me, carrying trays on both hands with decanters, glasses, and light refreshments. He stopped, pushed open a door with his foot, and I saw into the room. It was thick with tobacco-smoke and a merry group of men were sitting at a table. I noticed particularly a young giant of a man with a broad face, as red as raw meat; he had on a silk blouse with a massive gold chain running from one pocket to the other. From the smoke-filled room came noisy and apparently drunken talking, shouts, and laughter. By all appearances an all-night card-session was ending in the late morning.

Mr. Negri was not in our room. Seeing me standing in the open doorway, the waiter came into the room, flicked his serviette over the table and said, 'I'll tell him straight away. He's with the exciseman. He told me for you to wait and not go away.' And he disappeared.

A minute later the door opened and in came Mr. Negri. His face looked a little flabby and rather dejected. He came up to me without saying anything, shook me firmly and somehow meaningfully by the hand, and looked searchingly into my face for several seconds. Then he let go of my hand, took a few steps and sat down at the table with his head on his hands. A vague sense of alarm came over me. The strained and solemn silence of that moment was broken by noise from the neighbouring room. They were laughing, knocking, and calling someone. Negri turned his face towards me with a sarcastic and pained expression.

'Nice people, aren't they?' he asked.

I did not reply; I wasn't thinking about those people and hadn't formed any definite opinion about them, obviously from a lack of perspicacity. But Mr. Negri was thinking about them and had an opinion:

'What are they?' he asked with repressed anger and sadness. And he immediately answered briefly and expressively: 'Rrro-bbers.'

A pause ensued, full of acute, almost electric tension. Then, into this silence Mr. Negri let fall one sentence after another—distinct, quiet, burning hot.

'See! They are making merry. Carousing. You hear? Do you hear? Yet I! For my mission. For my noble mission. Oh!' He gave a dull groan and, turning to me suddenly, started to speak still more quietly and more distinctly, as if seeking to impress upon me an important and bitter secret.

'Why try to hide the truth? Do you know, my dear, unsullied young man, in what position I find myself? I haven't a kopeck! Credit! Lord above! What credit will a wandering missionary find in Russia? For the posters I ordered when you were here you have to pay in advance, or else the printer, a *kulak* and exploiter, won't issue them. So my concert won't take place! Tomorrow I, an artist with a cultural mission, will be flung out of this wretched hotel like a dog. But you . . . you still . . .'

My heart sank. Everything around was so awful and so criminal. One more second—and I would learn of my share in this joint crime. But Mr. Negri was looking at me through his gold-rimmed spectacles with tender affection.

'You asked yesterday: "Why? Did it have to be done?"' (I realized he was talking about Nechayev and Ivanov.) 'Yes! It did have to be done! Everything, you understand: *everything* is permissible and *everything* is necessary in this country, where fellows like that'—he poked his thumb over his shoulder—'can laugh a sated belly-laugh, while people like you and me can only weep; yes, weep tears of blood.'

His head dropped on to his hands again and he fell silent. His shoulders were shaking slightly. Could he—Mr. Negri, whom I had yesterday seen so magnificent—be actually crying? I stood, holding my breath, shocked and stunned. From behind the robbers' door shouting and laughter could again be heard.

I went timidly up to Mr. Negri and said, 'Teodor Mikhaylovich. I . . . forgive me, but I can't bear. . . . If you'd be willing to accept from me as much as you need for those posters and so on. Here . . . I've . . .' And I held out my thin purse. Negri raised his head and looked at me with a moist, moved expression.

'You . . . you would do that? No, no. I cannot, I must not.'

The purse was in his hands. He opened it and started reading out its contents, as if he were reading a touching epitaph on a gravestone:

'Luggage receipt. A note of an address, probably of friends in Petersburg. Ten, twenty, thirty-five, fifty . . .'. He looked at me inquiringly and continued in the same moved tone of voice, not taking his eyes off my face, 'Somewhere else, probably, a mother's loving hand has sewn in a bag a hundred or two roubles. And that is all. Yet this youth, himself a proletarian, stretches out a helping hand to a proletarian artist. Oh, thank you, thank you! Not for the money, of course, I still don't know whether I can take it, but for that pure faith in man, which . . .'

He blinked and wiped something under his gold-rimmed spectacles with the corner of a handkerchief. Then he said with a change of tone, 'Still, wait. If you really want to, then . . . money matters are not done this way. Sit down. That's it. Now let's get it clear: how much money have you altogether?'

I blushed so deeply that my face tingled. I felt as though I'd tricked a remarkable man who'd confided in me.

'It's all . . . there,' I said with some effort.

In Mr. Negri's eyes appeared a quick, complex expression of disappointment, a momentary cold gleam, as if he were really angry, then—humorous surprise, then simply puzzlement.

'All of it?' he queried. 'And you are going to Petersburg with that? I suppose you'll be sent money? No?'

'I'll give lessons,' I muttered in an altogether guilty voice.

He laughed.

'That's not so easy. You will have a bitter cup to drink. Never mind, don't blush, young man. I see that your means don't quite correspond to your generous impulses. Thank you all the more. Of course, we need to calculate. Let's see: to Kursk, Tula, Moscow, Petersburg.

Right, I'll take ten roubles for the posters; and also . . . yes, all right, all right: another five roubles. You are still saving me. The concert will take place. I shall have some money. Oh, your Petersburg address? It doesn't matter, though. I can write to you at the Institute. I shall probably be in Petersburg myself soon and shall look you up, my dear young friend. Then, perhaps, you in turn will not refuse a helping hand from a humble wandering artist. Right? You really wouldn't refuse me that, would you? Well, in the meantime . . .'

He stood up and took my hand. Holding it, he leaned back a little and looked into my face. An idea had suddenly occurred to him.

'One additional little request, my dear friend: you'd best not say anything to your uncle about . . . about our relations. Those people with hearts chilled by the prose of life, would they understand . . .'

'Of course I won't say anything,' I replied with conviction.

'Right we are, then.'

The door opened and the stupid face of the waiter appeared.

'The excise gentleman,' he began, but Negri made a pained face and said in an angry, suffering voice,

'I know, I know. Go and get lost, you and your excise men.'

The fellow disappeared. Mr. Negri again turned to me and began speaking in the way that affected me so easily, 'So, it's time to part. Believe me, my young friend. Yes, I know you will believe me. Teodor Negri is the Wandering Jew, a gipsy, a vagrant, but he will not forget that on his road, on the grim road of a travelling missionary, fate gave him a meeting with an unsullied youth, trustful, and with an unchilled, responsive heart. Farewell, farewell!'

Mr. Negri embraced me. I felt the touch of his soft moustache, and he pressed his lips to my cheek. I didn't have time to respond, for he let go of me and disappeared quickly, leaving me alone in the room. It was quiet. Only through the door of the robbers' room, that seemed to have been momentarily opened, there came a burst of particularly noisy exultation, laughter and shouting.

The streets of the unfamiliar town were dreary and dismal. There was a fine drizzle, grey bands of mist were moving over the sky, and the road was covered with thin, slippery mud. But in my heart there was music playing, rather sad music, but very inspiring. What a remarkable man! 'What are they? Rrrobbers!' Oh, how well he had said that! With one word he had characterized the vulgar group I had seen in the dirty room through a haze of smoke. That young man with the self-satisfied red face. That must have been the excise man? Of course it must; the waiter had said yesterday that only one room was occupied, and by an excise gentleman. And today he had again been coming from the excise man. Why? What could that vulgar fellow possibly have in common with the travelling missionary? Mr. Negri's pained expression at the very mention of the chap was perfectly understandable. He takes bribes, no doubt of that. Swanks in his gold chain. 'Yet I! For my mission. For my noble mission.' Where had he gone, after he'd said good-bye to me? Who was he talking to now? Who could it have been that the robbers met with such glee after we'd said good-bye? 'On my road, on the grim road of a travelling missionary, fate sent me an un-sullied youth.' Did he really say that about me? What was I for him? I was uninteresting, backward, ridiculously dressed. Yet his intelligent eyes had been looking at *me*, he had looked *up* at me with such deep sadness. Oh, Mr. Negri, dear, handsome, clever Mr. Negri! Artist, reciter, proletarian intellectual, wanderer with a mission. Would I never ever see you again!

At this thought my eyes became moist.

And yet, if the reader thinks that my contemporary was as hope-lessly stupid as it might appear from his mood as described here, he will, I think, be mistaken. Even at this moment the shy young man was not without some perspicacity. A solemn symphony was playing in his heart, but at the same time he was still aware that the streets were dirty and dreary, and that a mud-bespattered cab was rattling along the road. True, the charming and brilliant figure of Mr. Negri was floating before him in a golden haze, holding sway over the sunny side of his consciousness. But behind him, in the grey and dismal shadows, there loomed another figure, paler but still pretty distinct. If he had only been brought forward, he would have appeared in as much relief as his magnificent double. *This* Mr. Negri had been going to Kursk, probably after failures and with unformed plans. He had turned off to Sumy really because of me. I had paid for his dinner, for the horses, for the room, for the posters. There had been a gleam of disappointment in his eyes when my funds had been totalled up. He had thought I had more. He had purposely said that Ivanov *had* to be killed. He knew nothing about it really. Finally he had definitely come to me from the robbers and had gone back to them afterwards. Perhaps he was now continuing the game on the money he had had from me and would lose it all, right down to the last kopeck, to that chap with the red face. Yet I would scarcely have ten roubles left when I got to Petersburg.

But I have drawn this second figure too crudely and sharply. At the time, he was only trying to come forward in my consciousness—light, aerial, and so timid that he disappeared with every movement his magnificent double made. And when he made efforts to come from the shadows into the light, I felt hurt and aggrieved. I had only just parted from the live Mr. Negri. Surely I should not have to part with the memory too? No, no! At such moments the magnificent Mr. Negri would say one of his phrases that stabbed at my heart—and his despised double would dissolve in the mist.

In a word, even then I knew the real Mr. Negri, but my heart demanded the other Mr. Negri, whom I so admired. And that is exactly how he remained for me. As such he continued to hold sway over me. And had fate soon brought us together again, and had he again said some such stunning words and looked up at me with sad, suffering eyes, I should probably have followed him wherever he called me, without heeding the timid, warning voice of his double.

For a long time afterwards in Petersburg, at difficult moments that were as sad and dismal as that muddy street, the figure of the magnificent Mr. Negri, the professional reciter, would float out in all his fascination from a rosy haze. It seemed to me that he would open the door, come in, peer at me through his gold-rimmed spectacles and say,

'Here I am. A wanderer and gipsy. I have sought you out, knowing that things are hard for you. Yet, you, my young man, doubted me, did you not?'

My uncle once more started asking jokingly about my artist, but, seeing how I felt, he dropped the subject and instead undertook a thorough inspection of my financial and other resources. The results were rather sad. He himself was not well off and was in poor health. In his once twinkling dark eyes there was now reflected constant and serious concern about his children. Even so, he mended the breach in my finances made by the reciter and equipped me, besides, with his dark suit. He was very tall, and the tails of his frock-coat came down over my heels. My uncle burst out laughing and said, 'Never mind, never mind. In Petersburg you can call a tailor and get it altered. Goodness knows what you look like in your own suit.'

Towards evening, when I was driving out of the town, clouds were again hanging over it, and a fine drizzle was coming down on the dreary, muddy streets. On posts and fences I caught glimpses of large sheets of paper, on which I could make out the bold heading:

Teodor Negri, Professional Reciter.

They were being soaked by the rain, and I reflected sadly that the weather would spoil the concert of my remarkable friend.

13
Petersburg!

ON THE ROAD, ACCOMPANIED BY THE TINKLING OF THE horses' bells, and in the train to Kursk I felt very glum. In Kursk two passengers already familiar to me got into the carriage in which I was sitting: the man with a duck-like nose and his companion. The former proved to be Zubarevsky, a third-year student at the Technological Institute. (Somehow I can't recall the other's name or what he looked like.) They had spent those two or three days on various business matters in Kursk, and would also be stopping off in Moscow. I pretended to believe everything, but, really, it seemed unlikely to me that a man with such an undistinguished appearance and dressed in that way could in fact be a student. Still, I was now a man of experience and could not easily be tricked. When they proposed that we all stay together in Moscow at the Kokorevsky Hotel, I politely declined: I needed to stay somewhere near the Yakaterinsky Institute. I had a sister there.

At the old Kursk Station in Moscow I regretted this. When I found myself on the platform with my suitcase in my hand, I was immediately caught up in a whirlwind of shouting, cheeky faces and raised caps. They seized the flaps of my unfortunate cloak, tried to grab the case out of my hand, peered into my eyes, breathed in my face—their breath smelled of a variety of things, but mostly of wine—and seemed to be jeering. Far off I glimpsed the figures of Zubarevsky and his friend. They seemed pleasant to me now. Zubarevsky had kind eyes, really, and a far from stupid face. He could be a student at that. In any case he was no robber. I tore after him, but he had already disappeared. In my very ear came a husky, gentle voice:

'The Domnikov Lodging House, sir. Only forty kopecks. No need for a cab. I'll carry your things myself.'

I was tired of struggling and gave myself over to the will of fate.

The following morning this same man was off to the station again, and undertook to show me the way to the Institute. It was a holiday. Bells were ringing—slow, sad, and low. My short meeting with my sister did little to cheer me up. We sat in a huge, collonaded hall. I felt something within me longing to reach out to that little figure in her

Institute dress, and something else holding me back and smothering these impulses. My sister was soon called back, and when I went out of the Institute, Ivan the Great had joined the chorus of sadly conversing bells. There was grief in its measured, magnificent boom, and it seemed as though some age-old sadness were soaring and circling over Moscow.

All this made me feel such heart-ache that I stopped on the Samotyok, not knowing what to do with myself. Fortunately I remembered my fellow travellers—Zubarevsky and his friend. There was still quite some time left before the train went. I set off again, asking the way, and was soon at the Kokorevsky Hotel. The two students were in their room, very high up, almost in the attic. When I went in, they were a little embarrassed; they had been busy packing some books into a case. Zubarevsky stretched out his hand welcomingly:

'Marvellous to see you. Like some tea? The samovar is on the table there, pour yourself some. As you see, we're sorting through some literature. Do you know this?'

He handed me a book, I think it was Flerovsky's *Alphabet of the Social Sciences*. I had never heard of it.

'Do you know Lasalle? No? So, they haven't heard of socialism in your place yet.'

It was the first time I'd heard the word. One thing was now absolutely clear to me, and that was how short-sighted and foolish I'd been to have doubted Zubarevsky. Now, on the contrary, everything about him seemed exceptionally attractive. The two students kindly spent a long time telling me about Petersburg, and advised me as to where to stay initially. Then we said good-bye like good friends, and I came out feeling reassured, although the bells of Moscow were still slowly ringing out their age-old sadness.

It was strange: in the course of these two or three days I had several times been brought face to face with my own foolishness. The chap in the oilskin cap had nearly robbed me at the very time I had been suspicious of Zubarevsky and was on my guard against him. Mr. Negri . . . still, even now the figure of Mr. Negri remained brilliant and fascinating, and eclipsed his pale, real double. I sometimes caught myself giving my lips an intellectual set. Then the plain, kindly people in the place I'd stayed the previous night had seemed bandits, and, though I had thought I was in a dangerous trap, I had shamefully fallen asleep none the less. All this should obviously have greatly reduced my self-confidence. However, the opposite proved to be the case. Setting out to the station again, I felt as if I'd really survived all these dangers and had emerged triumphant solely due to my experience and unusual resourcefulness.

At the station, amid the crush, the shouting and the bustle, I once again walked about in a rose-coloured haze. At the ticket-office I bumped into Korzhenevsky, one of the Rovno lads. He had finished a year before, had been tutoring, and was now going to Petersburg with the money he'd earned. The poor fellow was quite bewildered by the commotion; he was looking around uneasily and clutching his bag convulsively with his left hand.

'Good Lord!' I thought. 'I was like that only two or three days ago.' And I immediately took him under my wing, behaving with such assurance and unconcern that the poor lad kept right at my heels, holding on to my coat like a sheet-anchor. When at last we took our seats in the tightly-crowded train, I felt as though Korzhenevsky was the person I had been in the train near Kiev, and I was his magnanimous protector like the magnificent Mr. Negri.

At this time passenger trains took exactly twenty-four hours from Moscow to Petersburg. Having left Moscow towards evening, it was dusk the following day when Korzhenevsky and I walked from the station on to the Nicholas Square. My heart raced with joy. Petersburg! Here was concentrated everything I considered best in life, because it was from here that the whole of Russian literature, so dear to my heart, issued forth. It was the time of year when summer has only just given way to autumn. The outlines of houses stood out massively and somehow dreamily against the indistinctly light background of the evening sky, while down below ran rows of street lamps, like bright-coloured beads. It is the time when they are usually lit again after the summer nights. They seem so bright, fresh, and young. It's as if they are going out to work for the first time after their holidays. Their work isn't very necessary as yet, for the air is still full of dreamy reflections of light floating up from somewhere beyond the horizon. The merry glitter of the street lamps under the fresh, gleaming sky, the clanging and ringing of a horse-drawn tram, the twilight fading in the distance, the distinctive, strong smell of the sea, brought to the square on the west wind—everything was in striking harmony with the way I felt.

We stood at the main entrance, waiting for the disorderly mass of carriages to thin out, and I eagerly drank in the sensation of Petersburg. So, I was now standing at last on the threshold of the great capital. There, to the left, was the opening of a broad street, like the mouth of a river. That, of course, was the Nevsky. I knew this, as I'd asked Suchkov about it in detail and had frequently imagined the first time I'd see it. So that was where Gogol's Lieutenant Pirogov[1] had once walked. And somewhere else, in that confused mass of houses, Belinsky had lived, and Dobrolyubov had worked and thought. Nekrasov was living here now, and so I was breathing the same air as he. Here, of course, Director Yermakov was waiting for me, and so was the new, fascinating life of a student. All this was beautiful and fresh and lovely to think about, and, like those lines of lamps, led into the mysteriously shimmering distance, full of dynamic life, as yet unfamiliar and unclear to me. And the lamps, flickering in the wind, seemed to be living and playing and saying something wonderfully kind and full of promise to me.

I am dwelling on this moment in such detail firstly because it stamped itself forever on my memory as one of the landmarks on the dimming horizons of my past. And, secondly, because those same streetlamps later spoke to me in a different language and even drove me from Petersburg with that same dreamy twinkling. At this moment I was happy with the consciousness of youth, health, strength, and expectations. When the cabs had dispersed, I set off across the square, accompanied by Korzhenevsky, who was literally holding on to my sleeve.

Only a small and really quite insignificant incident marred my feelings of delight. Right at the entrance of a humble boarding-house, sheltering at the back of the magnificent Northern Hotel, I noticed appetizing fresh loaves of bread in the window of a basement shop. I went down and asked for a French roll. The bearded broad-faced baker, who was cutting someone half a loaf, measured me with coldly mocking eyes and said, 'We don't have French rolls, sir. We sell Russian loaves.'

He and his two young assistants looked at me so derisively that I immediately felt as though I'd been slung out of Petersburg into far-off provincial Rovno with its stagnant ponds. And most clearly of all I remembered the tailor Shimko, since there was no doubt that it was partly to his efforts that I owed those looks of surprise and derision. But that was such a trifle! At all events, I was in Petersburg!

I woke up early, apparently from a sensation of almost unbearable delight. Korzhenevsky was still sleeping. I went barefoot to the window and looked out at the street. The Ligovka at this time was still a canal, or, more accurately, a foul ditch, across which there were wooden footbridges at fairly frequent intervals. The sky was overcast, grey. That was how it should be: it wasn't for nothing that it was

[1] In the story 'Nevsky Prospect'.

compared to a soldier's grey greatcoat. There it was. Very similar, indeed. From the Neva a creeping mist was nearing the top of the Znamensky Church. Excellent. These were the Petersburg mists that had been described so often. Everything was just so! There could be no doubt I was in Petersburg.

A little booklet with a plan of the city was lying on the table. I seized it excitedly and, still undressed, started studying the streets we would have to go through to find our Rovno friends. They were in Apartment 8, 4 Maliy Tsarskoselsky Prospect, Semyonovsky Regiment.[2] When Korzhenevsky had got up and we'd had some tea, I took him confidently along Nevsky Prospect. He frequently expressed surprise, and, not trusting my judgement, kept on stopping for fear of getting lost. At the beginning of Obukhovsky Prospect, on the Hay-Market, stood a horse-drawn tram. It had only just arrived, and the driver was changing the horses from the back end to the front. I boldly decided to sit on the top. Korzhenevsky was again reluctant.

'Listen, what are you doing! Look: no one's getting on,' he said quietly, pulling at my coat. But I recklessly waved him aside and began going up the stairway.

The tram moved off. On the right was the Institute of Communication Engineers. Which of our people had gone there? No one, I think. A bridge. The Fontanka.[3] We both stood up and, straining our necks, watched an unfamiliar sight: a barge, loaded with firewood, was drawing under a bridge. Further on was the long building of the Constantine Military School. The two Zabotin brothers and Zaverdyayev had gone there. Now on the left there was a long building with reddish-yellow walls. A young man in a dark blue blouse, spectacles, high boots, and a cap with a green band, who was sitting next to us, got up and went quickly down the stairs. 'Look, look! That's the Technological Institute.' It was a wide-fronted building on the corner of two streets. Buildings certainly have faces of their own. What a clever face this one had! Like—what? Like I imagined Director Yermakov. Impressive and serious. At the entrance I could see people going in, coming out and pausing to chat. Our fellow-passenger was walking towards it, as if it were his home, greeting people and exchanging remarks with them as he went.

'There's a typical student,' I said to Korzhenevsky. 'What an intelligent face he's got.'

[2] An area of Petersburg named after the famous Guards Regiment, which was quartered there. Some of the streets were numbered according to companies (*roty*). Another area bore the name of the Izmaylovsky Regiment.

[3] A branch of the Neva running through part of Petersburg.

Later I got to know him. Alas! once more I had to admit my lack of perspicacity. The young man was, indeed, very typical and not very bright. . . .

There were two young men in the large but very haphazardly furnished room. One was sitting on a chair, his legs stretched out and his head thrown back, so that only the tip of his nose was visible; he was ineptly strumming a guitar. The other was rolling a cigarette by the window, peering at a thick book. Our arrival did not make any particular impression on them. The guitarist went on running his fingers over the strings, then got up.

'You'll be Mirochka's friends?' he inquired. His face was a copper-red colour, none too clean, and he spoke with a peculiar sort of accent, as if he were squeezing out the words.

'Yes, we're from Rovno.'

'He was saying. Don't know where he's got to. We're waiting for him ourselves.'

'He's on the roam; been a bit long,' the one who was reading growled, and then buried his face in his book again. His face seemed very intellectual and serious to me: large features, a thin moustache over full lips, a cleft chin, and thick dark hair, which fell over his face when he leaned over the book. 'A real, serious student', I thought respectfully.

'Let's get acquainted,' said the young man who'd been strumming the guitar. 'Nikulin, Ardalion. Technological student.'

'Veselitsky,' said the other in a pleasant, deep voice.

We heard the bell ring, then Grinevetsky came into the room. He was tall and handsome, with golden-fair hair, which fell to his shoulders, and big, grey eyes. In a white chasuble he could have made an archangel in a passion-play. Now, in a plaid, flung carelessly over his shoulders, he looked like a German artist of the romantic period. At school he had been two classes ahead of me and had been regarded as a star pupil. I looked up to him, and was now touched by the open-hearted warmth with which he met us. All the same, a worried look soon replaced his animation. He threw off his plaid, tossed a bundle on to the bed and began striding about the room. He didn't make much sound at all, his heels not thudding but padding on the floor. I looked more closely and the sad truth became clear to me: there were no heels on his boots and there were wet marks on the floor.

'So, Mirochka?' drawled Ardalion Nikulin, looking inquiringly at Grinevetsky.

'So, not a damned thing!' Grinevetsky answered angrily.

'Still?'

'One and a half, there's your "still" for you.'

Ardalion gave a loud, angry snort.

'Ph-ew—the idea! You should have explained to him, you comedian, that you only redeemed them in the spring for eight.'

'He said: wear them through the summer and I won't give you a brass farthing.'

'That's a point,' Veselitsky said quietly. He was still reading, as if he were not interested in the conversation or the consequences of the failure. I had respectfully guessed that Grinevetsky must have been to a pawnshop with something. Their hopes had been dashed, and now they were in a desperate position. Very natural, too. How could it be otherwise: they were students, intellectual proletarians! It's also called 'Bohemia', I believe. In Paris there's the Latin Quarter. There, too, science and poverty live together like sisters. What if . . . I looked at my new friends. Only Nikulin was tolerably dressed. Veselitsky had no coat, one of his shirt-sleeves was undone, and the pockets of his wide trousers were broken and sticking out. I thought that it would not, perhaps, be too presumptuous of me to hope to come in with them.

The question really settled itself. The group was, indeed, going through a crisis. They'd already been refused the room. It was too dear and too luxurious for them. In the same house, right under the roof, accommodation for four had just become vacant—a place that could be described by the grand, literary word garret. But they still owed four roubles for this room, and they didn't have any money, or sugar, or tea. Grinevetsky had been to see Suchkov at his old flat, but he hadn't arrived yet.

My seventeen roubles seemed wealth indeed. In half an hour the samovar was boiling merrily, and there was white bread and sausage on the table. By the evening, we'd transferred our cases to the garret. Korzhenevsky did not join us. When he'd conquered his shyness and asked how to go about things, he set off around the Semyonovsky Regiment, read the advertisements, went carefully up staircases, haggled politely, and by the evening had already rented a cheap and suitable room.

'A careful young man,' said Ardalion, 'sensible. He has shunned evil and done well.'

'And why not?' Veselitsky said seriously. 'It's right enough. Here with us, old chap, you won't come to any good.'

And he gestured derisively with his hand. I liked these self-depre-cating words and the serious tone in which they were spoken. But, of course, I was not really in agreement with them and felt completely happy. Could anyone have found a better place so quickly?

The morning was simply a continuation of the same mood of delight. The sun was peeping obliquely and playfully through the little square windows, and the whole street echoed with a variety of very musical calls. At this time the streets of Petersburg were much more melodious than they are now. A woman's clear voice sang: 'Cran- berries, cranberries!' A baritone voice: 'Knives, scissors sharpened, razors stropped!' A strong, deep voice called something long and sad- sounding, ending with the words: 'Bru-ushes for your floors'. Finally, a Tartar called in a guttural voice, like an eagle's scream: 'Ro-obes, ro-obes!' And when heavy carts rumbled down the street, our whole house shivered, and there was a light ringing sound from the window- panes. After all, this was Petersburg, a city built on unstable marshes.

From the window there was a typical view of outer Petersburg— roofs, wasteland, courtyards, factory chimneys. Massive stone build- ings loomed above little wooden houses, and one could see the semi- circular tanks of the gas works, and the dreary fronts of factories. Farther away, on the horizon, there was a strip of trees, and the walls of churches gleamed among them in the sunlight. This was the Volkov Cemetery.[4] It seemed that all of this—the melodious calls of the pedlars, the factory hooters, the hurried whistles of locomotives on the branch line linking the Nicholas and Tsarskoye Selo railways[5]—bore some relation to my arrival. Everything seemed to be glad with me.

[4] The Volkov Cemetery: many of Russia's great writers were buried there.

[5] The Nicholas Railway runs between St. Petersburg and Moscow; it was built in 1851 and named after the Emperor Nicholas I. After the Revolution it was renamed 'The October Railway'. The Tsarskove Selo Railway was the first railway to be built in Russia. It was constructed in 1837, and was only about eighteen miles in length, running from Petersburg to Tsarskoye Selo.

At the outbreak of the Crimean War, these were the only railways in the whole of Russia. The war was followed by a period of intense railway construction.

14
Student Life

THE TECHNOLOGICAL INSTITUTE WAS SEETHING LIKE AN ant-hill, although lectures had not yet started. At this time batch after batch of boys was finishing at the Modern High Schools and pouring into the Technical Colleges, so that the centre of gravity of student life was noticeably shifting away from the University. That year 1500 men started in the Technological Institute alone, and before 15 August this whole mass filled the corridors, administrative offices, and technical-drawing classrooms. People from the same place arranged first meetings here, old friends met after the holidays, noted down addresses, got residence permits from the office, and reserved places in the drawing classrooms.

Students at this time did not resemble present-day students at all. There was no uniform. People wore all kinds of clothes, but there was a predominance of high boots and grey or dark blue blouses with leather belts. The blouses were sometimes very smart, with embroidered pockets, into which little gold chains descended, and tied round with broad sports-belts. Mostly, however, the blouses were plain ones, bought for sixty or seventy kopecks in the Aleksandrovsky Market, and tied with narrow thongs. As the Institute was under the Department of State Property, students sometimes also wore caps with green bands. But the Technological students could be recognized on the street without this cap. They had a generally 'democratic' look about them: long hair, spectacles, and plaids. In this variety of faces, figures, and clothes there seemed to emerge an overall type, in whom I joyfully discerned strangely familiar features. A sturdy and rather rough factory worker, with an intellectual's face and 'the stamp of thought'. The same, ideal young man I'd invented after reading Spielhagen's *Between the Hammer and the Anvil*,[1] a man descending from the heights of culture into the world of working men: the link between two worlds, a working intellectual or an intellectual workingman.

I walked along the corridor with Grinevetsky, and my eyes delightedly tried to catch every detail of this new world. Someone called

[1] Friedrich Spielhagen (1829–1911), German novelist who became very popular in Russia in the 1870s. His *Hammer und Amboss* first appeared in 1868.

out to Grinevetsky. It was a tall, fair-haired man with large features and the mannerisms of a good-natured bear. On his grey blouse there were traces of washed oil-stains. He shook Grinevetsky's hand firmly and said, 'Hello. How are you getting on? What did you do in the holidays?'

Grinevetsky blushed slightly. They had been together the first year. Now this fair-haired giant had passed to the third year.

'Nothing,' Grinevetsky answered, and asked in turn: 'How about you?'

'I worked on ballast trains to Polesye. For practical experience.'

'Hard?'

'Not so bad. I'm fit. First I was a stoker, then assistant driver. Interesting.'

A group had gathered round us. Other people had also done practical work: as plain workmen, timekeepers, fitters. At this time there was no 'movement to the people'[2] with political aims. Students were readily accepted, favourably treated, and had their paltry wages increased by moderate rewards. They came back with a great store of impressions and a small amount of money for the beginning of the new year. I listened with great interest to their stories, in which I sensed a sober spirit of pluckiness and echoes of my own dreams.

The whole enormous building seemed adapted to produce this very sort of man; it created the right atmosphere and environment for him. On the walls were plates with drawings of the plans and components of machines. Huge screws, drawn along exactly calculated curves, levers, cranks, shafts, fly-wheels, eccentrics. From figures were born lines, and from lines, forms. They are already turning into the colours of iron and copper, are assuming their metallic flesh, are becoming silent models. The imagination soars further, to where they are rumbling in factories and flying along rails. There is the heavy, measured breathing of steam-engines, pistons are moving backwards and forwards, pinions are juddering, and wind is coming from the fly-wheels, as trains speed across endless plains. And in this element people are moving—hundreds of thousands of them, the huge and mysterious mass of working people, in whose enigmatic face the whole of literature has become interested.

All this took strong hold of my imagination, but, of course, in a

_____

[2] In the summer of 1874 thousands of young people (largely students) spontaneously left the cities to spread socialism among the peasantry. In 1876 a second, smaller and more organized 'movement to the people' took place. See also Appendix.

vague, general way, not in such exact terms. The enormous building, filled with noise, laughter and the echo of voices, seemed a sort of factory, producing a new man for a new life. Somehow the black-coated figure of the barrister on the rostrum, appealing to the judges with eloquent gestures, paled straight away before the colourful figure of the technologist. Why, indeed, must I become a barrister? Was not everything I saw, sensed, and imagined here more interesting? The transformation of an abstract mathematical formula into a heavy machine, obedient to human will, was not that poetry in itself? The heavy working of metal-bound forces. The power of the mind over the blind power of nature and the vague but attractive idea of participating in the elemental life of the countless mass of workers. There were as yet no ready Populist programmes. This was part of the very air, it arose from the general intellectual atmosphere in which this generation lived.

Through corridors and then a small courtyard, where a pipe was smoking and jets of white steam were spurting into the air, Grinevetsky led me to the workshops. Students and ordinary workmen worked there under the guidance of specialists. The students were choosing places and making notes, talking with people they knew from the previous year. There was a smell of engine oil, shafts were turning, endless belts were running agitatedly through the air, and the lathe-stand was screeching slightly. Vices held beautifully cut screws, made from shapeless lumps of metal.

When we returned to the main building, I was struck by a new scene in one of the exhibition-rooms. A tall young man in a black coat and gold-rimmed spectacles was standing in the middle of a group of interested students and, holding his hand on the top of a cylindrical structure made of pig-iron, was explaining how it was made and how it worked. He looked exactly like a professor, and I was very surprised to learn that he was only a fourth-year student. He had invented some sort of furnace for special technical purposes. The model had been made in the workshop and there was soon to be a demonstration of the new invention. I didn't understand anything of what he was saying, but this handsome, purely intellectual figure with delicate features and unusually dark eyes set in a pale face took hold of my imagination in turn. I made some hasty alterations to my picture of my ideal self. What if in a few years' time I, just like that young man with the inspired face of a gifted inventor. . . . But my flight of fantasy now struck against a patent absurdity. In a few years' time—more precisely, in four years' time—no, it was completely inconceivable.

Such men were, obviously, made of different clay. In our school above the stagnant ponds we had studied any old how, without excitement, without a sincere thirst for knowledge. I again seemed so small and dull.

I went away from the Institute that first day with the highest opinion of students and the saddest opinion of myself. Right at the exit I bumped into a youth of about my age, obviously also a beginner. He was my height, had no moustache and was dressed ridiculously, like me. He had on a grey greatcoat, which the high-school buttons had been be replaced by black, leather ones. Our eyes met meaningfully. It seemed we both saw in each other, as in a mirror, our own reflection, and neither of us liked it. 'He's a student too!'—I read my own thought in his unfriendly look.

'No, it doesn't seem as if I'll ever make a real student,' I thought dejectedly. Grinevetsky had somehow quietened down as well: his meetings with old friends had reminded him of two lost years. A fine, penetrating drizzle was coming down. It had been warm in the morning, and I had gone out without a coat, in just my summer suit made by the honourable Shimko of Rovno. The jacket with its bouquet pattern became soaked and stuck to me like a rag. I cursed it. I recalled Heine's pathetic words about nankeen trousers: 'A young man is sitting, calmly drinking coffee, while in vast, far-off China his destruction is growing and coming to bloom. There it is spun and woven, and, despite the high wall, finds its way to the young man. He takes it for a pair of nankeen trousers, puts it on cheerfully and becomes unhappy.' Similarly, I had cheerfully put on this suit in Rovno, and the first thing everyone had noticed about me since then was how ridiculous I looked. It was as if it had been made with a spell: to make its owner an ugly duckling and prevent the transformation of a piteous Rovno schoolboy into an adult and typical Petersburg student.

By a stall, or it may even have been a hawker's tray, Grinevetsky stopped and said, 'Know what: buy yourself a Technological cap.'

We bought one for half a rouble. The man wrapped my wet hat in paper, and I put on a green-banded cap. 'I shouldn't do it,' I thought to myself, but I couldn't resist the temptation: it was plain now that I too belonged to a great body, and the rest didn't matter. We also bought a suitable, cheap grey blouse, I think for seventy-five kopecks. After this I no longer remember being depressed by the question of my clothes.

I continued to see Petersburg through rose-coloured spectacles. I liked everything here—even the Petersburg sky, because I'd known it earlier through descriptions, even the dreary brick walls that shut in that sky, because they were familiar to me through Dostoyevsky. I even liked the lack of money and the prospect of hunger. After all, this too was to be encountered in descriptions of student life, and I saw life through the prism of literature. The reader will probably recall the impressive figure of Teodor Negri, Professional Reciter, who on the way to Petersburg had rapped out the words: 'What are they? Rrrobbers!'— so expressively and so forcefully that my contemporary had immediately lightened his purse in his favour. This episode emerged as a kind of portent: real life responded in its own way to my literary ideas about it, and disappointments were naturally in store for me.

Our little group in the garret of 4 Maliy Tsarskoselsky Prospect finally came to consist of three people: myself, Grinevetsky, and Veselitsky. Their former co-tenant, Nikulin, had deemed it wiser to separate from us, though he still visited us frequently, and the three of us constituted a sort of friendly artel of poverty-stricken students.

As for classes, Grinevetsky and I were full of the very best intentions at the beginning and attended lectures conscientiously. I felt a shiver when a man in a black coat first appeared on the rostrum before a great, hushed audience, in which my humble figure was altogether lost. 'The Professor, the Professor . . .' It was Makarov, who lectured on visual geometry. He was a short, thin man with a delicate, nervous face and an intent look. He spoke standing up, and went to the board only in cases requiring a more or less complicated drawing. Mostly he contented himself with movements of his hands in space. With the thumb and index finger of his left hand he would hold a tightly pressed mathematical point, and with his right hand would draw imaginary lines from it, projected on to imaginary planes. It was said that he had measured his wife's figure with a compass, and from the drawings had made a dance dress for her that was regarded as a model by leading Petersburg tailors. This story stimulated my interest. If—I thought—through such projections and calculations one can reproduce such a delicate thing as the elegant figure of a beautiful woman, then, obviously, the mathematical sciences were not as dry and abstract as they had seemed in school, and I watched Makarov's thin fingers and the flights of the imaginary point very eagerly. It seemed that I could even see its traces in the air, like the delicate threads of a spider's web.

From this alone the reader may conclude that technology was not my vocation. I found pure maths hard, and I had to force myself to pay attention. But I went to the drawing class enthusiastically. There, along-side me on the same table, the youth in the grey coat with the black buttons had put his board—the youth to whom I had taken an immediate dislike because he had seemed my own reflection, just as shock-haired and, so it seemed to me, just as uninteresting. One further similarity emerged: we both drew keenly, quickly, and well, and the grey-haired teacher of technical drawing would come up to both of us with equal pleasure.

Anyway, for the time being I liked everything in the Institute and in our attic-room, and for a long time was even reconciled to hunger. Grinevetsky and I would begin the day with lectures, conscientiously listening and taking notes. In the second or third break we would go to the porter's lodge, to which the post would have been delivered. There was always the faint hope that there would be something for one of us. But the stout and indifferent porter invariably said, 'There's nothing for you, Mr. Grinevetsky. Nor for you, sir.'

'Perhaps there's something for Veselitsky ?'

'Nothing for him either, sir.'

Grinevetsky would heave a sigh, go to the cloakroom and thoughtfully pull on his coat. Somehow, worry about our daily bread fell naturally, as if by agreement, upon his shoulders. He had very wide connections among a certain section of students. These were rather a happy-go-lucky lot both as regards science and their own futures; men who once a month, anyway, after chronic periods of hunger, would go on a great spree as soon as they received money from home. The Institute porters did not even know the faces of many of these great chaps, but any billiard-marker within the limits of the Semyonovsky and Izmaylovsky Regiments could at any given moment provide very exact information as to which of them was on a spree, whom he was with and where he was to be found.

'Mr. Simansky played twelve games here, drank beer, and tore the cloth. He has money just now. He went from here to the White Swan with his friends.'

Grinevetsky would stride sadly off to the White Swan, where his appearance would be greeted with noisy delight. He was embraced, treated to beer, which he did not like, and invited to play billiards. He would answer the greetings, exchange jokes, walk round the billiard-table with a long cue on his shoulder and examine with his fine, protruding eyes which ball should be sunk in the middle or corner pocket. Tall and handsome, with a casually cocked Technological cap, he would seem carefree enough. But the thought of his friends starving in the garret on Maliy Tsarskoselsky Prospect never left him even for a minute. However attractive the suggestions made to him by the carousing party, he always declined most emphatically, borrowed two or three twenty-kopeck pieces and walked on long, tired legs to our attic, where Veselitsky and I would be languishing in hungry expectation. We knew his ring. He would come in, take off his plaid and silently toss the coins on to the table. His face would be tired and displeased: another senseless day had gone, more lectures had been missed, and the new life which he really had to start leading was receding further and further away. His legs were aching from walking around taverns and billiard tables. He had drunk a few glasses of beer, but he was just as hungry as we were.

I would jump cheerfully off my bed, put on my plaid and run to the usual sausage-shop on Klinsk Prospect. There, without my needing to ask, they would weigh me some dubious sausage with garlic for fourteen kopecks. We suspected that it was made from horse-meat and so was cheaper than all the other varieties. But that didn't put us off. For six kopecks I would get four pounds of the blackest, sourest bread in the neighbouring baker's. This was our usual supper. If there was anything left of Mirochka's catch, we would use it to buy a pinch of foul shop-tea, that smelled of birch-broom, and a quarter of a pound of sugar, which, of course, we nibbled, drinking our tea unsweetened. If we happened to get an odd job like, for example, copying out lectures and had a few roubles to spend, the régime didn't change. We gave two or three roubles for the room, and the rest went on reciprocal aid. One of Grinevetsky's recent creditors would drop in, give a worried look around and say, 'Hello. Where's Grinevetsky? Not here? Dash! It's two days since I've had a meal . . . Well, cheerio.'

And to Mirochka's constant concern about our little group there was added a new worry; he would adopt extreme measures, sometimes setting in motion the most surprising financial combinations, and bring his recently wealthy acquaintances home for tea and fourteen-kopeck sausage; sometimes, to console them in their tribulation, he even contrived to take them to the White Swan. This was a small, wooden tavern in a neighbouring lane—a very unpretentious-looking place with soiled walls and the reek of beer. Upstairs there was a single billiard-table. Its cloth, which had been torn and carefully darned countless times, gave it a look of self-respecting tidy poverty.

All this seemed interesting to me at first: it resembled student Bohemia. But we were beginning to be pulled and whirled around by a particular drift of student life. In this good-natured circle it was always easier to play a game of billiards and go for a drink of beer than to eat a proper dinner or get hold of lectures. It could be said with equal justice of every individual concerned that he was being led astray by bad companions. Ivanov would burst cheerfully in on Sidorov at the very moment Sidorov was opening his Mechanics or Chemistry notes with really serious intentions. It would turn out that the old folks had at last sent Ivanov some money and so it was an ideal time to go to the Gold Anchor. Sidorov in turn would invite Ivanov there at the very moment Ivanov had made up his mind to start a new life. Nobody kept strict accounts with anybody else; the one who had money at any given time would treat the others. It was the true communism of jolly idleness.

In the end, whoever had strength enough would, after a year or two, break away with horror from this vicious circle, move to another part of the city and transfer to another Institute. The parents of some came from the provinces and took their sons away to Moscow, Kiev, or Warsaw, as far as possible from the Gold Anchor, the White Swan, and their marvellous friends. Those who did not have strength enough, or did not have anxious parents to act as Providence, went round and round until the end—sometimes a very sad end. I began to feel the drawbacks of this order of life only gradually. It took time for the rose-coloured haze to dissolve. And when it had dissolved, the sad truth emerged clearly: a year had been lost.

For the present, however, all these disillusionments were still to come and being a student, even if not a 'real' one, was a new and wonderful experience. Hazy figures swarmed in my imagination. Naturally, the ideal figure of the 'real student' occupied first place among them, and I peered intently into the restless mass of young people surrounding me.

I have already mentioned my good friend Suchkov. He had gone to Petersburg a year before me, and I had expected him to come back completely transformed. But that hadn't happened. He was the same good old Suchkov I'd known and liked since childhood. Grinevetsky was older than both of us and it was his third year in Petersburg. At first, with his plaid and colourful appearance, he had seemed the real thing. Soon, however, I discerned in him the familiar features of a 'Rovno boy'. I got to like him immensely, but without any illusions, on an equal footing, so to speak.

Of our immediate group only Vasily Ivanovich Veselitsky continued to inspire a certain awe. I liked and was impressed by everything about him: his long hair, the pointed beard that framed his full cheeks, the barely perceptible smile of superiority that played around his full lips under a small moustache, and particularly his silent reserve that had, it seemed to me, a special and deep significance.

It was the third month, I think, when Vasily Ivanovich suddenly got rich. First of all, he was sent a brand-new, dark suit, made by a Kostroma tailor, and several pairs of pants and vests. A few days after that, the stout porter at the Technological Institute handed Grinevetsky a notification: 'For Vasily Ivanovich Veselitsky. Will you take it?'

Mirochka's face shone—it was an order for seventy-five roubles, real wealth! Our garret room seemed to brighten up. Of late our landlady had frequently been crying. We owed for the room, and a dispute was going on between her and her husband: he was insisting on stern measures, whereas the good woman felt sorry for us and couldn't bring herself to put us out. Now Vasily Ivanovich became the hero of the hour. However, when Ardalion heard the news, he gave a characteristic snort and said, 'You'd better watch him now, boys. Somebody go with him to the post office or he'll shoot off to his friend on the Bronitskaya, and that'll be the last you'll see of him. I know him.'

Veselitsky merely gave him a look of contempt and I seethed with indignation. The next morning when Grinevetsky mentioned Nikulin's warning, I objected so strongly at not trusting a friend that Mirochka gave way, though with some hesitation. Vasily Ivanovich, solemnly dressed in his new dark suit, set off to the post office alone, bearing with him our trust and our hopes. Mirochka went to the Institute while I stayed at home and read Flerovsky, which Zubarevsky had sent me.

I had been sitting reading for about an hour and a half when the bell rang. Instead of Vasily Ivanovich the landlady showed a stranger of the opposite sex into the room. She was a girl of about thirty with lively dark eyes and a noticeable moustache. She was dressed with the smartness of a professional milliner, and her manner was brisk and familiar. Looking round the room, she said, 'What? Hasn't he come yet?'

'Who?' I asked, immediately feeling embarrassed.

She took off her hat, put it on the table, shut the door in our landlady's inquisitive face and sat down without further ado.

'Vasily Ivanovich. I'll wait.'

Silence fell. I tried to go on reading, but without much success. I could feel the girl's pert dark eyes watching me all the time. The very silence became oppressive. The clock was ticking away, and from the kitchen came the noise of pots and pans as the landlady bustled about.

'Lord above, how dull,' the visitor suddenly said. I blushed deeply, I sensed a reproach in the exclamation: if I were a 'real student', and not just a boy, I'd be able to entertain her and we'd both be enjoying ourselves. But I didn't know what to say, and my face became scarlet.

All of a sudden the girl got up, walked lightly across the room, and with astonishment and alarm I felt her hands tousling my hair and her knees touching mine.

'What a lot of curls,' she said. 'My Znamensky was like that. I'm Nastya. I expect you've heard of me. The Technologists know me. I say! Are you going to go on reading!?'

She took the book out of my hands and tossed it on to the couch.

'Let's talk! And don't you be shy. What's this you've got? Pencil and paper? Good. I'm going to write you a note. I can write too, you know. I didn't live with a student for four years for nothing.'

She took the pencil, licked it, moved the paper nearer and bent over it, comically wrinkling her thick dark eyebrows.

I had heard a thing or two about this Nastya. She had lived on a free love basis with a student, Znamensky. The previous year Znamensky had finished, got a job and gone away, leaving Nastya just as unconcernedly as he'd taken up with her. They said she was free now, and many were not averse to the idea of taking Znamensky's place, especially as Nastaya had cost him almost nothing. She was an excellent dressmaker, and she and Znamensky had lived with all their resources pooled. Now this interesting person was sitting beside me, comically knitting her brows, and writing me a note. Naturally, I was curious. After considerable effort the girl finished and handed me the paper, with an arch look in her lively dark eyes.

I took it and was stunned: on it in uneven, childish, but fairly legible writing was a blatant piece of obscenity. Clearly, this was the only thing the happy-go-lucky student had tried to teach his mistress in four years. This did not correspond at all to my literary ideas of things, and I must have looked very foolish. Nastya burst out laughing, throwing back her head. Then she snatched the paper from my hands, tore it up and threw it into the corner, saying in a serious tone of voice, 'It wouldn't do for someone else to read it.'

At this point the bell rang again, and Grinevetsky came into the room. Nastya greeted him familiarly.

'Hello! I know you, you're Grinevetsky. I've come to see Vasily Ivanovich. We bumped into each other by Tarasov Lane. He promised to lend me some money. I have to pay the rent and I've nothing. He won't let me down, will he?'

Grinevetsky looked worried and scratched his head.

'The post office has been shut a long time,' he said, 'but there's no sign of him.'

There was another ring. Ardalion, Suchkov, and Suchkov's roommate Kuleshevich, a young man working on the Warsaw Railway, came in. When he learned that Vaska wasn't there, Ardalion let fly.

'You clever fellows! You let him out alone? Chumps. Blockheads. I suppose it was this little chap's idea.' He rudely rubbed his hand over my face. 'Well, maybe it won't matter! I know where to look for him. On the Bronitskaya, at his friend's, the civil servant's. Let's go together, shall we?'

They all went out and I was left with Nastya again. About an hour of wearisome waiting passed. What if Ardalion proved right? Impossible, I thought. Suddenly the bell rang and a noisy crowd burst into the room. In front, pushed by Ardalion, came Vasily Ivanovich. He was obviously embarrassed and partly drunk. Under his arms and in his coat pockets were bottles and parcels.

'Here, take him,' Ardalion laughed. 'We caught him at the wineshop on the Bronitskaya.'

On seeing Nastya, Veselitsky looked a bit taken aback, but recovered straight away.

'Ah, Nastasysa Ivanovna. Great. Let's have a bite to eat and put the samovar on. If we're going to have a good time, let's get on with it. You go and get some good tea from Shlyakov's, old chap. It's a long way, but no matter . . .'

I ran off to the shop for tea, which we didn't have. When I returned, I found Nastya and Veselitsky alone. The others had gone off to the White Swan for a game of billiards. Nastasya Ivanovna seemed tipsy to me: her eyes were moist, her cheeks flushed, and she was rocking and singing a country song. Veselitsky took me aside and said, handing me a banknote, 'Do me a favour, old chap. Go to the White Swan too.'

When I got there, however, I felt uneasy and, after talking to Grinevetsky, we decided to stop playing and go back all together for tea. I immediately noticed that something bad had happened in our absence: Nastasya Ivanovna was sitting at the far end of the table, while Vaska had occupied a chair at a respectful distance and was looking angrily and resentfully at her. He was completely drunk now—his whole person had somehow drooped and his face had grown flaccid. Nastya, on the other hand, seemed quite sobered up. She met us with a fixed, burning look from beneath knit brows.

'Hello, gentlemen! So you've come back at last? Why so soon?' She stood up suddenly and, leaning a hand on the table in a fine and forceful pose, continued, 'You laid a trap for a girl. You aren't students, you're just rotters!' Her lips with the little dark moustache quivered pathetically, like a child's. And suddenly her eyes fell on me. 'Ah, curly-tops is here. He's a smart boy, too. Before I could look round he'd disappeared as well. Knew what his friend wanted. What rotters you all are.'

Her head fell on her arms and her shoulders shook with sobs. I turned to where Veselitsky had been sitting, but he wasn't there: catching up his hat and coat, he had gone quickly through the landlady's room and disappeared. Ardalion rushed after him. I did not yet realize fully what had happened, and went down the stairs in turn and out on to the street. The figure of Ardalion was quickly disappearing in the mist in the direction of the Bronitskaya, but Vaska was in fact much closer at hand. On the ground floor of our tenement there was a dark and dirty little tavern. I happened to glance in at the window and saw a woman with a child in her arms behind the bar, and Vaska sitting on a chair, his head hanging down. I pushed the door, which gave a jarring ring. The woman looked up at me in fright and when I went up to her said, 'I thought it was the landlord coming back. Is that your friend there? I'm frightened of him. He just burst in, roaring drunk and demanding more. He talks funny.'

Vaska raised his head and said in an unusually biting tone of voice, 'Just a mo-oment. Who gave you the right to argue in such a way? Not an ounce of logic.' He attempted to stand up, but reeled and sank on to the dirty floor.

Just then the landlord, a sturdy, grim-looking man, came in. Casting an experienced glance around the room, he immediately summed up the situation and, without paying the slightest attention to me, raised Vaska off the floor with one hand, propelled him to the door and threw him into the street. I was just in time to prevent him bumping his head against a lamp-post and led him to our stairs. He was very unsteady and in the dim lamp-light his face was convulsed by pitiful sobs. It was hard to manage him, but Ardalion now arrived. He laughed as usual, took Vaska by the other arm, and we got him upstairs, where he immediately collapsed into a drunken sleep. Nastya was still there, quietly talking to Suchkov and Grinevetsky. Now she asked if someone would see her home. Suchkov and I put on our coats.

When I got back Vasily Ivanovich had gone, leaving a note addressed to me. In it he wrote that I had betrayed his best feelings by taking the side of a tart. Therefore, he was saying good-bye to me for ever. I couldn't collect my impressions. I understood Nastya, and the word 'tart' really upset me. What was I now to make of Vasily Ivanovich, whom I had so admired? Nikulin, who had warned us, had been right, then? Vaska was simply a drunkard, who'd let his friends down and tried to seduce a girl. Instead of the reserved, silent, profound Vasily Ivanovich there arose before me now the flaccid, drunken face of Vaska, whom Ardalion catches at one tavern and the landlord kicks out of another.

A few days later Vasily Ivanovich appeared in the strangest outfit. He wasn't wearing his coat or the new clothes sent from Kostroma. He and his friend, the civil servant, had sold them all. In some strange, drunken flight of fancy Vasily Ivanovich had bought my uncle's dark suit and was wearing it now. He was no taller than I, and so the waist-coat came down well below the waist and the tails of the frock-coat were flapping about his heels. In this guise, obviously after a drunken quarrel with his friend, he had come back from the Bronitskaya and immediately lay down to sleep.

I came home at dusk and heard whistling snores behind the parti-tion. I guessed who it was. I went to my own bed, lit the lamp and got out a book while waiting for Grinevetsky. After a time the snoring died down, and soon after there came dull groans. For a while I tried not to pay any attention to them, but couldn't endure it and went behind the partition with the lamp. Vasily Ivanovich was sitting on his bed, his hands in his hair, and groaning quietly.

In half an hour we were reconciled. Naturally, the former, magnifi-cent Vasily Ivanovich, the object of my admiration, was gone. Before me now was a weak man, a victim of student life, but still very dear to me. Once more we sat together on the bed, and in a voice rather hoarse from drink but still pleasantly melodious he told me a sad story. Yes, he too was infected with the dreadful moral affliction of his environment. He was struggling, he needed moral support (at this point he embraced me). He was already drinking himself into hallucinations. 'Little devils you understa-and,' he said in his Kostroma accent, prolonging the ends of the words, 'little ones, with moustaches. . . . But that's nothing. There's far worse . . .' His voice became thicker, and I even thought his face paled. 'Sometimes I dream I'm going up a sort of staircase. It's wide and so well-lit that you can see every speck of dust. I don't want to go up because I know that *he* is waiting for me on the top landing. He's pale, eyes like coals of fire, and . . . you understa-a-and, he's as like me as two peas. . . .'

'Well?'

'Well, I go up. I don't want to go but he's standing on the top step and pulling me towards him with his eyes, he's waiting. I go right up to him, eye to eye. And, you kno-ow, I seem to go into him and he goes into me. It's so terrifying that you think you'll go out of your mind . . .'

I felt uneasy. The lamp had been turned down. In the gloom I sensed the terribly pale face of Vaska or his double, and I felt a sense of terror for my friend, who was weak and had fallen in my estimation, but who was awfully dear to me none the less. This new figure, without any halo at all, stayed in my thoughts for a long time.

15
My First Secret Meeting

OUR LITTLE GROUP WAS POVERTY-STRICKEN. GRADUALLY, imperceptibly we became weak from starvation: our legs ached, our faces grew pale, our movements at times became heavy, our attention at lectures wandered, as if a curtain were hanging over our brains. Grinevetsky and I were still trying not to fall behind but we had fallen behind none the less. That year we had dinner in restaurants only five times. At first, the very smell of hot meals coming from hotels and restaurants irritated our nostrils awfully and made us feel hungry. In time, however, this passed, and the smell of roast meat or fatty cabbage-soup actually began to make us feel sick. Returning home after a hungry day in the drawing class or the Public Library, I would dream only of our sausage from Klinsk Prospect—the sausage and the black bread at a kopeck and a half. When after a long interval without proper food we once managed through some piece of luck to have dinner in one of Yelena Pavlovna's cheap restaurants,[1] we had something like an attack of cholera that same night. At this time I was attracted only by the windows of sweet-shops with their trays of sweets and cakes. Really, it was death by starvation, only protracted over a very long period of time.

But we were young and had iron constitutions. Though we now

[1] Princess Yelena Pavlovna organized a number of such establishments in Petersburg. She was well known for her philanthropic activities.

assimilated all external impressions through a sort of dim mist, this did not prevent occasional outbursts of excitement, which were then followed by reaction and depression.

Things didn't improve and our spirits kept on sinking. The rosy haze was lifting from everything around me, revealing a grey and prosaic reality. Grinevetsky also grew depressed: the third year was threatening to go the same way as the first two, whereas his parents thought that their son was in fact on the third-year course.

The first exam in advanced algebra was drawing near. It wasn't hard for Grinevetsky: maths came easily to him. For me it was much more difficult. Moreover, deficiencies in my clothes did not always allow me to attend the Institute and I had missed a term of technical drawing. Grinevetsky and I decided to apply to the Student Aid Fund for a grant. I tried to smarten myself up with the help of Suchkov or Ardalion, wrote an application and went off to the Institute.

That day the applicants were being received by Yermakov himself. He was a fairly tall man, with large, expressive features and a pale, unhealthy-coloured face, who reminded me of the description of Speransky in *War and Peace*. His face seemed rather sad and even disillusioned. Between him and the tight group of students standing behind the low barrier there lay, as it were, a faint shadow of mutual dislike. As he took applications he casually made short, morose comments. Finally my turn came. I stood before the man whose short notification, received ten months previously in Rovno, had cast such a glow over my life. Taking my application, he gave me a keen glance and asked, 'Have all your drawings been handed in?'

I was embarrassed and answered,

'Not all of them.'

'Thought as much,' Yermakov said with a nod of his head, as if to emphasize his perspicacity. I wanted to say that only one lot had not been handed in and that in fact I needed the grant to make up for lost time. However, I said nothing. Yermakov had already turned to someone else, and I went away feeling injured. 'Thought as much.' Why did he think as much? Because I was badly dressed, pale, and yellow from hunger? In my heart there was a bitter feeling of fresh disillusionment. I went up to the drawing class. At our table my double was finishing a superb drawing. My board wasn't on the table any more. The Institute was overcrowded, and the janitors had taken it away to give a place to someone else.

So, there too I had been formally put in the category of bad students. Hanging my head, I went downstairs, and noticed students of different years going into a lecture-hall. I followed the stream. In the lecture-hall a meeting was in progress. On a table stood a student in a blouse—a 'democratic' and awkward figure—who was reporting the result of a deputation to Yermakov. I remember it was about the demand for the Aid Fund to be put in the hands of the students themselves, since, as things stood, those really in need had difficulty in getting any money: advantage was taken of the grants by 'obedient lambs', often rich squires' sons. The speaker made his report, and every now and again exclamations of agreement came from the audience: 'Hear, hear!' Meanwhile Yermakov had refused point-blank to defend the students' demand in the Council.

'He doesn't understand young people any more,' concluded the orator.

'Hear, hear!' his audience noisily agreed. 'We must look for other ways!'

I naturally supported this decision wholeheartedly and eagerly caught echoes of my own feelings in the noisy exclamations of the crowd of students.

Towards the end of the meeting Zubarevsky came up to me. Ever since our first meeting on the train I had always been particularly pleased to see him. There was something plain, wholesome, and sincere about this unprepossessing figure with his high cheek-bones and duck's nose. I didn't put him in any literary category, but was simply glad whenever I met him.

'Well, how are things?' he asked. 'You look a bit down in the dumps. What's the matter?'

'Things aren't going well,' I answered, turning away. 'I'm feeling depressed.'

He didn't release my hand, but thought for a moment and said, 'Have you been at any meetings?'

'Yes, just now,' I replied.

'No, I'm not talking about things like that. Have you been in any groups? No? Well, would you like to? There's a group being organized here, very nice people. Right! Just wait a minute and I'll see about it straight away.'

He dashed after some student and took him by the arm. They started walking up and down the lecture-hall, talking about something and looking at me. I waited for the outcome with some trepidation: would these intelligent, serious people want to accept me? I still felt Yermakov's slighting glance. My board had been taken away from the drawing class. I felt knocked off the rails and unhappy. But the man Zubarevsky had been talking to, who was obviously in a great hurry, said good-bye to him and gave me a friendly nod through the thinning crowd. Zubarevsky came back to me.

'It's all arranged,' he said. 'On Sunday go to the 13th Company, Izmaylovsky Regiment. It's No. 163, flat No. such and such. When they open the door, ask for me or for so and so.' (I think he named Endaurov.) 'Even if we aren't there, they'll let you in. You go. They're a good crowd.'

I went happily home. It was spring. Every now and again great patches of bright blue sky would appear through scudding white clouds, and there was the freshness and distinctive stir of spring in the air. All these days I had been in the grip of that anguish of heart, peculiar to spring, which young people feel when they see their life speeding past to no purpose. This feeling had been with me when I'd gone to the Institute and it had come over me especially strongly in the drawing class. Someone opened two or three windows, and from the street had come the rattling of carriages, the melodious shouts of pedlars, the bustling noise of the quick moving life of the capital. But my life had stuck, as it were, in a sort of dark and dismal corner. My drawing-board had even been removed from the table. First the meeting in the Institute, then the invitation to the other meeting dispelled this mood to some extent. I sensed something new. It wouldn't be hard drinking or billiards in the White Swan. It would be something new. It was like a presentiment of a new revelation.

On Sunday towards evening I set off to the 13th Company. I had a long way to walk. Thick clouds had come in from the sea, it was drizzling, and the dim street lights (at that time I believe they still used oil) trembled on the unsteady surfaces of small puddles. By the light of one of these lamps I found No. 163. It was a huge, ugly house, which towered massively and stupidly above smaller houses in a lonely street in which employees of the Warsaw and Peterhof Railways, factory hands and students lived. I went in through the gateway, went up a staircase on the right to the very top, the fourth or fifth floor, and pulled the bell. There was a sound of footsteps behind the door, then some conversation. The door opened a little, I glimpsed a pair of young eyes, and a girl's voice asked:

'Whom do you want?'

'Zubarevsky,' I answered.

'He's not here.'

'Endaurov, then.'

'He's not here either.'

'Wait, wait,' another female voice interrupted hurriedly. 'What's your name? Ah, come in, please.' And the door opened.

I went into a hall, tossed my coat on to a pile of coats and not without embarrassment entered a large room.

'This, ladies and gentlemen, is Korolenko,' said the young girl who'd let me in. 'Recommended by Zubarevsky and Endaurov. Please sit down.'

I made my way to the far corner and looked around. There were about fifteen young men and women present, but every now and then the bell would rattle and new people come in. One could tell from the way they came in, bowed, and took their places that they were not yet a closely knit group. A shyness and awkwardness was in evidence. On catching sight of a familiar face among the young people sitting along the walls, newcomers would hasten there gladly, and the girls would embrace and start whispering. There was no general conversation. Through an open door another room could be seen, a smaller room with a table in the middle and a hanging lamp. At the table several students were sitting, including three or four women. I guessed that these were the hosts or organizers of the meeting and furthermore that they were in difficulty, not knowing what to do with us. They seemed to be waiting for someone.

The bell sounded. A big technological student in a blouse and spectacles came in. In his appearance and mannerisms he reminded me of the speaker at the meeting in the Institute, but he was more culti-vated. He started saying something to those sitting at the table, and then they spoke more quietly, as if conferring. Meanwhile in our room there was still the same tension. Something was lacking to unite those present.

I began looking with curiosity at the girls. Women students were completely new to me. At that time there was still no Girls' High School in Rovno, and the first high-school girl from Zhitomir, Dolinskaya, who'd come home for the holidays in her brown school uniform, had attracted everyone's attention. A certain Yekaterina Grigoryevna, a woman past thirty, had come to see Vaska a couple of times. She had short curly hair, held by a round comb, and wore a pince-nez. There was always a cigarette stuck between her large, ugly teeth. The first time she had come was when Vaska was still on a pedestal in my eyes, and I recall writing that same evening a rapturous, foolish letter to my brother, in which I described the first 'woman-nihilist' I had seen. Nevertheless, I remember that behind this literary impression there was a vague awareness of a pitiable, rather vulgar person with traces of schoolgirl manners and unhealthy passion in her eyes.

Before me now were modest-looking girls, like me—embarrassed and waiting for something. In the far corner I thought I saw my double. I would have liked to have gone up to him, but I should have had to cross the large room and, besides, I was too short-sighted to be sure it was he.

The rest of the evening I remember rather vaguely, for there were no interesting people or incidents. The serious student, who'd come last, spoke. I can't recall what he actually said, I only remember that both the speaker and his audience sensed that something wasn't quite right. In the strained atmosphere an attempt to strike a plain, genuine note was being made, but it wasn't coming off. There was talk, I recall, that, besides specialized knowledge, there also had to be the desire to apply it for the benefit of the people. This seemed to be true, but it didn't unite us there and then. It became a bit easier when we were invited into the next room, where a samovar was boiling. But a general, unconstrained conversation didn't get going here either; people went into the other room, broke up into little groups of friends and spoke in halfwhispers. Then they began to leave. It had been decided that people would be specially notified in the Institute and at the Courses for Women about the date of the next meeting.

I was among the last to leave. Into the square courtyard, enclosed by high walls, a fine drizzle was descending, as into a well. At the gates sat a motionless gate-keeper, and around him stood two or three figures in ordinary clothes. In the street the lamps were twinkling dimly and there were the same reflections in the trembling puddles. In my heart there was a dull feeling of disappointment.

At a near-by corner I was overtaken by my double. By a street lamp he looked at me and I looked at him. Yes, it was he all right. Until now the glances we had exchanged had been rather glances of dislike. Now I again felt an impulse to stop him and talk to him. The same desire seemed to show in his eyes, but he was walking quickly and went on, as if by inertia. I didn't call out to him either and he soon turned a corner. When I reached the corner a figure still loomed in the rainy darkness ahead. I wanted to catch him up and have a real talk about what we'd both been looking for in the meeting and had failed to find, and why it hadn't come off. But when I caught up with the man in front, he turned out to be wearing an ordinary black coat, not the grey greatcoat with the school-buttons removed. So, I did not catch up with my double, I do not know his name, and we never met again in our lives.

Grinevetsky was already asleep when I got home.

'Well, what was it like?' he asked, waking up. 'Was it worth going?'

'Nothing interesting,' I answered, and started indifferently to tell him about the boring meeting. He yawned, stretched and soon fell asleep.

The following day I was again gripped by spring-time anguish. All day I didn't know what to do with myself, and with Grinevetsky accepted an invitation from some chemistry students who had been distilling alcohol in the lab. At the same time they had prepared several bottles of 'liqueur' and had now invited a whole crowd for a solemn sampling of their product. We drank, sang songs, embraced one another, and finally collapsed side by side, poisoned by fusel oil. The next day, late, Grinevetsky and I returned home, our heads aching and with a bad taste not only in our mouths. Our alarmed landlady met us with the news that the police had been. Three of them had burst in together and frightened the poor woman to death.

'They were asking about you: where you'd been the evening before last and whether you'd come back late. Sinner that I am, I said you'd been at home all evening. "Mine are quiet boys," I said. "They study all the time." And this is how quiet you are! Haven't been in all night. You'll get into trouble.'

A few days later, in the Institute, the School of Building, the Semyonovsky and Izmaylovsky Regiments there was talk of nothing but our secret meeting. I recalled that when I'd gone about three or four blocks along the 13th Company I had chanced to look round and had seen movement by the big house. There was a flurry of vague shadows, some sort of commotion, and I think I even heard whistles. At the time I had not paid any attention to it. It turned out that the police had found out about the secret meeting late and had appeared when it was over, when the last of the people who'd been present were coming out of the gates. Among them, I remember, was a technologist, Kresto-vozdvizhensky, a huge, silent fellow. The whole evening he had sat in the other room and not said a word. But when some individuals in civilian clothes (whom I'd seen standing by the gate-keeper) went in and tried to detain the last people coming out, this silent giant suddenly deployed himself, performing great feats of courage, and put the panicking detectives to flight. He had then disappeared without trace. Our unsuccessful secret meeting became an event in itself. The police went from house to house, questioning, and there were fantastic stories about a meeting of a secret society and the extraordinary strength of the mysterious student. Even in my eyes the episode began to acquire a different colour. Something had taken place of which the government was afraid. So, in this there must be something that was growing and was important.

'Is it true you were there too?' students would ask me in a whisper, and I no longer felt like replying as I'd replied to Grinevetsky: nothing interesting, just a bore.

I subsequently recalled this episode many times. Who knows whether the revolutionary movement among Russian youth would have spread so quickly and so violently, had the government been more sensible and calm and had not panicked into using the crude and awkward apparatus of arbitrary power? It is quite clear now that the so-called 'movement to the people' was a naïve effort with useless methods. But the government itself provoked the dread phantom of terror. The mysterious and silent student who'd suddenly routed the police after the most innocent of secret meetings often comes back to my mind as a sort of portent.

16
The End of the Petersburg Dream

IT WAS BECOMING CLEAR THAT THE YEAR WAS NOW LOST FOR all of us. It was about this time I found work. In Ofitserskaya Street, far beyond the Lithuanian Castle[1] and the Demidov Garden, lived a teacher by the name of Zhivotovsky, who taught, I believe, in the Second High School. Besides teaching, he also did classroom charts and botanical atlases. I found out that he wanted a graphic artist and offered my services. As a try-out he gave me a botanical atlas to colour, consisting of nineteen drawings. They were turned out by the printing-press in outline only, the pages being completely covered with typographical oil colour. It was my task to colour in the rest.

This first atlas took me a whole week to colour. The printer's colour

---

[1] The Lithuanian Castle (*Litovsky ʒamok*) was built in the reign of Catherine the Great and altered under Nicholas I. It served as a prison. Korolenko was to become more closely acquainted with it later on.

hindered me because it wouldn't take water-colours. At last, after a week, I took my work to Zhivotovsky. He was very pleased with it, gave me five more atlases and a rouble for my work. This valuation of a week's work greatly depressed us all, but a rouble was still equivalent to five of our usual dinners. Anyway, in time I hoped to work more quickly. Indeed, the next atlas only took me three days, and then Grinevetsky had the idea of moistening the cursed print-colour with the aid of a tooth-brush, and that made the work so much easier that I was able to do an atlas a day. First, I made up my green, Grinevetsky gave me one sheet after another and I mechanically filled in the green. In this way the nineteen diagrams passed through carmine, orange, minium, vermilion and so on. After a time, admittedly by working for days on end, I could have earned as much as fifty or sixty roubles a month, had Zhivotovsky not set a limit to my greed. The poor chap had only his salary to support his family, and the atlases did not sell all that quickly. We remained well pleased with one another but Zhivotovsky limited my work to twenty atlases a month. Anyway, from this time on we had a regular income, and some of the worry about our subsistence was taken off poor Grinevetsky's shoulders.

Towards the end of this my first year in Petersburg we suddenly became rich. In our last years at school, after our father's death, my brother and I had received Imperial grants. Now my mother had written to tell me that, thanks to the efforts of a friend of my father's, the local priest Baranovich who knew Countess Bludovaya, this grant could be continued for higher education too. I would have to see Countess Bludovaya in the Winter Palace and she would tell me where I needed to apply. She had probably done everything already. 'You mind you go!' my mother added.

Two years later I would have rejected this project without any hesitation. At this time, however, my political ideas were vague and inconsistent. I saw nothing wrong in an Imperial grant, though I dreamed of a republic. My mother had written that it was absolutely essential to see Bludovaya. I didn't want to go at all, but I went. My friends got together to lend me decent clothes and, not really believing myself, I entered the Winter Palace by one of the small entrances facing the Neva. Broad, carpeted staircases, liveried footmen, and guardsmen, who stood with the butt of their rifle against their foot, every so often extending the arm which held it. The Countess was a small, stout and rather unattractive lady. She received me very cordially, told me that she'd received all the relevant information from Baranovich and had already taken certain steps. I was to go with her card to Prince Golitsyn in the Chancellery for Petitions submitted to His Imperial Majesty. The Chancellery was open just then and Prince Golitsyn was receiving petitions. He already knew about me and very kindly explained that I could not be given a grant at the moment. The funds were used up.

'However,' the Prince continued, 'we, that is a few of the Countess's good friends, learning of your father's services and the position of the family, have permitted ourselves (those were the words he used) 'to express our sympathy and concern by collecting a certain sum of money, which you may receive now.'

An official on duty handed the Prince an envelope, which he tendered to me.

Blood rushed to my face. I drew back my hand and said with some emotion that I was not asking for and not expecting charity, but only an official grant which imposed certain obligations with regard to my future work. I hurriedly took my leave and left with a certain feeling of relief.

'Well, there we are. I went and can write to my mother with a clear conscience that the matter is finished.'

But a few days later a Palace messenger came to our address and handed in an official invitation to appear on a certain day and at a certain time before the same Commission. There I was again met by Prince Golitsyn. He was a very handsome, tall, fair-haired man with soft features and gentle manners. On this occasion his appearance was official and somewhat stern. He immediately sat me at a table and dictated the text of an application, which I had to sign: 'Your Imperial Majesty's loyal subject, the student Korolenko'. Then he said in an official voice:

'Your petition is granted, and for a half-year. Give it out, Ivan Ivanovich, and you sign for it.'

I signed a receipt for 175 roubles.

Never in my life had I had such an enormous sum of money at one time. On the way back I went into a confectioner's and bought a whole lot of sweet stuff.

This good luck had come too late for us: the year had been lost anyway. We merely fitted ourselves out properly, paid up the room and certain other debts and went for some fairly innocent jaunts. Then we all went home for the holidays. Thus, my first year in Petersburg had ended. With what and how?

On the way home I again called in to see my uncle in Sumy, and the rest of the way we travelled together. During that year he had lost a lot of weight and his enormous eyes burned with an ominous, feverish light. He had always been very fond of me and once again was very pleased to see me. After a time, however, I became increasingly aware of his sad eyes looking at me searchingly and with concern.

'You've changed since I saw you,' he said.

Yes, I had changed. I was no longer the same person who a year before had been so foolishly moved by the words of Teodor Negri. I was no fool now, you wouldn't take me in that way! I had seen a lot of life, and the rosy hues had faded before me. Petersburg life had not raised me up. On the contrary, it seemed to me that it had come down to my level. I was colourless and uninteresting. So was it. All right, then . . . it was as if I was proud of my present cleverness. There were no real, ideal people. I was no worse, and perhaps, even cleverer than many.

One day, back at home, I accidentally overheard a snatch of conversation between my uncle and my mother in the garden.

'Yes, that's true,' my uncle was saying, 'he has grown up. He's lost his shyness and even become wittier, perhaps. He doesn't blush at every word, as he did before. But, like it or not, I liked him a lot better before. He's not so nice now.'

I felt hurt by these words. I liked this uncle of mine very much and had to admit sadly that he was right: I had been nicer when I'd seen life through rose-coloured spectacles. Only days before, Suchkov and I had gone to visit Grinevetsky in the country for a few days, and as Petersburg students had behaved as such swaggering asses—perhaps, indeed, from inborn shyness—that even now, more than forty years later, I feel ashamed when I think of it. And now there was this opinion of my uncle's, sad, stern and true.

'Well, never mind,' I said to myself, shaking my head. 'Next year will put all that right.'

Neither the next year nor the beginning of the third put anything right. That year our whole family moved north. We were very friendly with my cousin,[2] the artillery officer, who had for a long time lived with us. Now he had been transferred to the Kronstadt Garrison Artillery. My elder brother also decided to move to Petersburg, and then my mother decided to settle with her nephew in Kronstadt in order to be nearer us. My younger brother entered a Modern School[3] in Petersburg.

I had to think about earning some money. I continued to paint atlases, and also did draft drawings, geographical maps for publica-

[2] Vladimir Kazimirovich Tutsevich, see p. 75, note.
[3] Not a High School. By the decree of May 1871 the Modern High Schools (*real'nye gimnazii*) had been abolished, and Modern Schools (*real'nye uchilishchi*) set up in their place. See p. 52, notes 3 and 4.

tion, translated novels with my brother for Okreyts[4] for seven roubles per printed page, and did hackwork of that sort. Once a week my brothers and I boarded the Kronstadt steamer and spent Sunday with our mother. So passed the second year, and so began the third.

The autumn of that third year found me in the proof-reading bureau of a certain Studensky. This was the hardest time for me. It was my elder brother, I think, who had first got proof-reading work; he had begun working at Demakov's and then transferred full-time to Studensky. Studensky was an odd, purely Dickensian sort of character. He was tall, thin, and yellow, with a flaccid, almost moustacheless face which was covered in little wrinkles and furrows. He had light eyes of an indeterminate colour, which looked rather like dirty ice, and superb, wavy, light auburn hair, which provided an incongruous frame for his lifeless mask of a face. He had offered my brother a regular salary and a room. My brother had accepted, and then Studensky had made the same offer to me. As an introduction he brought us his own literary creation. It was a small brochure with a very long title, which was as follows (I think I remember it correctly):

> *Quotations and a volumization of the principles*
> *applied to the art of printing,*
> *and this work also suggests*
> *a new sequence of the heavenly bodies*
> *and the letters of the alphabet*

Another work of his bore the no less original title: *The philosopher, the coquette and the suppressed third man.*

As for the content of these two works, which were set out flawlessly from a grammatical and typographical point of view, it was a sort of intricate juggling with words, devoid of any sign of good sense.

'Did you read it?' he asked the next day.

I had read it, because the title had intrigued me, but hesitated to give any opinion.

'Yes, it requires a certain grounding in philosophy,' the author observed smugly.

At first I simply thought I was dealing with a raving lunatic, and had the creeps. Particularly when he informed us that, besides pay per page, we'd also have special work by the hour on a personal literary undertaking of his:

---

[4] Stanislav Stanislavovich Okreyts (Orlinsky), editor of the magazines *A cheap library of light reading* (*Deshyovaya biblioteka dlya lyogkogo chteniya*) and *Universal Work* (*Vsemirniy trud*).

'I am realizing a very original idea,' he said in his dreary, dead voice. 'I am preparing a Russian–French dictionary in which the words will be arranged not by their first letters but by their endings.'

However, this man with such weird and wonderful ideas proved to be a very good manager of his practical affairs. He had set up a bureau in which he had concentrated the proof-work of several more or less large-scale enterprises. He proofed *The Spring*, *The Week*, Makarov's *French–Russian Dictionary*, a scientific weekly, everything published by Demakov's huge press and several small presses besides. He himself was an excellent proof-reader, who adapted very quickly to the individual proof requirements of each publishing house and each individual author. But he worked extraordinarily slowly and, naturally, could not cope on his own with such a mass of work. And so he handed it out to needy young people, appraising very well the degree of desperate want that had put them in his hands. Rarely did he pay them a half of what he got himself.

I cannot recall without shuddering those two or three months that my brother and I lived at Studensky's. His apartment was in the narrow Demidov Lane, almost opposite the transit prison. Beneath it in the basement there was a chocolate factory. As well as a sweet, suffocating smell, there came from it a constant dull roar of machinery, which made the floors and windows tremble slightly. When we opened the windows on to the street, waves of sweet-smelling steam would sometimes pour into the room. Decorating the apartment according to his own strange taste, Studensky had had it papered in dark blue wallpaper. The doors and cornices were black, and even the ceiling was quite a dark colour. All in all the room was reminiscent of a coffin. Every so often the black door would open slightly, revealing a mask-like face and a long, thin arm with a proof-sheet standing out sharply and ominously against the dark background. I couldn't help feeling scared.

Taking out the rather high price of the room, my brother and I earned fifty roubles each. But for this we had to work from early morning till late at night, hardly snatching an hour to have a quick dinner in a cheap restaurant and glance through a newspaper. If there were any slack periods in the main work, Studensky immediately tried to fill them with work by the hour. This meant that he'd take down long pages of his dictionary arranged according to word-endings, and we would have to sweat at that endless, senseless drudgery. It was work for the boss, very poorly paid (six kopecks per hour, I think), completely nonsensical, and so particularly unpleasant. The man with a dead mask instead of a face and lustreless, icy eyes held us in his clutches all this time like a vampire. Moreover, his heart proved to be prone to the usual human weaknesses. Thus, he would sometimes send us as a reader a girl who was completely incapable even of that simple work. Under the influence of our environment our nerves were becoming very bad, and my brother, who was not a patient man at the best of times, frequently lost his temper.

Soon, in this heavy atmosphere, saturated with suffocating vapours and dull, shuddering noise, I had attacks of nervous asthma, to which I'd been subject since childhood. They always came at hard periods of my life, disappearing when my spirits improved . . . .

A bright, warm autumn had come, the time when in the half-darkness of the shortening evenings they begin lighting the lamps in the Petersburg streets. One day, I remember, I had just returned from my dinner. My brother was out, and as yet there was no work on the table. I opened the window and leaned out into the street. There was a pleasant freshness in the air from an off-shore wind, and it was good to breathe it in. A lamplighter with a ladder over his shoulder hurried past our window, and soon two little chains of lights stretched away in the pale dusk.

I was seized by a sudden, sharp pang of anguish that clearly bore relation to something. It happened every day at this time and I couldn't help wondering why. In the restaurant I'd been reading an issue of *Russian World* in which Leskov's story 'The Enchanted Wanderer'[5] was being serialized. It was full of the atmosphere of the vast steppes and the fanciful adventures of a naturally restless Russian soul. Perhaps it was from that story, from the contrast with my life in this coffin, that the anguish and the unsettling calls came? I looked along the street. The chain of lights had ended. They were now being lit further on, cutting across the Moyka and the Malaya Morskaya. I suddenly realized what it was: my anguish was from these street lamps, which had so struck me on my first arrival in Petersburg. There had been the same sort of evenings then, with the lamps being lit amid the Petersburg twilight. My old belief in the limitless horizons of life and all the expectations I had then harboured came suddenly flooding back to me. Then I quickly recalled the two intervening years: the garret on Maliy Tsarskoselsky, starvation, the senseless work on atlases, Veselitsky,

---

[5] Nikolay Semyonovich Leskov (1831–95), a leading writer of the 1870s and 1880s. He is remembered particularly for his tales, intensely Russian in character, of which 'The Enchanted Wanderer' ('*Ocharovanniy strannik*', 1873) is possibly the greatest.

my drawing-board in the Institute, Yermakov, a whole series of dis-illusionments. And now this coffin.

The door gave a gentle squeak and Studensky's deathly face appeared. He was holding out pages of his dictionary. I went up to the door and surprised myself by saying: 'Please settle up with me: I'm going to Moscow in a few days.'

Our group of my first year had dispersed. Grinevetsky had trans-ferred to the Mining Institute, had settled in the most distant part of Vasilyevsky Island, didn't come to see his old friends, and was working hard, receiving money once more from his parents. Suchkov had gone to Moscow and entered the Petrovsky Academy, where there were several other Rovno lads, including Mochalsky, one of my best friends. On receiving a gloomy letter from me, he had suggested that I throw up everything in Petersburg and come to the Academy. I would be accepted although the year had already started. To begin with I would stay with Rovno lads, and with my drawing would be sure to find some work again.

At first this had seemed completely out of the question, but now this aching longing after something dear and lost, and the strange language of that half-dark evening with its street lights said otherwise. A week later, having received a few dozen roubles from Studensky, I went to Kronstadt to say good-bye to my mother. She was actually glad at my plan. She pictured my career as a forester and a humble forestry house in which our family would gather once more under her roof.

A few days later I was in the Petrovsky Academy.[6]

[6] Korolenko entered the Petrovsky Academy on 1 February 1874.

PART FOUR
Student Years—Moscow: The Petrovsky Academy

17
First Impressions

AT THIS POINT IN MY MEMOIRS I FEEL A CURRENT OF
fresh air, and first and foremost in the literal, not the figurative sense.
From Moscow the road ran through cuttings in the forest with the
scent of fresh snow and pine. Empty *dachas* amid the trees, then the fine
building of the Academy, a little church, a path, a dam, a snow-
covered pond to the one side, and to the other open vistas and a quaint
village with the two-storey hostel. All around there were only the
figures of peasants and students. It is easy to understand what an impression all this made on me after Demidov Lane, the room with the
dark wallpaper and black doors, and Studensky's proof-reading bureau.
There now begins a new period in my life and a new frame of mind.

The Petrovsky Academy had been opened on 21 November 1865 in
a palace that had formerly belonged to Razumovsky.[1] The Academy
was a contemporary of the peasant reform, and its first statute reflected
the spirit of the time. The statute laid down that no preliminary tests or
certificates should be required for entry. Each person could attend
whatever and as many or as few lectures as he wished. As well as full-
time students, outsiders could be admitted at a charge of sixteen
kopecks per lecture. The first three lectures could, with the permission
of the Professor, be free of charge. There were not to be any yearly
exams, only final exams for persons wishing to receive a diploma. The

---

[1] The palace was in the village Petrovskoye-Razumovskoye. Hence the name
of the Academy.

course was a three-year one, but the exams could be sat at any time.
A group of students would declare their wish to be examined and the
Professor would fix an examination day. When a man had passed the
exams in all subjects, he was given a Bachelor's diploma. The students
were regarded as 'citizens consciously choosing a certain sphere of
activity and not requiring daily supervision'.

All the hopes enlivening the intelligentsia of the emancipation
period had been reflected in this statute, had found expression in it.
Freedom of study and faith in the young people of a country in the
process of self-renewal—that is what the statute had been based on.
Science did not seek diligence through compulsion. Unfolding all her
resources before thirsting minds, she proudly expected everything from
a love for knowledge and believed in this love, not chasing after it with
controls and regulations. The mysterious veil of Isis, which made
science rather like a professional secret for the initiated, was taken away.
All were called and it was up to each man to judge his own capability.
Diplomas did not give knowledge, and true knowledge could always be
used without an official diploma.

Such were the basic ideas of the statute. It only operated for seven
years. In 1872 there ensued a transformation that brought the Academy
closer to the usual type of Institution of Higher Education. The
excessively liberal statute had not passed the test.

A man from my home town, who was a student at Petersburg University and whose name was Grodsky, had come specially to see me in
order to tell me about the Petrovsky Academy. He was much older
than I, had earlier studied at Moscow University, and knew the
character of the Petrovsky students well. He was a humorist and his
stories made mock of the liberal statute. Layabouts who'd failed to cope
with the infinitude of wisdom in high school, scions of the gentry who'd
been expelled from the lower classes and whose parents wanted to give
them the title of 'student' in the easiest possible way had come flocking
to the Academy from all quarters. He drew very amusing pictures of
the free life of the Petrovsky students. On spring and summer nights
in the park, in the isolated *dachas* in the forest, above the ponds, songs
would echo and drinking parties go on from dusk till dawn. Moscow
was full of stories of the unusual escapades of these students. The
absence of control and compulsion led to some students sitting their
exams over and over again, when they knew only a part of the course,
in the hope that in the end they would pick a lucky question.[2] Grodsky

[2] Examinations were usually oral. A candidate would be asked to take one of a
number of slips of paper contained in a box, and would have to answer the question
written on it.

very amusingly told the story of a Cossack who, when asked about the centre of gravity, had thought for a while, then clasped his forehead and exclaimed excitedly, 'Ah, I know, I know. . . . The centre of gravity: that's when you hang a body on a thread . . .'

When the Professor expressed bewilderment, he confirmed categorically, 'Don't tell me. I've remembered it right now: if you suspend a body on a thread, that will be the centre of gravity. Look it up yourself in Gano.'[3]

Another student informed his examiners that cells multiplied through the agency of ovipositors, and insects through spontaneous generation from dirt, etc. Grodsky also told of how *The Moscow Gazette* had been waging a systematic campaign against the Academy, and the idealistic professors, who had participated in drawing up the statute, could not now find any arguments in its defence.

Only a short time before I would not have liked Grodsky's tone very much and would have called him a cynic. But now two years of living in Petersburg had made me feel rather cynical myself. The liberal statute had obviously been based on belief in the 'real' student. But I knew that there was no such ideal student; there were only Vaska Veselitskys and such uninteresting young people as myself. Now the statute had been changed, and a very good thing too. I would go there as a humble pupil, attend lectures regularly, receive my diploma and start work. An end to romantic dreams. Only somewhere deep in my heart there still lurked a hope: in my little forestry house I would write a story. And then. . . . All my distant dreams were hidden and concentrated in this, but in the meantime I was enjoying the new impressions and meeting friends.

I had sent my application for entry to the Academy while still in Petersburg. I had decided that, if I were turned down, I would prepare myself for six months and try for entry straight into the Second Year. But I had been accepted. My friends told me I would have to see the Director, Filipp Nikolayevich Korolyov. In the Director's study I was received by a small, grey-haired old man with a big head, large features, and a stern expression. Before his appointment to this post he had been headmaster of a Moscow high school that had been well known for its strict discipline. Apparently, he had been favoured by Katkov as a man who would be able to tighten up the Academy. He met me just like a real headmaster. He informed me sternly and coldly that the Council had agreed to enrol me in the middle of the academic year conditionally: if I didn't pass to the Second Year, I would be

[3] Author of a textbook on physics.

thrown out. I bowed and left, feeling exactly like a schoolboy.

When I came out on to the well-kept path to the park with one of my friends, a group of people was coming in our direction. An old man with thick grey curls and a young-looking face stood out among them. My companion bowed. The old man acknowledged him, his alert, sad eyes casting a fleeting glance over us.

'That's the Professor of Agricultural Chemistry, Ilyenkov,' my companion said. 'One of the architects of the old statute.'

I looked back with curiosity at this figure of a typical man of the sixties, and couldn't help remembering Yermakov. And, indeed, in Ilyenkov's attitude to the students, polite and cold, one sensed a certain estrangement. When I later went to be examined by him, I was afraid that he would suddenly look at me like Yermakov and say: 'I thought as much.'

I was nevertheless very pleased that I had been accepted. During those years I had got to miss proper studies, and it was nice to attend lectures regularly again, make notes, swot and feel at last that I was not a bad student. My whole environment really delighted me. Everything around was different and interesting, and particularly interesting was the contiguity of the student way of life and the simple life of the village. Immediately beyond the dam was the large two-story hostel. It was a rather ramshackle building, the walls of which had become permeated for ever with the smell of tobacco and beer. In it there were two corridors (upstairs and downstairs), on to which the doors of the separate rooms opened. The acoustics were such that a word uttered loudly in one room rang out everywhere. As well as this hostel, the students also took shelter in little *dachas*, and the entire life of the student-body and that of the villagers ran parallel and open for all to see.

Naturally, I soon got to know my fellow students. Life in the Petrovsky Academy was still quite different from life in other colleges. After a time three of us moved from the village on to the highway, taking a room in the so-called Bishop's *dacha*. Directly opposite its gates there was a thick pine forest, and on one occasion a wolf brazenly dragged off one of the dogs. The *dacha* itself was, strictly speaking, not habitable in winter. We covered ourselves with everything we could lay our hands on, but still shivered dreadfully. Similar *dachas*, only better adapted for winter, were scattered about in other places off the road and in the forest. Two gendarmes lived in the village but obviously it was quite impossible for them to keep an eye on these isolated *dachas* and meetings were frequently held in them. I remember the interest with which I made my way for the first time along a forest path thinly covered with fresh-fallen snow. A light shone between the trunks of the trees, and in the frozen windows I could see the outlines of many figures. Nobody was afraid of being shadowed: it would not have been exactly safe for detectives to get there. I remember being struck on this first occasion by the picturesque figure of the student Vladimirov, who appeared with a revolver. At first sight, with his long, shaggy hair, beard, long boots and this weapon, he looked like a real bandit. In fact, he was a very good-natured man, who later dutifully occupied a prominent position in the Department of Forestry. He himself, it would seem, treated his bellicose appearance as a joke, and, when asked why he did it, he would give a smile and answer with quotations about the Carbonari,[4] who used to go to meetings in the forests 'armed to the teeth'. He had an exceptional bibliographical memory, and even argued with quotations.

Really, nothing serious happened at these meetings. On this occasion they talked about the fact that Korolyov was trying to introduce school-type discipline and treated the students like the pupils of the high school where he had been headmaster. A few speakers appealed for a protest, but everyone realized that it wasn't in earnest, just like Vladimirov's revolver, which would never be fired. At parties they would loudly sing revolutionary songs, which carried far, echoing in the park. Revolutionary publications were passed round, like Sokolov's *Renegades* or Bakunin's *Anarchy according to Proudhon*. There was much here that was very extreme, even savage. Bakunin[5] directly advocated uniting with the robbers and brigands of Russia, as with an instinctively revolutionary and anarchic element. It seems to me now that this too was a relic of the former Nihilist period and had no support whatsoever in the psychology of the new generation. The students read books on anarchy, sang revolutionary songs, delivered incendiary speeches, and then gained their diplomas and merged with society, as though all this did not oblige them to anything. And the meetings in the snow-covered *dacha* did not make any greater an impression on me than the secret meeting in the Izmaylovsky Regiment had done.

The year came to an end, and all our group from Rovno, including Suchkov who, like me, had wasted his time in the Technological Institute, passed our exams with distinction. Not only did I pass to the Second Year but also received a grant (of which there were many at

[4] Members of a secret society in Italy at the beginning of the nineteenth century. Its chief aim was the unification of Italy under a liberal republican government.

[5] Mikhayl Aleksandrovich Bakunin (1814–76), the great apostle of anarchism. He had no use for reform and placed all his hopes upon a great revolution of the Russian peasantry.

that time), and was preparing to visit my mother in Kronstadt. Before I left, however, I happened to meet someone: this meeting had a very definite influence upon my outlook and marked the beginning of a deep friendship that was to last all my life.

One hot day in early summer I was walking across the ground past the Academy and noticed a young officer arm in arm with a little old lady. He had just come out of the office and was looking around with the air of a man completely unacquainted with the place. Seeing me, he bowed politely and asked whether he could look round the Academy. I didn't have anything to do, so I offered to go with them. I conducted the two of them through the empty lecture-halls and rooms, and then suggested having a look at the park as well. The park was also virtually empty and we got into conversation. His name was Vasily Nikolaye-vich Grigoryev, and the old lady was his mother. He was an officer at the Engineering Academy, in his second year, but had just now applied to be accepted at the Petrovsky Academy. His friend Konstantin Antonovich Verner was also entering with him.

This aroused sudden interest and deep sympathy in me. These officers were not satisfied with their situation and were looking for something, just as I had once looked. Would they find it? My heart suddenly turned cold. We had come up to the Ivanov grotto.[6] It was only a ruin now. The roof had fallen in and filled up a part of the cave. It was a remote spot, away from the main paths. Nearby a stream was trickling and trees rustling. Every time I went there a strange feeling of anguish came over me. Under the rustling of the trees and the quiet gur-gling of the stream I used to try to guess at the meaning of the grim drama that had taken place there. The personality of the dead Ivanov evoked a strange echo in me. Perhaps he had lost faith as I had done.

This sensation came over me again; and before this stranger, who had roused a sudden feeling of sympathy in me, I unexpectedly poured out all the bitterness that had accumulated during those years. I told him about the old students, and about our generation, which seemed so small and uninteresting to me. Grigoryev listened attentively, and in his grey eyes that looked at me from beneath a steep forehead I saw deep interest and concern. But it seemed to me that his interest was roused not so much by what I actually said as by my mood. I felt that everything I told him was not new to him, that he understood me, but that he already had some answer of his own to all this. I in turn passed to questions, but Grigoryev was very reserved. He simply said that after finishing the engineering school he had served several years in the

[6] The place where Ivanov was murdered. See p. 109, note.

army. Army service had not satisfied him. He had entered the Engineering Academy, but had come to the conclusion that that was not his true road either. And so—he was coming to us.

There was something about this new acquaintance that attracted me to him and at the same time commanded my respect. Despite my twenty years I had not seen anything of life as yet and at times I felt a boy. Before me was a man, not much older, but who had seen life. I sensed my own mood in him, only . . . he, as it were, could see something else that I could not see, and it was this that gave such firmness and definition to the expression of his grey eyes.

At one of our subsequent meetings Grigoryev quoted from Pisarev in some context or other: 'Scepticism, once it goes beyond certain limits, becomes shabbiness'. Pisarev said it somewhat differently, but the idea was the same, and in the actual form it was expressed by Grigoryev it made a strong and ineradicable impression on me. It also seemed to me that I had given him lessons in my own precocious disillusionment far too presumptuously.

Grigoryev entered the Academy, and, as I was going to Petersburg and Kronstadt, he asked me to be sure to call on his friend, K. A. Verner, and give him the syllabus and a letter. I found Verner in a garret on Pushkin Street. He was a young officer in the uniform of the Engineering Academy; he was wearing a frayed tunic with a disproportionately short waist, had wild hair and an altogether ummilitary appearance. It seemed to me that on reading the letter he glanced at me with curiosity. I took a liking to him. Verner also entered the Academy and when I came back from the summer holidays I became good friends with both of them, especially with Grigoryev. From this time on, many of the striking things that happened in the future we experienced together.

This second year in the Academy is marked for me by close participation in student life. Several men from Archangel had entered the Academy, among them the two Prugavin brothers and Lichkov. Living in exile in Archangel during these years was Vasily Vasilyevich Bervi (Flerovsky).[7] Many young people used to go to see him, and the Archangel men appeared with a quite definite outlook. Furthermore, Grigoryev had a special talent for getting to know people, and after a time he informed me that he had met several very interesting people among our students; and he told me exactly what was interesting about

[7] V. V. Bervi (1829–1918), author of *The position of the working class in Russia* (1869) and *An alphabet of the Social Sciences* (1872). Wrote under the pseudonym N. Flerovsky.

them. I hadn't noticed them before because of my prejudiced view, and they now appeared to me in a different light. Therefore interest in student life grew as well. I went to meetings, which continued as before, but they were much livelier now. Contributions to the student fund had trebled and our unofficial library became considerably richer. At the meetings concrete questions of daily life were discussed, and this gave them a lively interest that attracted considerable numbers of hitherto indifferent students. But it didn't stop at that.

One day Grigoryev gave me an issue of an illegal paper that was published abroad (I think it was *The Tocsin*) with an article by Tkachev[8] to read. Tkachev was a fairly well-known writer, who had emigrated after the Nechayev trial, in which he had been involved together with his common-law wife Dementyeva. In the Nechayev trial they had both occupied a special place, and there had been a lot of talk about them at the time and, *inter alia*, about civil marriage. The article Grigoryev had given me was polemical and directed at Lavrov[9] who had also fled from exile (in Vologda Province) and founded the publication *Forward* abroad. I knew Lavrov from his *Historical Letters*, which had been published in *The Week* and had then come out as a separate book that had been taken out of circulation by the censorship (in our unofficial library it was stitched together from *The Week*). Tkachev argued against Lavrov's programme, which called on young men and women to go 'into the people' for the propagation of socialist ideas. In so doing, he required from propagandists preliminary intellectual preparation demanding considerable work and time. Tkachev considered this superfluous. His point of view was different. He also called on men to go to the people, but to go in revolutionary passion to preach immediate rebellion. At the centre of his article, finely written and very fervent, was the image of the martyred people, put on a cross. And now—he wrote—we are urged to study chemistry in order to analyse the chemical composition of the cross, botany in order to determine the type of wood, anatomy in order to discover what tissues have been damaged by the nails. No, we are in no mood to investigate. We

[8] For Tkachev and the Nechayev trial, see pp. 109 and 110, notes.
[9] Pyotr Lavrovich Lavrov (1823–1900). His *Historical Letters* were serialized in *The Week* in 1868–9 and were written as an attack on the Nihilism of Pisarev and his followers. Lavrov stressed the intellectual's 'debt to the people'. Only the toil and privations of the masses has made possible the leisure necessary for individual intellectual development. Educated men thus have a moral debt to repay—they must dedicate themselves to the enlightenment of the people and the creation of a just socialist order. This was their moral duty. It was Lavrov's appeal to the conscience of the intelligentsia that made such a strong impression.

are seized with one passionate desire—to take the victim off the cross now, straight away, without preliminary and unnecessary investigations.

I am quoting from memory and, naturally, cannot convey Tkachev's passionate pathos. I remember that at first the article impressed me through this pathos. It seemed to me that a true revolutionary should talk like that. Grigoryev made no objection, but soon after gave me *Forward*, which contained Lavrov's programme and also an article: 'A conversation of consistent people'.[10] I read it all in one go and was completely carried away by the well-ordered system of revolutionary Populism. I liked Tkachev's small article simply as a fine piece of literature. The programme and articles of *Forward* immediately stirred thoughts and feelings deep inside me that had been formed from the direct impressions of life and literature.

I shall not say a great deal about Populism. It is easy now to recognize its moral truth (which many people nevertheless tend to deny) and its mistakes too. Among the latter, the chief mistake of course was the naïve idea of 'the people' (at that time the word referred mainly to the peasantry), of its potential wisdom, which was slumbering in its consciousness and waiting only for a final formula in order to manifest itself and crystallize the whole of life in its image.

From the time of the Emancipation the idea of 'the people' (*narod*) loomed very large in the mind of Russian society as a whole. The people lay on our horizon like a cloud into which men peered, trying to discern or guess the shapes swarming within it. In so doing, different men saw different things, but they all peered anxiously, with great interest, and they all invoked popular wisdom. Without dealing with the Slavophiles, in whose system the people played such an important part, one might mention that even Katkov and the conservatives pointed to 'the wisdom of the people': in their view the people consciously upheld the foundations of the existing order. For Dostoyevsky the people was '*bogonosets*' ('God-bearer'), while Ivan Aksakov[11] even in the 1880s loved to make use in his paper in various contexts of the pronouncements of Russian *moujhiks*, even though those '*moujhiks* of ours' were really money-bags who had long since left the peasantry for the merchant class. That did not matter. The very fact of peasant origin conferred a sort of patent on the possession of true popular

[10] Korolenko must have in mind the articles 'Our Programme' (1873) and 'To whom does the future belong? A conversation of consistent people' (1874).

[11] Ivan Sergeyevich Aksakov (1823–86); with his brother Konstantin he was one of the leaders of the younger Slavophiles. He published several papers in the course of his life, the last being *Russia* (*Rus'*), started in 1881.

wisdom. In a story by Zlatovratsky[12] ('Hearts of Gold') there is an intellectual of peasant origin, the medical student Bashkirtsev. He is almost inarticulate, but everyone feels that he knows something the restless intellectuals do not know, and that when he does speak at the proper time, he will say something new and of great moment.

A comparison automatically suggests itself between this hero of a rather feeble populist story and Karatayev in *War and Peace*. Karatayev can't put a sentence together correctly either, but Pyotr Bezukhov remembers his short pronouncements all his life, trying to grasp some mysterious and almost mystical meaning in them. This same attitude to what Karatayev represented was doubtless characteristic of Tolstoy himself and of almost all Russian critics who have written about *War and Peace*.

That is why the ideas of revolutionary Populism took such a quick and complete hold on the minds of people of our generation. Social injustice was a fact that hit one in the eyes. Those suffered most from it who had the heaviest work to do. And everyone, without distinction of viewpoint, recognized that in those peasant masses there was ripening, or perhaps had already ripened, some Word that would resolve all doubts. This is what was so widespread in the consciousness of Russian society at that time, and from which our generation—which in the 1870s was approaching the cross-roads of life—merely drew the most logical and honest deductions. If the overall premise was correct, then the deduction was clear indeed: one had to renounce the old world, one had to depart 'from those that exulted, idly chattered, stained their hands with blood'[13] to where 'rough hands were working' and where, besides, some kind of formula for a new life was ripening.

Was this naïve? Yes, it was naïve, but this naïvety was shared by the least romantic representatives of Russian educated society at that time. Part of the legal and all the illegal press drew the logical and most moral deductions, while the younger generation contributed its characteristic enthusiasm. And so revolutionary Populism was ready. It offered our generation what the previous generation of thinking realists had lacked: it brought faith not in mere formulas and abstractions. It gave our aspirations a kind of wide, vital foundation.

Circles now met in Moscow and at the Academy and passionately discussed Lavrov's programme. At this time I was won over by Mikhaylovsky's articles and spread them among the students, pointing

12 Nikolay Nikoleyevich Zlatovratsky (1845–1911); his novels and stories idealized the peasantry and reflected his Populist views.
13 From Nekrasov's poem 'A knight for an hour' ('*Rytsar' na chas*'), 1860.

to the direct link between his ideas and what we had been discussing only in secret meetings. I had now found what I had looked for in vain in Petersburg: at our secret meetings we talked in a friendly and straightforward way about how we could live honourably and what we could do. I no longer looked for the real ideal student. That elusive image had been replaced by the wider and more alluring image of the great 'people', mysterious in its wisdom—the object of new searchings and, possibly, of new illusions.

18
Valuyev's Visit to the Academy

MY SECOND YEAR IN THE ACADEMY ENDED IN THE AT-mosphere I have described. I began my third year. Secret meetings in the forest *dachas* went on as before, and sometimes there were also meetings in Moscow with the Technical and University students. The feeling of the movement 'to the people' was quite definitely in the air. Every now and then someone would leave the Academy and disappear. Every so often people from Petersburg arrived, organized small meetings in Moscow or in the Academy itself, inviting men to join them and establishing connections. Along with this the number of arrests increased and among the students as a body there developed a peculiar mood of unrest.

It must have been around the beginning of the summer holidays that the Minister P. A. Valuyev[1] suddenly visited the Academy. We had already had the pleasure and honour of seeing this famous statesman in our midst. On one occasion during examinations a very unexpected

[1] Count Pyotr Aleksandrovich Valuyev (1814–90), Minister of the Interior (1861–8), Minister of State Property (1872–8), Chairman of the Council of Ministers (1877–80).

thing had happened; Professor Ilyenkov, who was examining us in Agricultural Chemistry, suddenly broke off the exam and gave us a lecture on a new method of puddling steel, which had recently been used in works in the Urals. We all looked at one another: special methods of puddling steel had nothing to do with agricultural chemistry or with our future activity as agriculturalists or foresters. Without going into any explanations, Ilyenkov simply asked us to remember what he had said, then proceeded with the exam.

Shortly afterwards, the door of the chemistry lecture-hall opened and Valuyev entered, accompanied by the academic staff and his own officials. Tall, spare, grand, and even rather pompous, he took a seat at the professor's table, the members of his escort sat on the benches, and the examination went on in the usual way. Suddenly Valuyev politely requested Ilyenkov's permission to ask a few questions himself. Ilyenkov bowed, a barely perceptible ironic smile appearing fleetingly on his serious face. The reason for the strange lecture became clear to us. His Excellency immediately interested himself in whether the students were aware of the usual methods of puddling steel. It proved that they were. But were they also aware of the most recent methods, that had been used in the steel-mills in the Urals? A student repeated what he had just heard from Ilyenkov, making a few mistakes at the same time. This gave the Minister obvious pleasure. He authoritatively corrected the mistakes and departed, clearly satisfied, whereupon Ilyenkov went on once more with the exam. It seemed to me that the old professor felt a little ashamed to look at his young audience.

Valuyev's visits did not always end so happily. One day he put in an appearance at one of Professor Tsvetkov's physics exams. Yakov Yakovlevich Tsvetkov was an extraordinarily original figure. As well as being a professor in the Academy he also fulfilled the duties of a tutor in the Katkov Lycée[2] and always came to his lectures in the Academy (eight miles away) on foot, regardless of the weather. He was considered terribly stingy, but when he died it was discovered that he had spent his money on endowing grants. So, again, at an examination by this eccentric professor, Valuyev suddenly asked a student a question. The student didn't open his mouth. Valuyev put the same question in a different form. There was the same puzzled silence. The Minister turned to the professor, obviously expecting him to extricate the student from his difficulty with some leading questions, but Tsvetkov's bird-like

---

[2] Its real name was The Imperial Lycée, in memory of the Tsarevich Nicholas. It was founded in 1868 on money donated by various people, including M. N. Katkov.

face with its long nose, rather reminiscent of the profile of a young be-spectacled jackdaw, preserved a dispassionate silence.

'The students don't know this?' the Minister finally asked, looking hard at Tsvetkov.

Tsvetkov shrugged his shoulders and said off-handedly, 'I don't know either. If Your Excellency knows, please tell us.'

Not deeming it necessary to hide his sense of injury, the Minister got up and walked out of the hall.

Now Valuyev had come to us at an unusual time. The exams were already over, and a large proportion of the students had gone away for the holidays. There remained only those who never went home and those who had practical work to do. The wardens ran through the fields, grounds, and forest huts, summoning the students to the recreation hall straight away. We presented ourselves in the Academy in our high boots and blouses, just as we were, straight from our work. After a while the door opened and Valuyev came in. Behind the Minister, and rather to one side, like a little boat roped behind a ship, his whole figure leaning in His Excellency's direction, came a Special Duties' Secretary, and behind him, in uniform and wearing his sword, F. N. Korolyov and the senior staff. Valuyev walked straight in with a majestic step, and after three or four paces stopped in front of the crowd of students. Then, turning rather superciliously to the Director and senior staff, he said, 'Gentlemen, please leave me alone with the students.'

F. N. Korolyov, a venerable-looking old gentleman with a white beard, withdrew respectfully, even timidly, on tip-toe, along with the senior staff. The figure of the Ministerial Secretary, in tight-fitting uniform, assumed a truly ballet-like pose: the upper part of his body was launched towards the Minister, while his legs were ready to carry him out after the Director. This was so comical that a wave of tittering ran through the disrespectful students. Valuyev no doubt thought it was directed at our Academy authorities. He gave the Secretary a condescending nod and said, 'You stay . . .'

The Secretary's body froze in the same graceful leaning position. His face expressed rapt attention. He gave us a glance which seemed to say: 'We are witnessing an historical occasion.'

The Minister began. He had purposely asked our staff to withdraw in order to have the opportunity of speaking freely with us. He understood young people and hoped that we too would understand him. Lately he had been informed of lamentable events in the life of the Academy. It was no secret to him that the Academy was no exception in this respect: among students in general an anti-government mood had developed, and was leading to the most regrettable results. Students were being arrested and exiled. Careers were being interrupted and even destroyed. The state was being deprived of useful workers. And so he had come specially to have a friendly chat with us about these things.

Valuyev's voice was rich, deep, and permeated with self-satisfaction. He clearly admired himself and liked showing off his rhetorical skill. To a man accustomed to speaking in front of Tsars, the present task seemed an easy one indeed. He continued:

'Gentlemen, as you see, my beard has grown grey in labours which, believe me, I have by no means always found pleasant.'

And now a little hitch occurred: at this point in his speech the eminent orator raised his hand to his supposed beard, but it proved to have been freshly shaven-off. Once more a titter rose from the crowd of students. An expression of alarm, anger, and horror appeared on the face of the Secretary. The Minister proceeded.

He wasn't going to tell us that, as people receiving education in institutions maintained by the government, we owed a debt of gratitude to the Tsar, as the head of that government. We might reply that it was the Russian people that gave the money for educational institutions and that, therefore, we owed a debt of thanks only to it and not to the government.[3] Neither was he going to talk about the expectations our parents, tutors, and guardians placed on our studies, on the diploma, which constituted the formal goal of the course. We might again object that a man could serve the people in fields other than those that demanded diplomas.

The orator's speech flowed smooth, rich, irrepressible. However, whether it was because his ear had caught the sniggers that had twice run through his scarcely respectful audience, or whether simply, like a nightingale, he had got carried away by the sound of his own voice, the fact was that negative figures of speech had taken him too far. He had rejected one argument after another, making big play of his familiarity with our point of view and paving the way for some final invincible argument. But when at last the time came for him to move to the positive part of his speech and deliver that final blow, it became obvious that he had used up all his arguments, refuting them all 'from our point of view'. Nothing remained for the positive part. The orator stopped in obvious difficulty. On the Secretary's expressive face suffering was

[3] Here Valuyev is demonstrating his familiarity with Populist thinking. The idea that the educated individual, as a member of the privileged sections of society, had a moral debt to the Russian people, by whose labours all privileges had been bought, was central to the Populist outlook.

written. A quarter of a minute of painful silence elapsed, and the orator realized that, accustomed as he was to speaking in high places, it would be hard for him to carry things off on this occasion and, most important of all, he couldn't possibly end in the same liberal vein. Therefore he suddenly said with a kind of harsh ferocity:

'It is nevertheless my duty to tell you, gentlemen, that as you are being educated in an institution which owes its very existence to His Majesty the Emperor, that fact alone obliges you to respect his government and obey it.'

A slight, cold bow, and the Minister majestically withdrew. His listeners were certainly not disposed on this occasion to any kind of demonstration, but an ironic movement again passed noticeably through the young audience. The Minister had already gone through the doorway, but the graceful Secretary was still with us and he gave us a reproachful and even hostile look. No doubt, he would take back to Petersburg the most awful impression of those blouses, high boots and the dreadful lack of respect.

19
My First Arrest

POSSIBLY INFLUENCED BY THE MINISTER'S VISIT, KOROLYOV decided to adopt measures against the rising discontent of the students. These measures he understood purely in terms of school discipline: in his talks with students in his office or when he met them in the park, on the farm, or the experimental grounds he started rebuking them more frequently for long hair, untidiness in their dress, for adopting a dis-respectful stance when speaking to him and his colleagues. This was the worst thing he could have done in his position. This sort of carping was liable to agitate the mass of the student body that was neutral in all other respects. I remember a gathering at which a student by the name of Berdnikov told about one such collision with the Director. The crowd grew angry and noisy. Yet Berdnikov, a plump and rather smug fellow, with chubby red cheeks, was a most inoffensive being, who later, no doubt, made a very efficient civil-servant.

There was a great accumulation of such irritating details, which united the mass of the students in defence of their self-esteem as a body. At the entrance to the hostel the caretaker rather rudely stopped a lady, who had come to see a relative among the students. Women were not allowed into the rooms, only into the common reception-room, and in our present mood that seemed humiliating: we were sure that we ourselves would be able to prevent any disgraceful incidents. Some students in the hostel began noticing that someone was searching their things in their absence. The wardens started watching that lectures were regularly attended, which there was not really any need for. Finally, something occurred which stirred up the section of the students more deeply affected by the revolutionary movement.

Some of the students who were being looked for were living unregistered in Moscow. In the lobby of the Academy, false notifications began to appear to the effect that money or parcels had been received for these people living in hiding. When they came for them, they were kept waiting and handed over to the gendarmes. In one case an arrest of this sort in the office was made successfully and fairly unobtrusively, but in another case the student (seemingly, Voinov) suspected a trap, managed to get out of the building in time and started running across the yard towards the park. A luckless, long-legged old warden jumped out after him and ran over the yard, summoning the janitors. It was a pitiful and revolting scene. I remember that eye-witness reports of this occurrence made an impression on me before which the purely school questions of haircuts, Korolyov's rebukes, the non-admission of female relatives to the hostel, and the refectory, which the students were demanding to run themselves, all faded completely.

Meetings were now held all the time. The students gathered fairly openly in the hostel, and when on one occasion a sub-warden appeared accompanied by janitors, the door was barricaded against him. A collective address of protest was being drawn up. It had been going on for about two weeks, but they couldn't work out the actual text of the address. Everybody wanted to state that relations with the academic administration were provoking indignation. However, only the purely school questions united the vast majority. Our group was not satisfied with this. We also demanded a declaration concerning the detective activities of the wardens, but the majority would not go as far as that.

The matter dragged on painfully; nobody thought about classes, the crisis had somehow to be resolved. After one stormy meeting Grigoryev and I declared that we would take no further part in debates, but would compose our own address and hand it in, even if there were only two signatures on it. Somebody had to tell the truth. We then withdrew to my room, where I quickly drew up a declaration and signed it. Grigoryev, obviously not ascribing importance to niceties (which subsequently caused us some trouble), gave his complete approval to the basic theme: relations between the administration and the students were based on deep distrust and mutual lack of esteem, and had latterly taken completely unworthy forms: the incident involving the attempt to arrest the student so-and-so made us regard the Academy office as a department of the Moscow Political Police, and the representatives of the academic administration as its obedient agents. When we had signed the declaration, we jointly announced that without further discussion we invited everyone to sign who agreed with it, but that we would hand it in anyway, however many or few signatures there were. Names began to cover the paper. The first to sign were the members of our own circle from Archangel—Aleksey and Viktor Prugavin, Nikolsky and Lichkov. Verner, who was living in Moscow, came specially to add his signature. Soon there were ninety-six signatures, and there it stopped. The majority, judging that the mention of the arrests introduced dangerous political undertones, shrank back immediately. The signatories elected Grigoryev, Verner, and myself as deputies to present the address. The meetings ceased. A hush fell over the Academy.

The three of us went to see the Director. He received us seriously and rather coldly, took the paper and began reading it with a somewhat disdainful air, shrugging his shoulders at certain places. But when he came to the part about the arrests, his pale, aged face suddenly flushed a deep red, which spread in a sharply defined line over his forehead and began rising quickly up his high skull. I actually grew alarmed, afraid that he might have a stroke. However, he controlled himself and said morosely, 'You are touching on things that I have no right to discuss with you. Your declaration will be handed to the Council.' We bowed and went out.

In the Academy classes took their normal course, the lecture-halls were full again, but the student-body was buzzing like a disturbed hive. At this time there were about 250 students in the Academy; so, less than half had signed. Some attacked us bitterly: there was even talk of a counter-declaration, which that same Berdnikov who had so stirred a meeting with the story of his purely schoolboy confrontation with

Korolyov, was supposedly going to hand in with a number of people of
like mind. Many would stop us outside and in the lecture-halls, hotly
disputing the address. I remember particularly a student called Arshenevsky. He agreed passionately with the purely school protest, but
objected just as passionately to 'the waging of politics'. Grigoryev and I
replied that it was the same thing in principle, but on a deeper moral
level. In the West universities were inviolate from the police, whereas
here the inspectors catch their pupils with their own hands and deliver
them to the political police.

Two weeks passed. Late one evening a janitor brought me an official
paper, in which I was informed that the Deputy Minister of State
Property, His Excellency Prince Liven was summoning me for an
interview. I was to appear the following day, at eight in the morning, at
a certain hotel on Lubyansky Square. Grigoryev and Verner, who were
living in Moscow at the time, received similar notices.

The summons produced a great stir among the students. Despite the
late hour, people hurried to see me with questions and reports. It had
been heard from the professors that Liven had arrived in Moscow that
day and had already conferred with the Governor-General. He was
expected in the Academy tomorrow. As I was rather unconcerned about
clothes, my friends lent me a brand-new dark suit. I put on a shirt with
a starched collar, a smart tie, and glossy boots—all from various con-
tributors. I was decked out as for a celebration, and at six o'clock the next
morning Grigoryev and I set out for Moscow in the village cab,
jokingly called a *fiacre*. Towards the appointed time we went into the
hotel entrance, and a few minutes later Verner drove up.

Although it was so early, the prince had already left the hotel. The
porter showed us to his room and suggested we wait. We waited for an
hour. The streets had come to life, but the prince had not arrived.
Grigoryev then suggested writing a note on a sheet of paper lying to
hand to the effect that we had appeared at the appointed time but, finding
no one but the porters and having waited more than an hour, we were
leaving. We signed the note and returned to the Academy. Later a story
went about that Liven had returned shortly after our departure and, on
reading our very original visiting-card, had made his way to the Governor-General, Dolgorukov, declaring that he could see quite clearly
from the insolent action of the students' spokesmen that the Academy
was about to flare into open revolt. The unnerved prince was therefore
demanding troops to restore order. They managed to calm him down.

Meanwhile in the Academy an instruction had been received that
all the students should gather in the assembly hall. A rumour that we

had been arrested scarcely helped to calm the atmosphere. Uncertainty about our fate made the mass of the students very nervous and greatly heightened the strong, generous feeling of comradeship. When we drove up to the entrance of the Academy in a cab, the students poured out of the building and gave us a really rapturous welcome. They shook our hands, embraced us, bombarded us with questions. When he'd heard our story, the stout Arshenevsky embraced me fervently and said, 'Wonderful. That's the way: you have upheld the honour of the students. Now we are all with you.'

It transpired that during the anxious period of uncertainty someone had provided a sheet of paper for additional signatures. Now this sheet was filled: the whole Academy, with one or two exceptions, had backed our declaration.

About twelve o'clock we were all asked to go to the recreation hall. A carriage drew up outside the Director's door. We three were summoned first as the spokesmen. Prince Liven received us in the Director's study in the presence of Korolyov and, I think, the Dean, Professor Sobichevsky, and his own official. He declared that he had been sent on the instructions of His Imperial Majesty. The Emperor had been most grieved by our collective declaration. We must be aware that by our statutes the students did not constitute a corporation. A collective declaration was thus an offence in itself. He required first of all that we should apologize for this unlawful action. He was sure that the mass of the students had merely followed the leaders blindly, and it now depended upon us to bring them back to the path of legality. He then turned to each of us separately, requiring an answer.

The general mood of the students, expressed when we had met them, had made us feel so happy and had filled us with such certainty in complete unanimity that we replied without hesitating and with utter sincerity that we were not the leaders, but only the spokesmen of the opinions and feelings of all our comrades. I added that to deny the corporate spirit of the student body was a great mistake: where there is a certain mass of people, united by common intellectual and daily interests, there, undoubtedly, a corporation exists. This was a fact of life, whether it was recognized by statutes or not. Liven affected to be horrified by this seditious declaration and, turning slightly towards Korolyov, said, 'If such, indeed, is the spirit prevailing amongst the students, I do not know how I shall dare inform the Emperor of it. It will only remain to close the Academy.'

He turned to us again and added that he hoped we would honourably give him the opportunity of ascertaining that our comrades were acting fully consciously, and not blindly following us. To that end he expected our word of honour that we, though certainly not under arrest—he emphasized that—would remain in the Director's apartment during the course of the talks with the students, not trying to influence them in any way. We readily gave our word, as required. I remember that during these minutes I felt great affection for the whole agitated young mass of comrades standing behind us. I felt affection for them all together, I now loved and respected that collective being, called 'the Petrovsky student', 'the Petrovets'. We believed fully in the sincerity and depth of the general feeling. Therefore we willingly promised not to try to influence the decision of the other students.

We were then taken to a separate room, on which a watch was put. After a short time we heard the agitated voice of Professor Kliment Arkadyevich Timiryazev[1] outside the locked doors.

'You dare not refuse me entrance: I am a professor and am going to my students.'

The door opened and Timiryazev entered quickly. Shaking our hands hurriedly, he said straight away, 'You know, gentlemen, there is much in your declaration I cannot agree with.'

He was tall, thin, fair-haired, and still a young man, with fine large eyes. He was energetic and nervous, and there was a distinctive sort of elegance in everything about him. Even his experiments on chlorophyl, which had brought him European fame, were set up with artistic taste. To begin with he would not speak very well, sometimes drawling and stuttering. But when he became carried away, which happened especially in his lectures on the physiology of plants, all his defects of speech disappeared, and he held his audience completely captive. I used to draw demonstration plates for his lectures, and every time went to his little wooden house right at the entrance to the Academy farm with the same feeling with which I had gone to Avdiyev in Rovno. There were peculiar threads of sympathy between him and the students, though very frequently his conversations outside lectures would become arguments on extra-curricular subjects. We felt that the subjects that concerned us also interested him. Furthermore, in his nervous speech we detected sincere and fervent beliefs. It related to science and culture, which he defended from our tendency to simplify everything, and in this belief there was a great deal of idealistic sincerity. Our young generation valued this. Besides, we were certain that the detective role of the

[1] Kliment Arkadyevich Timiryazev (1843–1920), a great Russian botanist. The Petrovsky Academy now bears the name 'The K. A. Timiryazev Agricultural Academy of Moscow'.

wardens revolted him no less than us. We therefore prepared to hear him out, but the chat was cut short before it had even started. A sub-warden came running in on Timiryazev's heels and informed him that the Council had gathered and that they were waiting for him in the Director's study. Apparently his visit had provoked some anxiety among the short-sighted members of the administration; though, of course, if anything was capable of shaking our certainty, it would have been the words of Timiryazev. We subsequently learned that Timiryazev had protested strongly against the fact that Liven had interrogated the administration, and even policemen who had nothing to do with the Academy, before turning to the Council. The meeting soon started, and from time to time we could hear Timiryazev's ringing voice, though it was impossible to distinguish the words.

When Timiryazev had gone, the door opened again. The local Inspector of Police came in, whose name, if I'm not mistaken, was Rzhevsky. He was an elderly man with fair hair that was turning grey; he had a whitish sort of look about him which made him seem good-natured. On coming in, he unfastened his sabre and undid the buttons of his tunic, which made him look even more good-natured. Then he asked us to let him sit with us, and started speaking straight away with the air of a condescending uncle chatting with his nephews.

'Oh dear! You've worn me out. What's to be done?! I was young myself, was a student once and used to get carried away. . . .'

Endless stories poured from his lips. He told them all as an old card who'd seen a great deal in life, and who couldn't have wool pulled over his eyes.

'Take you gentlemen. You're keen on Shchedrin.[2] Of course, he's a clever satirist, lampoons bureaucrats and landowners, and you like that sort of thing. But what of the man himself? He is nothing other than a former Counsellor of the administration of Vyatsk Province. He has an estate in Tver Province, and I personally had occasion in the performance of my official duties to pacify the peasants on his estate.'

He told some story in which M. Y. Saltykov-Shchedrin allegedly figured in the role of a despotic serf-owner. After this tale there followed another, and a third, and they were all of the same kind, revealing the ugly hidden side of 'popular celebrities'. After some time he had talked so much that the story about Saltykov was told about Turgenev: he had had to pacify the peasants in Spasskoye. Grigoryev gave him to

[2] Mikhayl Yevgrafovich Saltykov (1826–89), a great radical satirist. He wrote under the pen-name of N. Shchedrin, and is often referred to as Saltykov-Shchedrin.

understand with characteristic bluntness that he was talking rot, and the Inspector effaced himself.

Meanwhile in the Academy events were proceeding apace. After the meeting of the Council the authorities went to the assembly hall, where Liven addressed a short speech to the students, in which he said the same as he had said to us. He threatened the closure of the Academy, suggested an apology from each year, and withdrew, leaving further persuasion to the professors. We were again summoned to him and he demanded a continuance of our undertaking until the next day. Of course, he wasn't even thinking in terms of arrest. If, for example, we agreed to withdraw to Moscow for the day and not to enter either directly or indirectly into any relations with our comrades until two o'clock the next afternoon, that would be quite enough for him. He would accept our word of honour and ask us to come to see him in the morning at the apartment of relatives of his, at such-and-such an address. We agreed and were given a cab. When we got into it, a number of students ran out of the building and surrounded it. They thought that we were being arrested. Had that been so, then without any doubt comradely feeling would have flared up like powder and we would have been rescued. We explained what was happening: we had not been arrested but were merely being discharged on our word of honour until the next day. The students stepped back, and we drove off.

In educated circles in Moscow that day there was talk of nothing but what had happened in the Petrovsky Academy. By the evening it became known that the students were delivering an apology, the main reason for which was their concern about our fate: we would suffer badly if the disorders continued. I remember how grieved we were by this news. We had somehow completely disregarded the consequences to ourselves. We considered that we had spoken the truth, and we wanted to stand by it to the end. It grieved us that personal considerations for us were able to destroy the comradely unanimity and spoil the moral significance of the whole affair.

By twelve o'clock the next day we were at Liven's. This time he received us immediately in his relative's modest study. His manner was extremely cordial and mild. Later we realized that he had been afraid of us at the time: we might still, even then, spoil the whole business. He told us that the vast majoirty of the students had already realized the unlawfulness of their action, and he was sure it would all end safely for the Academy. He was merely asking us to prolong for one more day the promise we had given and to remain in Moscow. Grigoryev answered this with a firm refusal.

'If, of course, we won't be arrested . . .' he began, but Liven quickly cut him short.

'You don't think I came here with police measures of that sort, do you ? Believe me, there can be no question of any arrest.' Then, taking me by the arm (I was sitting nearer him than the others), he started saying in an almost moved tone of voice that in us he had met opponents, but honourable opponents: we had chivalrously kept our word, and he had no cause to regret that he had trusted in our honour . . .

'That gives us grounds to suppose that in your person we are dealing with a similar opponent,' said Grigoryev.

The prince turned to him and replied hurriedly, with a shade of surprise at the student's boldness. 'Oh, of course, of course. So, you agree to remain twenty-four hours more in Moscow? Where will you be staying during this time ? In the same apartments ?'

Grigoryev was again the first to answer.

'My obligation expires at two o'clock. After that I shall return to the Academy.'

Verner and I said the same, after which we bowed and left.

'They are certain to arrest us before two o'clock,' Grigoryev said with conviction. Verner, mild, good humoured, trusting, reproached him: 'You never trust people.'

In two hours we had, in fact, all been arrested and escorted to the Basmanny district police station, beyond the Red Gates. We were taken in two cabs, Grigoryev arriving considerably sooner than Verner and I. We found him in the office. In his usual open way he was asking on whose authority we had been arrested and could we not see the order.

'I am not permitted to do that,' the officer replied.

'Well, at least tell me by whom the order is signed.'

'The Ober-Chief of Police.'

'Is that all ?'

The officer looked at the paper brought by the policemen who had arrested us and, lowering his voice, said, 'By order of His Excellency Prince Liven, specially commissioned by His Imperial Majesty.'

I recall that this disclosure gave me a feeling of a sort of moral victory: the government in the person of Liven had stooped to cunning and sly deception. Liven had been playing a part for our benefit.

Our escorts received their receipts and left. We were taken off to a cell. The police-officer apologized that he was forced to put former army-officers in a basement cell (he was referring to Grigoryev and Verner): there was no room upstairs. A few minutes later we found ourselves in a stinking basement-corridor of the Basmanny district police station.

Verner had already once experienced the delights of arrest in Moscow police stations and, as an experienced man, tried to prepare us for the worst. But when we were shown into a cell with damp walls and a small window on a level with the ground, he turned out to be the most surprised of the three of us. From his words we had prepared for the worst, while for him this cellar proved to be the worst possible surprise. Along the wall under the window were plank-beds, on which lay three dirty narrow mattresses, stuffed with straw. The mattresses were covered with thick sackcloth-sheets. But what made Verner really shudder were the grey prison blankets over which huge lice were crawling, catching the eye immediately on the dark grey background. Moving this bedding aside, we sat down on the edge of the beds and began drinking tea from the tin mugs brought by the man on duty.

We sat like this for quite a long time, listening to the various sounds from neighbouring cells. There was drunken singing, shouting, swearing. Every now and then they brought drunks in from the street. At first they were noisy and resisted, and the policemen would start beating them up. The corridor would echo with piercing screams, which soon changed to piteous moans. Then a door would open and the pacified prisoner would be thrown into some common-cell. Subsequently I wrote many times about the murders committed everywhere in our police stations, and each time I recalled that first evening of my first arrest.

Weariness from these two anxious days was telling on us. We could hardly keep our eyes open. At last Grigoryev decided to straighten his bed; he jokingly made the sign of the cross three times and threw himself on it as if he were plunging into cold water. I followed his example. Only poor, fastidious Verner remained sitting on the edge of his bed, leaning his shoulder against the wall, and nodding, unable to force himself to this heroic action. So passed my first night as a prisoner.

PART FIVE

Vologda-Kronstadt-Petersburg

20

A State Criminal in Exile

TWO DAYS LATER[1] I WAS THE FIRST TO BE SUMMONED TO THE station office.

By putting our little table on a bed and climbing up to the window, we could see what was going on in the courtyard. I had been looking out of the window when a carriage had rumbled into the courtyard and two gendarmes had stepped out of it. From this we realized why I had been sent for. I was being exiled. Thanks to Liven's 'open way of doing things' we had not been prepared for this: we should have to go away without money or a change of clothing. I was wearing a loaned suit and a light overcoat, and my stiffly starched collar chafed my neck.

The preparations did not take long. We said a warm good-bye to one another, and in half an hour the gendarmes had taken me to the Yaroslavl Station. I hadn't reckoned on such speed, and I felt particularly sad to be going away without saying good-bye to my sister in the Institute.

I was led into an overcrowded third-class carriage. Right in the corner sat a shortish man with a long, black beard, who reminded me of the fairy-tale Chernomor.[2] He was between two gendarmes as well, and we introduced ourselves. He was Bochkaryov, a *zemstvo* man from I. I. Petrunkevich's[3] circle. Just as the train was about to leave there was a bit of a commotion on the platform. Apparently, some Petrovsky stu-

---

[1] 24 March 1876.

[2] A wizard with great powers in Pushkin's *Ruslan and Lyudmila*.

[3] I. I. Petrunkevich was a leading and outspoken *zemstvo* liberal. The *zemstva* were elective rural district and provincial councils, established in 1864. They did not have police or military authority, but were responsible for such things as roads, public health, and education. Many enlightened men willingly entered the new service.

dents had kept a watch on the police station and had now tried to get into our carriage, but were stopped from entering. The train soon moved off.

During a short stop at Pushkino station a young and beautiful brunette with an expressive, even dramatic face came up to the window. She fixed her eyes on Bochkaryov as on an icon. It was not possible to talk through the double windows, and she remained standing motionless, with a tragic expression on her face, until the train started. Bochkaryov bowed good-bye to her and sighed.

In the middle of the night I suddenly woke up with a jolt and for a long time I couldn't grasp where I was. I had dreamed about my mother, and my heart was now gripped with a sharp sense of anguish. The carriage was stuffy and filled with tobacco smoke, which shrouded the dim light of the lamp. Opposite and alongside me four gendarmes were nodding. I finally remembered where I was, and the thought of my mother rose clearly in my mind. All this time I had thought little about her. She was not well, and how would she receive the news of my exile, should it appear in the papers? The nervous exhaustion of those past days told: I felt tears welling into my eyes. The sooner I got where I was going, the better, so as to be able to write and tell her something definite. In the meantime there was no point in giving in to fear: other thoughts replaced and drove out my anguish. I wasn't sorry for what I had done. Despite my twenty-two years I felt a boyish sense of pride: in the police station they had formally announced that I was being exiled 'by Imperial order' to Ust-Sysolsk in Vologda Province. I recalled my first secret meeting in the Izmaylovsky Regiment. At that time the forces of one police station had been mobilized. Now the apparatus of supreme power had been put into motion against me.

I don't remember exactly where Bochkaryov and I parted, but when we separated we embraced each other just like members of a fraternal order, united by common persecution. The gendarmes took me from the station to the Yaroslavl Police Department, the windows of which looked out on to the Volga. The ice had begun to break up and large ice-floes were moving slowly down the river. Everyone in the Police Department was at the windows, watching the gallant Public Prosecutor, President of the local Lifeboat Society, bringing the post from Vologda across the river in the lifeboat. When the crossing had been safely completed, the assistant Chief of Police, a kindly looking old man, received me from the gendarmes, and it was from him I first learned that I was a 'state criminal'.

'You're mistaken,' I said. 'I'm only a student and am being exiled for a collective declaration to our academic authorities.'

'Come, come,' he replied with positive certainty. 'It's down here. "By Imperial order", old chap. You must be a state criminal, mustn't you?'

Once again I have to admit there was something in this that tickled my vanity.

The Chief of Police arrived shortly after, a dark-haired man of military appearance, with imperious manners. He had already been to see the Governor and brought an instruction from His Excellency to send me straight to the prison. I made a very earnest request not to be held up on my journey, to be sent on today, if possible. I had started thinking about my mother again, and once more I felt watery about the eyes. The 'state criminal' must have looked rather pathetic, and the Chief of Police treated my request with obvious sympathy. He cast his eyes over my best suit, noticed the complete absence of any sort of luggage, and realized that I really ought not to be held up.

'If you're not afraid of the breaking ice,' he said, 'I'll have a word with the Prosecutor and ask him to take you across with the post tomorrow. Meantime—there's nothing for it, you'll have to spend the night in the prison. . . . Let's have a decent-looking escort,' he said to one of his subordinates.

A local constable appeared but proved to be the very reverse of 'decent-looking'. At this time policemen in provincial capitals had not yet acquired any semblance of smartness, and the constable who'd come in looked like one of the subordinates of Gogol's Derzhimorda:[4] his greatcoat was all in shreds with multi-coloured patches, and his sabre was simply hanging on an old bit of string.

'Get him out of here. Send in another, more decent-looking,' the Chief said fastidiously.

Another came in. His patches were the same colour as his greatcoat, and his sabre was hanging partly on a thong, partly on string. The Chief took a look at him and gave a wave of the hand.

'Well, sorry. You'll have to take the best we've got. There's nothing else for it.'

I thanked him for his kind thoughts and set out on foot through the town to the prison.

There were four of us: the rejected constable was escorting some unfortunate fellow in a short convict's jacket with an ace of diamonds on the back. On the way I heard him squabbling with his escort about something and, looking round, saw the constable grab him by the seat of his wide trousers and try to pull him back.

[4] In the Comedy *The Government Inspector* (*Reviзor*).

'What's the matter ?' I asked.

'The usual ignorance,' my constable explained. 'He wants to walk beside you. He thinks you and he are comrades.'

Taking advantage of a halt the fellow jumped forward and asked pertly, 'You're being exiled ?'

'Yes.'

'Under police subveillance ?'

'I expect so.'

He turned triumphantly to his constable and said, 'Well, I'm under police subveillance too. We must be comrades.'

From there on we walked side by side—I in my light, borrowed, but very smart suit, and with an erect starched collar and round hat, he in his convict's jacket with an ace of diamonds on the back. The constables walked behind. Passers-by looked round with ironic curiosity.

Yaroslavl Prison was the first I became acquainted with. I was put in a cell, which was left unlocked. Soon afterwards, a short bespectacled prisoner in an imperial cloak came in to me. He was my neighbour, one of the privileged common criminals. It transpired that I had been put in the nobles' corridor. Introducing himself, he asked, 'You must be in for the Ivanchin-Pisarev and Countess Pototskaya affair ?'

The name of Ivanchin-Pisarev was new to me. My new acquaintance told me that in Yaroslavl Province they had unearthed a circle of revolutionaries, at the centre of which was Ivanchin-Pisarev. Many had been arrested and some were in that very prison then. Ivanchin had disappeared. The prisoner mentioned the name of Countess Pototskaya frequently, hinting that he knew her and offering, should I so wish, to give her a note. I had nothing to tell Countess Pototskaya and I declined, to the great disappointment of my affable neighbour.

I remember it was some sort of holiday, and after the usual dinner the head prisoner, a fine-looking man, by no means old, brought in a mug of tea and a whole pile of buns and rolls.

'There was almsgiving today,' he explained. 'Eat your fill.'

The corridor was almost empty. I went into my cell early and slept almost the whole of the day and night. At six o'clock in the morning I was woken up. The Chief of Police had kept his promise: the lifeboat that took the Vologda post was already waiting for me on the bank of the Volga. Together with a policeman-escort and the postmen I got into the boat, which was standing on runners. The movement of the ice had stopped; only in the middle, colliding and rustling, little floes and broad fields of ice were quietly floating. The boat was dragged on its runners across the ice and, gathering speed, splashed into the water and moved through the ice sludge until, propelled by the oars, it beached on a large mass of ice. The crossing was not without considerable excitement. The rest of the way we travelled smoothly along the narrow-gauge Vologda railway.

The Governor in Vologda at this time was an old Pole, Khominsky, fairly liberal and very benign. Probably because of this I was put not in the prison but in a duty room in the Police department. It was Holy Week, and when I asked to be sent on quickly the Chief of Police replied that I would leave on the third or fourth day of the holiday.

The Chief also turned out to be a kindly man; he told me to make myself at home in the duty room and asked if I wanted to go to the baths. I declined: I didn't have any clean clothes. Towards evening he sent me clean underclothes, suggesting I gave mine in to be washed. His attitude impressed me very favourably. In my career as an exile I got to know three very amiable Police Chiefs, all of whom, by some strange accident, were prosecuted.

On the first day of Easter I received an unexpected visit from the Governor, Khominsky. It transpired that his sons, students in the Communications Institute in Petersburg, had been informed of events by Petrovsky friends and had telegraphed their father. The kind-hearted old man had come to reassure me and ask if I needed anything. Shortly after him his office secretary arrived. He was an enormous man, still young. He stayed about an hour and told me the notorious story of the despoliation of the northern forests. There was a great deal being written about it in the papers at the time. The young official was appalled at the collusion between the Forestry Department and a certain foreign company. A special Commission of Investigation was at work, but it was unlikely to uncover anything: very important people and enormous foreign capital were involved.

The visit of the Governor and his Secretary evidently made quite an impression on the staff of the Police Department, not excluding the Chief of Police himself. Greeting me with the customary triple embrace (it was Easter Sunday), he suggested I take a walk through the town.

'With escorts, you mean?'

'With me, if you've no objection.'

I had no objection, and off we went.

'Would you care to take a look at our House of Arrest?' he asked, and, without waiting for an answer, went up a flight of stairs into a building under a watch-tower. I was rather surprised to see that they had apparently been expecting us there. The corridors had been swept clean and ventilated. Walking along the corridor with me and inviting me to look into the cells through the peep-holes, he unexpectedly said to the warder, 'Is there an empty cell?'

'Yes, sir: number nine.'

'Open it. Care to take a look inside?' And, like a polite host, he indicated for me to go first.

I recalled the scene between the Mayor and Khlestakov[5] and, like Ivan Aleksandrovich, I'd have been glad enough to have declined the kind invitation. But, plucking up courage, I crossed the threshold and a little later emerged safely from the cell. Obviously, the Chief had merely wanted to show off the cleanliness of the building. My surprise increased still further when, on coming out on to the steps, I saw the fire brigade drawn up in full order.

'Is there a fire somewhere?' I asked.

'No, I arranged it specially: I thought perhaps you'd be interested to have a look at our new engines?'

He gave a signal and the brigade started off. The well-fed horses pulled eagerly, the little bells were tinkling, the brigade flag unfurled in the breeze, the new pumps, painted bright red, glistened, and the men's bronze helmets gleamed, while I stood on the steps with the Chief, blushing and feeling for all the world like Khlestakov: so many men and horses had been disturbed on such a big holiday just for me.

It was a strange period to be in exile and one that soon came to an end. In the more remote places of exile there obviously still survived memories of the times when men had found themselves exiled only to rise even higher later on, when circumstances changed. The telegram from the Governor's sons, and the visit of the Governor himself had obviously evoked that very idea in the mind of the good-hearted Chief of Police, who judged it would be as well to show his household in model order just in case.

As we were returning along the front of the Police Department building, an unexpected little incident occurred: all of a sudden one of the doors half opened and out of it came a smallish figure. Somebody's hand was holding him firmly by the scruff of the neck and then gave him a strong jerk that sent him tumbling down the steps. The man might well have had a nasty fall if, waving his arms like a windmill and staggering from side to side, he had not collided headfirst into the Chief's paunch. The Chief seized him by the collar, shook him a couple of times, set him firmly on his legs and asked rather threateningly, 'What's this? Are you drunk?'

The man was, in fact, drunk, but still tried to justify himself: he had

[5] In Gogol's comedy *The Government Inspector* (*Reviẓor*).

come to the Department for a form, and that's the form they'd given him—seized by the neck, and pushed down the steps.

And suddenly inspired, he exclaimed with real pathos, 'Your Excellency . . . what sort of practices are these? What's this we've got, a republic?'

'Off with you now, off with you. Come for your form sober and on a working day.' And, giving a sad, condescending smile, he turned to me and said, 'I ask you . . . what a notion of a republic.'

One could guess that his own notions of a republic were different. All in all, I repeat, I retained a pleasant memory of this man's benevolence, and I should like to think that the official troubles that overtook him later on were not of a particularly serious nature.

I didn't have to wait long before moving off again. Spring was coming quickly from the south. In Yaroslavl the Volga was already moving, but the Middle Dvina was still lying under ice. There was deep snow, but the days were warm and everywhere spring streams were gurgling under the snow. We hurried, but unfortunately by the time we were approaching Totma the road had broken up completely and in places was nothing but a sea of mud.

Fate had sent me a very original sort of man as my escort. He was a constable whose name, I think, was Fyodorov, very short and squat, with a spherical head and fat cheeks between which his small nose was almost buried. A real Quasimodo in his ugliness, he proved to be a good-natured and talkative fellow. For some reason he also harboured a passionate hatred of gendarmes.

'I can't stand them,' he would say. 'A gendarme is the lowest of men: a slanderer, informer, sneak. He'll not only inform on his comrade, but on his own father.' We shared this disapproval, though for different reasons.

At the post station in Totma I was told the Inspector of Police wanted to see me. He informed me that he had received a telegram from the Governor that morning telling him to give the student Korolenko the choice of going on to Ust-Sysolsk or of returning to his hometown under the surveillance of the police. After considering for a short time, I wrote that I preferred to serve my term of exile 'in Kronstadt where my mother was'. Back in Zhitomir I no longer had anybody. Moreover, I still remembered how I had yearned to get away, and so decided to take a chance: perhaps I'd get to Kronstadt. The Inspector took the paper and there and then issued the policeman a written order to take me back to Vologda.

There were no horses in the station as the Archangel post had gone through not long before. Se we had to wait. We were sitting amicably on the station steps, chatting, when my Quasimodo's face suddenly darkened.

'Look, look, there's a gendarme. He's poking about for something, the swine. Must have got wind of you. Look at him, you'd think he hasn't seen us, but he'll stop just now. You'll see.'

The gendarme was walking along the other side of the street, which was a sea of watery mud. With his unbuttoned greatcoat and cocked cap he had the air of a man simply out for a stroll and was looking unconcernedly around. Then suddenly, as if by pure chance, his gaze fell upon us. He stopped, pleasantly surprised.

'Ah, travellers. We're always delighted to see strangers here. Allow me to join you for a chat. Where are you from? Moscow?'

He looked to the right and to the left, but there was no way across. So he braced himself and waded through the deep mud, extricating his feet with some difficulty.

'So you're travelling from Moscow? A student? The Petrovsky Academy? You don't say! What a pleasant surprise! I've a friend there —in fact, a relation: do you know Surovtsev? Is he well? He hasn't written for some time.'

My escort was making signs to me. Surovtsev was in hiding at this time, and the gendarme was investigating. I calmly replied, 'Yes, I know Surovtsev. We're friends. I saw him just before I left. He's well and asked me to remember him to his relations, if I met them.'

'It can't be true!' the gendarme said in astonishment, and his eyes started shifting. 'Where's he living then, do you know?'

'Of course I do: he's living in the Academy, in the village, where he lived before.'

'You've made me really happy. I'll go and tell my wife straight away. Good-bye and thank you.' And he went quickly off.

'What on earth did you tell him for?' my escort said with an expression of extreme reproach. 'They're looking for Surovtsev. He's just run off to the telegraph office to send a telegram.'

I started to laugh and told him that it had been a joke: Surovtsev was in hiding and his address wasn't known. The constable fell into a rapture of delight, his face contorted in unimaginable grimaces, and he swayed from side to side in such convulsions of laughter that I thought he would fall off the steps.

As I was waiting for horses I received an unexpected invitation. An official of the Forestry Department, a former student of the Petersburg Institute of Forestry, was living in the town. He considered me, as a

Petrovsky student, to be his friend and asked me to go and have some tea with him. I willingly agreed, and my constable had no objection. My host turned out to be a forestry valuation officer, whose name, I think, was Uspensky. He was a likeable, but extremely doleful-looking, even grim-looking man. He was living in a cold, comfortless place with a junior forestry officer. As it was a holiday they were both slightly tipsy, but the alcohol had had opposite effects on them: the valuer was obviously depressed and gloomy beyond measure, his co-tenant talkative, bright, and breezy. As soon as I arrived, Uspensky took his companion to one side and began whispering something to him. The other answered complacently, 'Well, so what? We don't care about that,' and, demonstratively taking out his purse, he immediately set off 'to see to things'.

Uspensky's swarthy face seemed to darken even more. Seeing that his secret had been revealed, he looked down and said, 'He's a good sort, and a colleague, but corrupt and so he prospers. You see, I hold to the old, student ideas. I oppose graft, and so they pick on me. They made a deficit and for three months now I've only been getting a third of my salary.' And he told me that he hadn't agreed to sign some deal, and his immediate superiors were taking their revenge on him.

'And you're a fool,' the other, who'd just come back, said with unpleasant familiarity. 'Just tell us whom you want to impress with your honesty. I'll tell you, sir, in our line the main thing is to be able to observe the irregularities. Then you can make a living, ha-ha-ha-ha.'

Uspensky's face twitched in a martyr's grimace.

'Keep quiet. You're drunk,' he said.

'And you're awfully sober. Only I'm drunk on my own money, and you get into debt,' the familiar young man replied.

After an hour a postal troika arrived at the apartment. Grabbing some bottles, my hosts got into the roomy sledge to take me as far as the next station. On the way they went on drinking, Uspensky sinking deeper and deeper into depression, his co-tenant becoming merrier and more and more familiar. He tossed empty bottles at passing peasants, roared with laughter, bawled out songs, and became altogether insufferable. At one spot he suddenly stopped the driver. By the roadside lay stacks of good, freshly-cut timber. Despite the drink, he walked briskly, if unsteadily, through the deep snow, and took a look at something. He then took out a note-book and cheerfully made a note.

'The ends are pointing in different directions. It's against the rules. A fine on the contractor, or he can buy me off,' he said cheerily, climbing back into the sledge.

'He ought to be ashamed to face the man,' Uspensky uttered with sad reproach.

At the next station we parted. Uspensky embraced me warmly and began to cry. 'I envy you. You have chosen a good way,' he said in a slightly blurred voice, 'and I'm perishing here. See: a triumphant swine for a colleague.'

'Come off it. What are you swearing for ? Who's to blame if you are stupid and can't observe the irregularities ?'

And he also came forward to say good-bye. I went on alone, carrying with me a strong impression.

Youth is inclined towards swift generalizations. Behind me I had left His Excellency Prince Liven, the highest representative of the Department in which I had been going to work. At this time, after his perfidious dealings with us, he seemed to me an absolute scoundrel. Then there'd been the stories from the Governor's Secretary about the grand-scale plundering in the Forestry Department, encompassing virtually the whole North, and with which justice was powerless to cope. Then, finally, that vivid illustration of sad, suffering virtue in the person of Uspensky and of triumphant vice in the person of the little cheat—all this was merging together into a firm attitude of mind. No, I would not now go for work to that State with its Livens and Valuyevs at the top, and a mesh of petty, insuperable corruption below. All that was the past that was rotting away. I would go into an unknown future.

21

Vologda-Moscow-Petersburg-Kronstadt

ALL THESE THOUGHTS WERE IN MY MIND AS WE TRAVELLED along to the squeak of the runners and the tinkling of the bell. Towards evening we were driving between two walls of thick, dark forest. It stretched away on both sides of the road, mysterious and silent, and my talkative constable told me how, when younger, he'd gone through the forests with a detachment under the command of the District Inspector and had destroyed the cells of the hermits. They had gone on skis into the depths of the forest, where there were quaint little huts, the occupants of which mostly managed to disappear in time. Sometimes a lamp would still be burning before an icon. They would destroy the hut, make a fire out of the beams and throw on it all the household effects, the icons, and the lamp, and then go away.

'And what about the people who lived in them,' I asked, 'what happened to them?'

'That was in God's hands. Some would reach a village or a dwelling —they were lucky. Those who didn't would be caught by frost in the forest or by a blizzard in the open, and freeze to death. We found one such man: he was sitting under a tree, encrusted in hoar-frost. His eyes were open and had snow on them. Two fingers were together for the sign of the cross.'

'And you didn't feel that this was a sin?' I asked, upset by his story.

He gave a little sigh. 'It was an order. Perhaps it was a sin, of course. My superiors'll have to answer for it. But they couldn't help it either. They also had their orders, because many of those hermits were tramps without passports, runaway soldiers, and even escaped convicts.'

We drove the whole night, so as to catch what was left of the road, already breaking up in the thaw. The next day, after leaving one of the stations, we made a stop in a big village. The driver who had taken over at the last station lived here, and he ran into his house for a minute or two. It was a bright, sunny, warm day. Down the long, wide street stood roomy, mostly two-storey peasant-houses. Snow was still lying on them, but here and there one could already see dark patches of the plank roofs, and along the whole street, bathed in the warm light of the spring morning, drops of water were sparkling merrily. Nowhere was there a little garden or a long fence. I recalled that someone had called the nature of our north scrofulous.

The constable had followed the driver into the house, and from it now emerged the master of the house, probably the driver's father. He was tall and young-looking for his age. He had light reddish hair, and a small reddish moustache and beard. He was broad-shouldered and obviously strong, with large labourer's hands; but his chest was sunken, and his whole figure was in strange harmony with the nature of the north, bursting with life and yet scrofulous. He had no coat or hat on, and he was carrying a big jug in his hands. He came up to the sledge and greeted me with a sort of earnest and imposing kindliness.

'Have a drink, my friend, don't scorn it: we made it for the holiday.' And he handed me the jug of home-brewed beer.

I drank it and thanked him gratefully. When he'd gone, I was suddenly seized by a feeling of deep tenderness and affection towards this man—no, towards all these people, towards the whole village with its tattered, snow-covered roofs, towards the whole of this poor northern land with its white fields and dark forests, its murky winter cold, sparkling spring thaw, and the hidden melancholy of its boundless spaces. It was my fate to experience this deep and thrilling emotion in the north. Had such a moment occurred in similar circumstances in my homeland, in Volhynia or the Ukraine, perhaps I would have felt more a Ukrainian. But, later too, such decisive moments were linked with Great Russian and Siberian impressions.

Now, everything I'd read in Nekrasov, Turgenev, and in all Populist literature, suddenly burst into flame, illuminating the experiences of those days, particularly of that road between two walls of forest, with the stories of the hermits and their persecutors. And over all this there rose the figure of that tall, powerful, yet somehow exhausted peasant who had come with a majestic bow and welcoming word to a persecuted stranger.

We arrived in Vologda. Again the same duty-room in the Police Department and the same affable Chief of Police. I arrived towards evening, and in the night my brother[1] unexpectedly burst into my room. Learning of the disturbances in the Academy and that I had been a spokesman, he had rushed to Moscow straight away. My friends in the Academy had given him particulars and he had come to Vologda. Here he had made such an onslaught on the officer on duty that he had completely bewildered him, and I unexpectedly woke up in my brother's arms. When the Chief appeared in the morning he merely shook his head at what had happened. This again illustrates the comparatively easy-going attitudes towards political exiles at that time and would have been quite impossible later on.

That same day the Governor Khominsky came to see me with my declaration that I wished to return to Kronstadt.

'But surely Kronstadt isn't your home-town, is it?'

I told him frankly why I had put down Kronstadt. If I couldn't go there, I'd prefer Ust-Sysolsk. Khominsky thought for a moment, then gave a wave of the hand.

'All right, I'll content myself with your answer and send you to

[1] His younger brother Illarion.

Petersburg. Whether they'll agree there is another question. They may still send you to Volhynia.'

Two days later we set out on the return journey on the narrow-gauge Vologda railway, accompanied by a decently-equipped, even smart-looking constable. My brother, of course, travelled with me in the same carriage. We arrived in Moscow in the morning. The Petersburg train was leaving at four o'clock, I think, and my good-natured constable and I had already agreed that I'd go to see my sister at the Institute, while he would see relatives in Moscow and then go on to the station. This is what we did but, apparently, doubts crept into his mind, for, instead of going to the station, he called for me earlier at the Institute. His appearance and my departure in the company of a policeman created a real sensation. The inquisitive faces of girls appeared fleetingly in the windows, and the venerable porter gave me a surprised and seemingly shocked look. This must have been the first visit of the sort in the annals of the Institute.

My brother rejoined me at the Petrovsky Academy halt, seven miles from Moscow. A crowd of Petrovsky students, who'd learned I was passing, burst into the carriage with him. We embraced one another warmly, but I noticed they were somewhat dispirited. I remember a Pole, Kersnovsky, was there. He had had fine wavy hair, but it was now cut very short. When I jokingly remarked on this, he turned his head away morosely and a deep blush appeared on his sensitive and nervous face.

'I should have had my head shaved completely,' he said. 'We let ourselves be taken in like proper idiots.'

They told me what had happened in the Academy after our departure from Moscow. The Professors tried to persuade the students to submit. Seeing that it was difficult to deal with the whole mass of the students, since some sections were influencing the others, the administration demanded the students disperse and decide separately, according to years. One of the chief arguments of the advocates of submission was the uncertain fate of the spokesmen. It was a well-calculated argument, to which the students finally yielded: they dispersed, and then one section after another sent a deputation to Liven with an apology. The result had been achieved, but at what price? When we were, nevertheless, exiled, all these young men felt they had been tricked, and the representatives of the State, for which they would soon be working, appeared in their eyes as deceivers and cheats.

The students accompanied me for two or three stops. If I was a 'harmful trouble-maker', then this meeting and the fervent emotions it evoked reflected the unquestionable moral triumph of trouble over official order. They told me that Verner had been exiled to Glazov, Vyatsk Province, and Grigoryev to Pudozh, Olenets Province. It seems, in mitigating my punishment, as if the Sovereign (Alexander II) had wished to stress the difference between them and me: as former officers they had to bear a harsher punishment. To this I owed the offer of serving my exile in my home town.

My train was a slow one, and in Petersburg I was brought to the City Prefect's building rather late. The office had been empty for some hours and I was taken through passages to a room on the ground floor. Here I had to wait quite a long time while my papers were taken to the City Prefect's Secretary, Fursov—if I'm not mistaken.

My brother was an enterprising young fellow: he had gone straight from the station to one of our close friends, Brzhozovsky, and they had come hard on my heels to the Prefect's building. Here, I don't know how, they had managed to get to the room where I was waiting, and the three of us were having a friendly chat when the door unexpectedly opened and the Secretary came into the room. He was a tall man, dressed in civilian clothes, with a large fluffy moustache. It was obvious he had been got out of bed and was displeased, even angry about it. Coming in, he stopped in astonishment.

'And what little gathering is this? How did you get here, who let you in? I'm going to arrest you.'

He quickly opened the door to call someone while I ushered my brother and Brzhozovsky out through the other door. When Fursov reappeared with a policeman there was no trace of them. He went for my Vologda constable, who could only say that one of the visitors was my brother and had travelled with me, and that he didn't know the other one. In answer to an angry question addressed to me I calmly said that I saw no necessity to give him my friend's name. This absolutely infuriated him. Quickly reading my paper from the Vologda Governor, he said:

'Some hope! How can Kronstadt be your place of exile? No, my dear fellow, you were born in Volyn Province, weren't you? Right then, straight to the transit-prison and off to Zhitomir.'

He went up a narrow spiral staircase.

'He's gone to Trepov,' whispered the policeman Fursov had brought in to arrest my visitors. 'It looks bad for you: he'll wake him up, the General will be angry. He'll send you to the transit-prison, definitely.'

However, half an hour later the angry gentleman came back down the spiral staircase and, walking across the room, disclosed with a shrug: 'Strange. The General doesn't mind. The Kronstadt steamer leaves at nine o'clock tomorrow morning, but an Oranienbaum train goes earlier. Take your choice. You,' he turned to the Vologda police-man, 'take him to his destination and hand him over to the Kronstadt Chief of Police. You'll get your paper straight away.'

I decided to go to Oranienbaum, and we set out to the station to wait for the train. Early next morning[2] we disembarked from the Oranienbaum steamer on to the quay in Kronstadt. And so my first road of exile was finished.

I need to add a few words in order to finish with our Academy story. After the well-known, large-scale student disturbances at the end of the 'sixties and the Nechayev trial noticeable movements among the younger generation had subsided, and there had not been any student disturbances. Something had started up in the Academy of Surgical Medicine but had quickly died away. Amidst this hush our really quite insignificant story burst like thunder in a clear sky. There was a lot of talk about it in society at large, but the papers did not dare to write about it. There appeared only the briefest reports with the mention of our three names. The papers were probably waiting for an official report, but it was not forthcoming. Finally, Krayevsky's *Voice* decided to publish a note about the affair, presumably because it came from the most reliable of sources: it had been sent by the old fool we have already met, the District Police Inspector Rzhevsky. He gave his own special version of it. The students had presented a childish declaration in which, *inter alia*, 'they demanded women'. They were excited and unwilling to apologize, but, fortunately, the local Police Inspector was on the spot—a man of experience, who was well acquainted with the ways of young people. This old gentleman, who loved young people and was loved by them in return, had had only to say a few simple and heartfelt words for the disturbances to die down immediately.

My brother procured this note for me when I was already in Kronstadt. He and some other students had gone to the editorial office for an explanation, and had been informed that the note had in fact been published because it had been written by a Police Inspector. In society there was only talk and rumours, and nothing could be printed. The paper had therefore risked putting in a report from a reliable source. As the surnames of the spokesmen had been mentioned, I con-sidered it my formal right to send a letter to the editor, in which with the indignation of youth I refuted the fabrications of the Inspector. They replied, however, that there had followed a categorical prohibi-tion to touch the affair.

[2] 10 April 1867 (according to the archives of the Third Section).

This episode left me with nothing but scorn and anger towards Krayevsky's 'liberal' paper. I wrote another letter, not this time for publication, in which I said that a paper that had printed 'heinous slander from a police source' was morally obliged to refute it, regardless of the prohibition. I need hardly say there was no reply.

Kronstadt at this time too was in a special position: it was governed by the navy. The Chief of Police was Captain Golovachyov, and the Commandant, a sort of Governor, was Admiral Kozakevich. In the town Golovachyov was known as 'Captain Nose', because on the end of his nose he had big blue swellings. He was not an old man, wore a naval uniform with a dirk,[3] was lively, energetic, effusive, and so enterprising that it was not long before he found himself arraigned on thirty-two charges. One of them had to do with the fact that, coming out on to the market-place five minutes before the end of the Church service and seeing that the tradesmen, despite his order, had already hastened to open their shops, he had stood in the middle of the square and shouted in a stentorian voice:

'Sailor lads! Loot them so they'll remember the law.'

The crowd didn't need to hear this order twice. Sailors of various nationalities rushed at the stalls, shouting, 'Hurrah! Captain Nose's orders!' and the market was apparently ransacked before the service ended.

This was going a bit too far and the decisive Police Chief was finally put on trial. When I arrived in Kronstadt, however, he was still flourishing, and his temperament harmonized completely with the views of the High Naval Administration. Navy men were a liberal lot at this time. Golovachyov quickly read my paper, gallantly shook my hand and said, 'Ah, I know. Your name has been in the papers. Right then, welcome to Kronstadt. We'll go and see the Admiral straight away.'

My constable was released, and the Chief and I drove to the Admiral's palace. It was still quite early, and I had to wait in the reception-room, where the furniture was draped in covers. Finally the Admiral entered with Golovachyov, who looked as if he'd brought him something of a rarity that was bound to give him pleasure. The Admiral had obviously been got out of bed and looked rather sleepy, but he greeted me cordially.

'Welcome,' he said. 'Very pleased to meet you. I'm sorry our acquaintanceship should come about in such circumstances. Still, perhaps it won't be for long. I hope we won't quarrel. You are free now.'

I ran out of the palace and took a cab to my cousin's apartment.

[3] The dirk was worn by admirals and high-ranking officers in the navy.

My mother was unwell and in bed. The trouble was of a purely nervous order, and latterly she had noticed they were hiding something from her and guessed that it had to do with me. Her eyes opened wide when, accompanied by my cousin and his wife, I rushed into her room and hugged her, laughing happily. She was surprised and delighted. Taking advantage of her happy excitement, I told her straight away that her dreams of living in a forester's house had come to nothing but that we would be living together. She laughed and cried at the same time.

And so I was living 'under subveillance', as my Yaroslavl convict had put it, in Kronstadt. My sister had finished at the Institute, and we decided to move from my cousin's to a place of our own. At this time my younger brother had entered the Building School as an external student and was living in Petersburg. My elder brother continued to work as a proof-reader, but on his own now (he too had escaped from Studensky's tenacious clutches). My youngest sister was living with mother. I had to find work in Kronstadt and put an advertisement in the local *Herald* that 'a student wants work', and listed: lessons, plans, drawings, and proof-reading. That same day I received an urgent summons to Golovachyov.

'My dear fellow. What are you doing to me ?' And he pointed to the advertisement. I expressed surprise. What was there to disapprove of—lessons, plans, proof-reading ?

'That's it, the very thing. Lessons are all right, but proof-reading is out of the question. Plans are quite another thing. By the way, can you draw a fire-engine—a new model—for our Police Department ?'

The impetuous Chief took me off to a police-station where a new fire-engine was standing—the sort I'd already had demonstrated to me in Vologda. I sketched and measured it, and a week later the finished drawing, complete with barrels, pumps, the cart for the ladder and hooks, was delivered to Golovachyov. A week after that it was in an elegant frame, decorating the Chief's room in the Police Department.

'That's the style,' Golovachyov said delightedly, 'that's not proof-reading. Do as much of this sort of work as you like. Can you draw us a plan of a lifeboat-station ?'

'That isn't really my line,' I said. 'I'm not an architect.'

'Fiddlesticks. Take a trip to Oranienbaum, draw the lifeboat-station there like you drew the fire-engine, and there you are.'

'But I've given a written undertaking not to go outside the town.'

'Don't worry about that. Go as much as you like, only don't get mixed up in anything. A little brush with the police over something, and there'd be trouble, of course. Now let's go and have a look at the site I've chosen. I've already had it fenced off. The scoundrels in the Duma have put in a report about arbitrary appropriation. Pettifoggers!' He gave a sigh. 'You think we don't struggle? My dear fellow, we struggle just as much as you.'

On this occasion the Duma pettifoggers triumphed, and our station was not built.

One day Golovachyov summoned me and said, 'I've got a friend, Vladimir Pavlovich Verkhovsky, who's in charge of the officers' mine-class. I've spoken to him about you and shown him the drawings of the fire-engine. Would you like to go to the mine-class as a draughtsman?'

I was rather surprised at this unexpected suggestion: Golovachyov had been alarmed at the idea of proof-reading, yet now he was offering me work in an establishment of that sort. Still, perhaps I am surprised in retrospect: terrorism had not yet flared up, chemistry and explosive substances played no part in revolution, and soon I started spending my mornings behind a drawing-board in the officers' mine-class.

The establishment, its work and the man in charge presented a great deal that was interesting. In my desk there were drawings of all sorts of mines, including the marvel of contemporary torpedo design— Whitehead's torpedo[4]—which could travel at a speed of twenty miles per hour at any depth, blow up the underside of a ship, and in cases of failure come back again. In the room where I worked officers gave lectures to sailors, and in the next room there was a large concrete tank in which experiments involving small underwater explosions were carried out. Explosive cartridges with Howard's mercury[5] were also made there. One day there was a sudden explosion in that room and a torpedo-man had his hand and wrist blown off. He was taken to hospital, and an officer immediately gathered the men together and gave them a lecture about the preparation of the cartridges. He enumerated all the precautions that should be taken and concluded: 'But since, despite all precautions, Howard's mercury sometimes explodes for unknown reasons, every man working with it must only have enough at any one time for thirty cartridges. Then in the event of an explosion the man will be killed, perhaps the room will suffer, but the building will remain intact.'

From that I drew the pleasant conclusion that I too was working

[4] Robert Whitehead (1823–1905) developed a successful torpedo in 1866. In 1868, after some modifications, he was able to offer it for sale, and it was bought by the Austrian, and then other European governments. The speed of his torpedo was, in fact, about six knots, its range was not more than 700 yards, and it did not return home in the event of a miss!

[5] Mercury fulminate, discovered by E. C. Howard in 1799.

amid such risks. The Russian is a happy-go-lucky fellow. Every day I used to go to bathe along one of the dikes that jutted far out into the sea. At the end of it a hut had been built for drying gun-cotton, and several times I had the opportunity of observing sailors filling cylindrical mines with gun-cotton, holding lit pipes of tobacco in their teeth.

'God's providence,' a sailor said confidently in answer to my comment.

This theory was soon strikingly confirmed: the gun-cotton had somehow got over-dried and it flared. I should point out that an explosion and a simple burning of gun-cotton produce different results. On this occasion the gun-cotton simply flared. Even so, the little building was shattered as a result of the pressure of the quickly developing gases, but the sailor who was standing at the time by the open window (perhaps it was the one who had uttered the philosophical maxim) was merely thrown forty yards or so into the sea and escaped with nothing worse than a scare and a soaking.

I thus found myself in a new environment and examined it with interest. The man in charge of the mine-class, V. P. Verkhovsky, seemed a remarkable man to me. He was short and stout, and his face and hair reminded me to some extent of Napoleon. He was a remarkable mathematician and a superb administrator. His directions were always quick, precise and clear. It seemed to me that a great future lay before him. However he was a Russian and was living in Russian conditions that reminded me of Totma, the gloomy valuation officer Uspensky and his cheery, corrupt co-tenant.

One day Verkhovsky instructed me to draw all the separate components of a cylindrical brass mine, so as to place a big order with the artillery factory in Kronstadt. The drawings came back from the factory with the estimates. Looking at them, I was simply astonished at the blatant and colossal profiteering: ordinary brass screws an inch long were priced at seven roubles. I was young and naïve. Verkhovsky seemed a very decent man and I didn't refrain from expressing my surprise. His face flushed slightly and he immediately sent a sailor to fetch the expert who had done the estimates. An individual in the uniform of an official of the War Department, with Jewish features, appeared. The other side of the door I heard Verkhovsky shouting in a rage: 'I'll take you to court. I'll go personally to the Admiral-General. This is robbery.'

The fellow made some excuse in a slightly shrill and meek voice. When he came out of the room his face was red and covered in perspiration, but an ironic and, so it seemed to me, triumphant smile was playing on his lips. A day or two later the prices came back altered, but the alterations were a mere mockery. Verkhovsky must have again noticed bewilderment in my eyes. He understood the feelings of the inexperienced student and, looking at me with his intelligent and steady eyes, said, 'I could have had that scoundrel before a court ten times already, but I know full well that in his place they'd appoint a favourite of General X. He'd be a Russian, but a thief ten times as bold. With him it would be even harder. And I,' he concluded, speaking firmly and distinctly, 'want my work to proceed. I haven't time to fight universal abuses. My work comes first.'

The whole atmosphere in Kronstadt was permeated by this 'professional' philosophy. It conquered and swallowed up even men of principle. At this time there was a lot of talk about a new captain of a certain warship. He was a young, talented man with an excellent professional record, who was idolized by his crew and was very high-principled. At the very outset he refused to accept a large consignment of coal because it utterly failed to conform to standards. The contractor had a big pull in the Department and among officers. People, and not only in naval circles, waited with interest to see how this clash between a man well known for his principles and a notorious swindler would end.

It ended unexpectedly: one fine day the Admiral-General Grand Duke Konstantin Nikolayevich (a liberal and supporter of reforms, as is well known) appeared on board. Everything on the ship proved to be in exemplary order. The Grand Duke went round the ship from the deck to the hold with a reserved air and said, on leaving, 'Good. But they say you're very hard on a contractor. There's no need for that.'

The officer was left with taking a truly revolutionary step—resigning as a mark of protest—or submitting. Apparently, the officer submitted to established practice.

All in all, I, 'an exiled student', was well treated by navy men. One day a crowd of officers came into the drawing office where I was working, sprawled over a large drawing-board. In front, accompanied by Verkhovsky, was an old admiral, shortish, very stout and with a coarse insensitive face. I stood up when they entered, greeted those I knew, and then got down to work again. Obviously, this was an infringement of the respect the admiral was accustomed to: a draughtsman should remain standing all the time he was in the room. The admiral was the then famous Popov,[6] all-powerful in the Navy Depart-

[6] Andrey Aleksandrovich Popov (1821-98).

ment, and the builder of the no less famous *popovki*,[7] which proved utterly useless in practice. He was well known as a coarse, self-willed chump. If I'm not mistaken, he was later portrayed by Stanyukovich in the story entitled *The Dread Admiral*. The whole party stopped by a cylindrical Whitehead torpedo, but, before proceeding to examine it, the admiral turned his attention to the disrespectful draughtsman.

'Who's that?' he said loudly, giving a nod in my direction.

'A draughtsman, a student,' Verkhovsky answered, and added a few words in a low voice.

'Ah,' and the dread admiral calmed down. They examined the way the torpedo was constructed and went further on.

Some time later Verkhovsky came running to me from another room and, making a hurried sketch, asked me to make a drawing of a structure resembling short, wide iron ladders. These were the so-called 'crinolines', a Popov invention that was supposed to protect moving battleships from enemy mines. Verkhovsky argued hotly against the project, contending that the crinolines would slow down the speed of the ships terribly. In a month's time they were tested on the Sevastopol Roads, and Verkhovsky informed me (confidentially) of the results. They had been very impressive, and a large order was made for them. But a friend of Verkhovsky said in a letter that the results of the test were nothing but a servile piece of fraud: the ship with the crinolines allegedly went very fast while Admiral Popov was on board. However, as soon as he left the deck, the battleship immediately started going almost half as fast. 'Corruption and decay,' I concluded privately. 'Fraud from top to bottom.'

---

[7] Ironclads designed by Vice-Admiral Popov. There were two such ships—*Novgorod* (1873) and *Vice-Admiral Popov* (1875)—both of which belonged to the Black Sea Fleet. Built after Russia acquired the right to station a fleet in the Black Sea (1871), the ships were chiefly designated for the defence of two strategic points—the estuary of the Dnieper and the Kerch Straits, where the depth of water was $15\frac{1}{2}$ feet and 14 feet respectively. They were very thickly armoured and very heavily armed, but unsuccessful. The ships were round in shape, which made them very difficult to manoeuvre or hold on course, and they rocked so much that it was impossible to fire accurately.

22

Petersburg—The Gloom Deepens

IN A YEAR OUR TERM OF EXILE (MINE, GRIGORYEV'S AND Verner's) was coming to an end, and it was I who first reminded them of this in the Ministry of the Interior.[1] The reminder met with success and Grigoryev followed my example. Verner had even earlier applied to enter the army. He was sent as an officer to the Caucasus, distinguished himself in the Russo–Turkish War, and after the war returned to Russia a free man. He entered the Academy again and subsequently became a professor there.

I recall one of my last evenings in Kronstadt. I had come out of the Navy Club library, where I'd returned books for the last time. I was gripped by the awareness that my carefree life of exile in Kronstadt was ending and responsibility for the family's future was falling on me. It was a quiet summer evening and there was a bright moon over the trees on the boulevard. I sat on a bench and remained there for about two hours. Many thoughts passed through my mind. I had simultaneously to combine serious family responsibilities, perfectly clear and well-defined, with dreams of working for society—dreams that were alluring, but unclear, ill-defined. I came home late but without having made any clear decision. In the end we moved to Petersburg,[2] I passed a competitive examination to the Mining Institute and started looking for work.

We found a place on the Fontanka, not far from the Izmaylovsky Bridge, and bought the cheapest furniture we could. One day my brother came hurrying to tell us that he had bought a lovely couch at the Hay-Market, but that it had to be collected straight away. The two of us ran off and carried it home—to the surprise and scorn of the gate-keeper.

I had to turn to proof-reading again. At this time Ivan Vasilevich Vernadsky, the once famous editor of *The Economist* who had disputed with Chernyshevsky, decided to publish a new, weekly *Economic Index*.

[1] Korolenko was freed from police surveillance on 14 May 1877. He then applied to the Council of the Petrovsky Academy to be re-admitted as a third-year student. The Council agreed, but the Director did not ratify the decision in view of Korolenko's political 'unreliability'.

[2] Autumn 1877.

It was a small, rather sorry-looking publication, full of figures. My brother and I did the proof work for it. The wage was miserable, somewhere around twenty roubles a month, and the work was hard, all figures. Still, it was a sort of *point d'appui*: *The Index* was printed in Vernadsky's own printing works, which was called The Slavonic Book Press, and other work could be found there. In fact, I was soon invited to be second proof-reader for the paper *News* and worked for it until my new exile from Petersburg. It was night-work and thus did not prevent me attending the Mining Institute in the day.

I must say, however, that this time I again failed to become a good student. In Petersburg the movement was on the boil. Those who had taken part in the demonstration on the Kazan Square[3] had been brought to trial. Some of our friends had been involved, and my younger brother had come forward as a witness. The prosecutor, analysing his depositions, remarked caustically that it was only through an oversight on the part of the police that this witness was sitting on the witness-bench: his real place was beside the defendants. I was down as a former exile, and the police immediately began keeping an eye on us.

Then started the memorable 'trial of the 193'. These were the victims of the first wave of the so-called 'movement to the people'. Now, of course, the whole movement has been sufficiently illuminated by the memoirs of many men who took part in it. Based on a completely illusory idea of the 'permanent revolutionariness' of the people, of its constant readiness to overthrow the existing order and create a new one founded on the most idealistic principles, the movement was not really dangerous. The revolutionary intelligentsia and the people had neither a common language nor mutual understanding. As always, however, the Tsarist government was frightened to death.[4] The alarm spread through the whole of Russia: people suspected of sympathy or unreliability were seized right and left, brought to Petersburg and held for three or four years before being tried. During the trial the prosecutor Zhelekhovsky said with idiotic frankness that the vast majority of the defendants had been put in the dock merely 'to provide a background' against which the figures of the chief malefactors would stand out. And, indeed, some of these young men and women were sentenced by the court to terms of one or two months' imprisonment after having been held for four years 'to provide a background'.

[3] 6 December 1876.
[4] The inquiry into 'revolutionary propaganda in the Empire' began in 1874 and lasted three years. In the course of the inquiry as many as 2,000 people were arrested in various parts of Russia. The 'trial of the 193' lasted from 18 October 1877 until 23 January 1878.

Long before the actual trial this whole affair had created an under-
current of agitation among young people, which expressed itself in an
unexpected demonstration of unprecedented proportions. In March
1876 the student Chernyshyov had died. He was one of the victims of the
mass trial. He was being held in the Remand Prison as part of 'the background' and had contracted tuberculosis. He had been transferred to a
clinic, where he had died. On 30 March a fairly small number of students
appeared at the carrying-out of the body, but then, as the procession
moved through the streets, the crowd grew. At the Remand Prison the
procession stopped. The coffin was raised on high and a requiem sung.
The demonstration had been organized so successfully that even after
this the police didn't realize what was happening and the huge crowd
reached the cemetery unimpeded, on the way explaining the meaning
of the demonstration to the interested public. Only when openly
revolutionary speeches started being delivered over the grave did the
local police wake up to the situation—but were unable to do anything
about it. When police detachments and mounted gendarmes arrived,
everything was, apparently, already over, and nobody was even
arrested.

All this had excited public opinion and in Petersburg there was a
great deal of talk about the impending mass trial. To begin with it was
proposed to try them all together, but the authorities grew afraid of this
crowd of defendants, embittered by years in prison and the obvious
injustice of 'justice'. So it was decided to divide the mass of the
accused into separate groups. When they were informed of this, stormy
scenes broke out in the Senate-House. The accused resisted being taken
away and made passionate speeches of protest. The public was admitted in very limited numbers, newspaper accounts were strictly
censored, but even so news of the proceedings flew round Petersburg
every day like the wind. People told of how Rogachyov, a man of massive build and a former officer, had terrified the Senators by breaking
through to the railing and shaking it in his hands. Myshkin, a fanatical,
passionate and not wholly balanced man who possessed an exceptional gift for oratory, delivered a speech in which he compared the
Senator-judges to prostitutes. 'Those poor women sell their bodies out
of need, while you sell your souls for rank and decorations.' The effect
of this speech was all the greater in that it ended amid a struggle between the orator, the gendarmes who rushed to take him out, and the
other defendants.

All this was eagerly seized upon. When I visited Kronstadt at this
time, officers of our acquaintance and their ladies would come to my

cousin's to hear the latest news. I would tell them what I knew myself. Even military society felt indignation, and the ladies would weep. The ideals of socialism expressed in general formulas attracted passionate sympathy, particularly among women. One officer, a great sceptic, once drew the practical deduction:

'But in that case, madam, everybody will be equal.'

'What of it? that's so fine,' women's voices interrupted.

'Excuse me, I've not finished. That means there'll not be any cooks or maids, for example . . .'

The women's faces fell.

'No-o? That really is awkward in practice . . .'

The court petitioned for a significant mitigation of the sentences of all the defendants, but Alexander II not only did not mitigate them, but even increased the sentences of some, with the result that many, who had been released in anticipation that the plea for mitigation would be acted upon, were re-arrested and put in prison. This produced an impression most unfavourable to the Tsar.

At the end of 1877 Nekrasov died. He had been ailing in health for a long time, and that winter had been literally fading away. Yet, even in those last months of his life his poems had appeared in *Fatherland Notes*. Dostoyevsky in his *Diary of a Writer* says that these last poems are not inferior to the works of Nekrasov's best years. One can easily imagine what effect they had on young people. Everyone knew that the poet's days were numbered, and expressions of sincere and deep sympathy were presented to Nekrasov from all sides.

I had a friend at this time who was a student in the Mining Institute. He was very radical, very good-natured, and comically ingenuous in his radicalism. He told me that signatures were being collected for an address to Nekrasov from the students of all the institutions of higher education. In his expressive, naïve language he thus summarized the content of the address:

'Listen, Nekrasov. You haven't long to live anyway. So write those scoundrels the whole truth and we'll spread it throughout Russia, you can depend on it.'

I merely laughed, and, of course, the address the students presented to the sick poet was written very finely, with deep and sincere feeling. Nekrasov was said to have been very moved by it.

When he died (on 27 December 1877), his funeral naturally could not pass without an impressive demonstration. In this case the feelings of young people and of educated society as a whole coincided, and Petersburg had never seen anything like it before. The body was carried

out at nine o'clock in the morning and the enormous crowd of people
did not disperse from the cemetery until dusk. The police, of course
were very worried. In his *Journey to Erzerum* Pushkin tells how on some
road on the border of Georgia and Armenia he met a simple cart on
which lay a wooden coffin. 'We are bringing back Griboyed,'[5] the
Georgian carters explained. Pushkin's own body was taken out of
Petersburg in similar fashion, dishonourably and secretly, as is well-
known. Those times had long passed, and the authorities were no longer
able to hold back manifestations of public sympathy. Nekrasov was
buried very solemnly and a great many speeches were made over the
grave. I remember the verses read by Panyutin, then Zasodimsky[6] spoke
and several others besides, but the real event was Dostoyevsky's speech.

With two or three friends I had managed to make my way along the
top of a stone wall almost to the grave itself and, holding on to the
branches of a tree, I heard everything. Dostoyevsky spoke quietly, but
with great force and feeling. His speech provoked a lot of noise in the
press. When he put Nekrasov's name after Pushkin and Lermontov,
some of those present felt that this was belittling Nekrasov.

'He is greater,' someone shouted, and two or three voices supported
him.

'Yes, greater . . . they were only Byronists.'

Skabichevsky[7] made the characteristically sweeping statement in
The Stock Exchange Gazette that 'the young people in their thousands
proclaimed the superiority of Nekrasov'. Dostoyevsky replied to this in
his *Diary of a Writer*. However, when I subsequently re-read the con-
troversy in the *Diary* I didn't find any mention of what had made a
much stronger impression upon me and on many of my direct contemporaries than the argument about superiority, which many people
had not noticed at the time. This was the point where Dostoyevsky,
speaking in what seemed to me a moved and prophetic voice, called
Nekrasov the last great 'gentleman-poet'. The time would come, and it
was already near, when a new poet, equal to Pushkin, Lermontov,
Nekrasov, would appear from the people itself.

'True, true . . .' we shouted in delight, and I almost fell off the wall.

[5] Aleksandr Sergeyevich Griboyedov (1795–1829) author of the great classic
of the Russian theatre *Woe from Wit* (*Gore ot uma*). Griboyedov had been appointed Russian Ambassador to Persia, and was hacked to death by a mob in
Teheran.

[6] Pavel Vladimirovich Zasodimsky (1843–1912), a novelist of Populist per-
suasions.

[7] Aleksandr Mikhaylovich Skabichevsky (1838–1910), literary critic and
journalist. His article on Nekrasov appeared in the sixth issue of *The Stock
Exchange Gazette* (*Birzhevye vedomosti*) for 1878.

Yes, it seemed so near and such a cause for joy. All present-day culture had a false orientation. It occasionally reached a very high degree of development, but its basic character, one-sided and narrow now, would only with the advent of the people become immeasurably fuller and thus higher.

Dostoyevsky, of course, differed from his enraptured listeners in a great many and very important respects. Later he said that the people would recognize as its own only a poet who respected the same things as it respected, that is, of course, the autocracy and the official church. But all this was now only commentary. I was to remember Dostyevsky's words for a long time thereafter as a foretelling of the imminence of a fundamental social revolution, as a sort of prophecy about the people's entry on to the arena of history.

During these years even my old dream of becoming a writer faded. Was it worth it, after all, if even the Pushkins, Lermontovs, and Nekrasovs were only large beacons on an old and travelled road? I had never been sufficiently influenced by the 'Pisarev school' to reject Pushkin, and realized that Nekrasov as a poet was considerably lower than both Pushkin and Lermontov, but the time would come, and it seemed to be near, when there would be 'a new heaven and a new earth', different Pushkins and different Nekrasovs. It was our generation's task to contribute to its coming, and not to repeat the one-sidedness of the old culture, which had reached a splendid and one-sided flowering out of injustice and slavery.

23
An Odd Character

THE PAPER *News* WAS PRINTED IN THE SLAVONIC BOOK PRESS. Its proof-reader was F. K. Dolinin, who also did a little article-writing. One proof-reader proved to be not enough, and Notovich invited me to become second proof-reader. Dolinin and I worked alternate days, and so I had time enough left over.

The paper was not enjoying much success, and I had some difficulty obtaining my money, which was paid to me in instalments as cash came in. To get any money I had to go two or three times a week to the office. Every time the cashier would send me to Notovich. He would try to draw me away from talking about money, waiting until twenty or thirty roubles had accumulated in the cash-box, and thus I spent many hours talking with the editor of *News*.

He was still a young man, with delicate, aristrocratic Jewish features, a lawyer by training. He had published a popular summary of Buckle's book which he was very proud of, saying that he had only 'squeezed the water out of Buckle'. He had a special editorial talent: a few abridgements, a few corrections—and often a completely illiterate manuscript would acquire a literary polish. With remarkable skill he would make use of every piece of paper with writing on it that found its way into the editorial office. He had to do so all the more assiduously as he paid nothing at all for correspondence.

In this connection the following little curiosity appeared in print. At one time *News* published brisk, witty articles from Saratov by S. Gusev, who subsequently became widely known under the pen-name of Slovo-Glagolya. At this time he had only just begun his literary career. Notovich quickly appraised the young beginner and readily published everything he sent, but systematically paid not so much as a single kopeck. After persistent demands the unfortunate author lost patience and sent the editor a very passionate and expressively written letter of abuse in which he depicted the hard position of a provincial contributor, and called Notovich a spider, grasping exploiter, and other such names. Notovich was true to form even here. Immediately recognizing the literary merit of the abusive letter, he entitled it: 'Provincial corre-spondents and Petersburg editors', skilfully altering the text so that it referred not to him but to a third person, and in *News* there appeared a striking little piece, whose author again received not a kopeck.

One should say, however, that the newspaper's position at this time was an exceptionally hard one. There were very few advertisements. In order to hide this sad fact which adversely affected the inflow of new advertising, the paper resorted to a ruse: it began to reprint advertise-ments from other papers. It seemed this could only be to the advantage of the clients: an advertisement put in one paper was repeated for nothing in another. One day, however, coming as usual to procure at least some part of my wages, I found traces of a great uproar in the editor's office. A sporting man, apparently a Baltic baron, had advertised a racehorse for sale. At a race-meeting another sportsman had come up to him and said he'd read his advertisement in *News*.

'You couldn't have read it in *News*,' the owner of the horse said. The other insisted that he had. 'Would you care to make a bet on it?' said the first.

'Certainly'.

Quite a large sum of money was staked. The owner of the horse lost: *News* had reprinted his advertisement. The infuriated baron burst into the editor's office demanding that his loss be made good. Notovich stood by his right to reprint within legal limits. A furious argument arose and the baron began chasing the editor around the table with his stick.

Another story had rather an elegiac flavour. 'A respectable elderly widower' wished to find a middle-aged lady companion, as far as possible of pleasing appearance, and put an advertisement to that effect in *New Time*. *News* obligingly reprinted the notice. Everything went well for the elderly widower, a companion of pleasing appearance was found, and he settled down to married life again. Then suddenly his doorbell started ringing as a crowd of nice-looking, middle-aged women began to turn up at his apartment. It transpired that the *News* compositor, finding a shortage of advertisements, had pulled out an old type-block and the advertisement had appeared again. The unfortunate widower did not become violent, he merely asked tearfully for his notice not to be printed any more. Notovich magnanimously agreed.

Notovich also had a special nose for that philistine vulgarity that makes for success among the street public supporting the retail sale of newspapers. The memorable trial of Yukhantsev, a bank-cashier who had embezzled an enormous sum of money, had been going on in Petersburg. At the time an American by the name of Gillin was living there. He had published a small collection of rather feeble stories, in the preface to which he had expressed the hope that 'the Russian public will support a young American who has dedicated his pen to Russian literature'. This Gillin offered for a modest fee to write Notovich a sensational novel based on the famous trial. Notovich seized on the idea and several times sent someone to the printing-shop to inquire if the first chapters of the novel had arrived. At last, I read the first proof of the opening chapters. It was an unbelievably coarse, banal piece of writing, and I thought how disappointed Notovich would be. Late at night Notovich came to the printing-shop.

'Well?' he asked briskly.

'You're surely not going to print this stuff?' I asked. 'You can't call it literature.'

Notovich's face darkened, and be began to examine the proof with a worried look. As he read, however, the expression on his face changed: his face shone with a smile of approval that remained right to the end. When he'd finished, he got up with obvious satisfaction.

'You don't understand a thing,' he said. ' A superb piece of work!'

A few days later he said to me triumphantly, 'Well, Mr. Critic, which of us was right? The newspaper vendors are saying: "If you've got Gillin, give us fifty copies. If you haven't, twenty-five will do."'

I realized that this wasn't just an editor's viewpoint: he himself shared the tastes of the masses, for whom he published his paper. He was a man with a university education in law, but I was struck by his profound ignorance in other fields. The idea that the exact sciences were pitifully insignificant was Notovich's perpetual hobby-horse. For several weeks he had been publishing essays (apparently written by Hieroglyphov) in the Sunday Supplement to *News*, in which the author contended that in the schools the young generation was being crammed with all sorts of prejudices in the guise of such things as physics. One such prejudice was the 'fact' that air possesses weight. The writer made great fun of this, analysing and refuting what he called 'that obvious absurdity'.

'It's clever, isn't it? What twaddle those naturalists and physicists are filling our children's heads with,' Notovich said with the same self-satisfaction as when he had read Gillin's novels. I told him that the whole 'criticism' was founded on a complete ignorance of the text-books the writer was trying to refute, and proved it there and then with a few convincing examples.

'Well, all right . . .' Notovich agreed. 'Still, it's witty, it makes you think.'

'Yes,' I replied, 'but if it's taken up in the pages of *The Stock Exchange Gazette*, you'll look a real fool.'

This consideration had visible effect. Notovich sat down at his desk and wrote in the margin: 'Responsibility for the argument rests with the author.'

24
Vera Zasulich—My Second Arrest

ON 24 JANUARY 1878 I GOT INTO A WAGONETTE GOING FROM the Mining Institute to, I believe, Isaac Square. Professor Bek, the Director of the Institute, sat down directly opposite me. He knew me by sight because after I'd been accepted at the Institute he had called me for a special talk about the Petrovsky affair. Now, replying to my, bow, he said, 'Did you know Trepov has been killed ?[1] It was some girl, they say, a real beauty. She's been arrested, of course.'

Everybody in the wagonette was very interested. In July 1877 Trepov had ordered Bogolyubov, convicted for the demonstration on the Kazan Square, to be flogged. It was said that during the exercise-period Bogolyubov had not taken off his hat when passing the City Prefect. This was the first case of corporal punishment being inflicted on a political prisoner. It had made an enormous impression. Society at large was appalled by it, and in the Remand Prison there had been large-scale disorders followed by beatings and solitary confinement. A particular mood had developed, as much in society as in revolutionary circles, which had given rise to a general anticipation that this would not pass unanswered.

However, six months had passed. It later became known that people had continually been coming to Petersburg from the provinces, intend-ing to kill Trepov. But the 'trial of the 193' was not yet finished, and central revolutionary circles held the avengers back for fear that an attempt of Trepov's life might affect the fate of the mass of prisoners on trial. People were thus beginning to forget about the Bogolyubov affair when Zasulich's shot rang out—the first terrorist act in answer to the first case of corporal punishment.

This affair is still well remembered by everybody. A great deal has been written about it, and I do not propose to go into details. I shall merely say that Zasulich became a heroine immediately. The very fact that she was given a trial by jury doubtless reflected the attitude of governing circles to Trepov and to Zasulich herself. She was tried in a district court on 31 March. The President of the Court was Anatoly Fyodorovich Koni, whose summing-up halted his brilliant juridical

[1] Trepov was severely wounded, not killed.

career for a time. After a short withdrawal the jury returned a verdict of 'not guilty'.

This was so unexpected that an order for the administrative detention of Zasulich in case of an acquittal had not even been issued. Koni therefore pronounced her free, the governor of the Remand Prison did not detain her, and she walked out to freedom. At the gates a carriage was waiting. Outside the court and the prison a fairly large crowd had gathered to welcome the acquitted girl, but a small detachment of gendarmes was already moving to re-arrest her. A clash occurred. The crowd would not allow the arrest, and one man was killed—Sidoratsky. At first everyone in Petersburg was convinced that Sidoratsky had been killed by a gendarme's bullet, but later considerable doubts arose. A friend of mine told me that during the demonstration and the uproar it produced he had seen a young man run out on to the pavement a few yards from him, put a revolver to his temple, and fire. As no one else was killed, it must have been Sidoratsky. It was said that when the gendarmes stopped the carriage Sidoratsky had fired at them, but so badly that he had wounded someone in the carriage or on the box. Someone shouted that Zasulich had been hit, and that was the reason for his suicide.

The very unexpectedness of the acquittal made an even stronger impression than Zasulich's shot itself and brought the general delight to boiling point. It seemed that revolutionary currents and the broad aspirations of society were beginning to merge together. As well as *News*, the Slavonic Book Press also printed *The Northern Herald*, edited by E. Korsh, son of the famous writer and a lawyer by training. The paper was losing a lot of money. It was probably because of this that Korsh took a risk and published a letter from Zasulich in hiding. The paper, of course, was closed, and I remember how cheerfully Korsh met the news of its closure. The issue containing the letter had been snatched up like hot cakes. Zasulich had written that she was not hiding from trial and that in the event of a legal cassation she was ready to stand once again before a court of public conscience. She was hiding only from administrative punishment without trial.

The shot fired by Vera Zasulich was one of those events that alter, at least for a time, an established alignment of forces. The censorship immediately lost its head and weakened. With the barriers weakened, public opinion burst through. Eulogies of the court, comparisons, allusions, and sometimes even open praise of Zasulich's action kept on appearing in the papers. Particularly bold articles appeared in Korsh's *Northern Herald*, and this stimulated Notovich. He even wrote a big article himself. It began very affectingly with the exclamation: 'Reader, Vera Zasulich has been acquitted . . .'. There then followed sentences in the most elevated style. However, when *The Northern Herald* was wrecked and inspectors started appearing in the printing-shop, the editor of *News* lost his nerve. The eloquent article was put away in a drawer. Even so, Notovich ordered that the type of the article should not be distributed.

'Perhaps it will still come in handy,' he said.

And it really did come in handy. A few months after the Zasulich affair the trial of Yenkuvatov was going on, I think, in Odessa. It was very characteristic of the times. Yenkuvatov and his wife had married for love. Unfortunately, Yenkuvatov's brother had fallen passionately in love with his sister-in-law. They were all young radicals and one of the brothers (or even both) was in exile. They were devoted to each other, and as a result came to a very original kind of agreement: the husband temporarily renounced his marital rights, and his brother tried to win the wife's heart. The young woman loved her husband and declared so openly, but before the expiry of the peculiar agreement her position became intolerable. The wildly infatuated elder brother went beyond the bounds of the agreement. One night the husband, sleeping in a 'neutral' room, heard his brother going into his wife's bedroom. Then came shouts for help. This went beyond the limits of 'high-principled' long-suffering. The husband ran into the bedroom and shot his rival. The jury acquitted him.

Accounts of the trial were printed in all newspapers, including *News*. After the telegram about the acquittal had been received, I was pleasantly surprised to meet an old acquaintance: the article Notovich had put aside had come to light again. It began just as affectingly: 'Reader Yenkuvatov has been acquitted . . .'. Then followed the same eolquent sentences, only with Yenkuvatov's name instead of that of Zasulich.

'The big trial' (that was the other name for the 'trial of the 193') not only failed to weaken the movement to the people, but for a time even strengthened it. This was natural: its direct and completely negative results and their lessons could not be discussed widely or freely, and the events of the trial itself had given the participants a halo. Our closely-knit Petersburg circle shared this general feeling, and my brother and I, and Grigoryev too, decided to organize our lives along new lines. Grigoryev was free of family responsibilities, but for my younger brother and myself the problem was much more complicated. We were 'Lavrists'[2] and viewed going to the people not as a revolutionary excur-

2 For Lavrov see p. 176, note 9.

sion with temporary progagandist aims, but as an alteration of our whole life. Grigoryev not only shared these plans, but, perhaps more than anyone else, determined them. For the immediate future my brother and I solved the problem in this way: if there were an opportunity to take part in any venture entailing danger of arrest, only one of us would participate, the other remaining in charge of the family.

Such an opportunity presented itself shortly after the Zasulich affair. It was proposed to hold a requiem for Sidoratsky in the Vladimir Church.[3] Fighting and arrests could be expected. We tossed up and my brother won. After he'd gone, Grigoryev came running into our apartment and said, 'Dusha Ivanovskaya[4] has arrived from Moscow. I thought you'd be going to the requiem. She'll be there too. It was your brother's turn? Well, that's it then. Good-bye for now.' And he hurried away.

We both knew Ivanovskaya. In the last year at the Academy our circle had grown considerably, and we had had regular meetings in the rooms of the married student Markovsky. We had also met in various places in Moscow. At one such meeting I couldn't help noticing a tall girl who was simply called Dusha by her friends. One evening, arriving rather late at a meeting at Markovsky's, I said hallo to a few people I knew and stopped. I had seen Ivanovskaya nearby. By now we had been together at two or three meetings, but no one had introduced us, I had never spoken to her and didn't know how to act. Perhaps noticing my slight embarrassment, she came up to me, stretched out her hand and said simply: 'Hello, Korolenko.' This won me over immediately and from then on we met informally. I learned that she had two sisters and that her brother, a *zemstvo* doctor, had been arrested and had escaped from the Basmanny district police station in Moscow. All the sisters were under observation by the police, and Ivanovskaya was arrested a little later on. There were rumours that she had fallen ill in prison, and the news had wrung my heart.

Now I had suddenly learned that she was here in Petersburg, and decided to go to the Vladimir Church, find my brother, and change turns with him. As I approached the church I saw a detachment of mounted gendarmes trot up the street and ride into one of the courtyards opposite the church, after which the gates were shut tight. The gates of the neighbouring buildings were also closed: one must suppose that police were lying in ambush there too. I decided to make a little reconnaissance. Further away from the church, in the neighbouring lanes, along the walls and in the passages beneath gates stood groups of

[3] 2 April 1878.   [4] Korolenko married her in 1886.

people in Siberian coats and high boots. Some were wearing aprons and held brooms in their hands. They were all standing as if on some sort of duty. I realized what it was: the police had found out about the requiem and had got its own people ready to help deal with the seditious gathering.

When I entered the crowded church, the requiem was coming to an end. In the waves of incense and the solemn sounds of the superb singing I seemed to sense a special mood: few of these young men and women had known the late Sidoratsky. Yet shortly, perhaps, more than one of this crowd would meet his fate.

Not far from the entrance, at the back wall I caught sight of Grigoryev signalling to me, and I made my way to him through the crush. Dusha was standing next to him. She greeted me just as simply and warmly, and after a time said, 'Listen, Korolenko, you can't stand like that in church.' I was standing facing her, with my back to the altar.

When the requiem was over, the congregation poured out of the church, but stopped at the parvis, obviously waiting for something. The dark crowd of people, about five hundred strong, seemed so small on that square under the imposing portal of the church. Strangers in aprons and armed with brooms would soon come running from the side-streets, and all around were the blind eyes of closed gates, hiding armed men in ambush.

A young man got up above the crowd and began speaking from the church steps. He said a few words about Sidoratsky and the significance of the requiem, and began urging the crowd to restrict itself to this peaceful expression of its attitude to the dead victim and disperse and go home without further demonstrations. The speech was well delivered and had effect: after a little hesitation the dense crowd seemed to shiver. They had been expecting objections, and a few isolated shouts of displeasure were heard, but, probably as a result of the organizers' preliminary plan, there were no other speeches. Group after group of people started leaving the compact mass, and soon the crowd had dispersed in various directions. As far as Nevsky Prospect and the beginning of Liteyny Prospect it was still fairly thick, but after that began to merge with people at large, though in places it still attracted surprised glances from the people who met it. At the end of Liteyny Prospect, where it slopes to the river, a small incident occurred. Someone noticed or just simply suspected a spy, and a number of students looked as though they might throw him into an unfrozen patch of water near the bank of The Neva. However, it ended all right.

I was seeing Ivanovskaya off and said good-bye to her at this spot. When I'd walked a few steps, I looked round. A very well-dressed

woman had just passed the girl and also looked round. A mocking smile
appeared on her face, and I knew what it meant: the figure of the tall,
thin girl was anything but smart, she had on a dark coat that looked as
if it had belonged to somebody else, and a round oilskin hat with a
ribbon that fell back on her shoulders together with her plait.

'Yes,' I thought, 'those oilskin hats are terrible, but how I love her!'

'The big trial', Zasulich's shot, which had evoked such wide sympathy, her acquittal, her declaration of respect for trial by jury and her
readiness to submit to it again were all things that seemed to establish
some interaction between broad social currents and the aspirations of
revolutionary youth. But this didn't last long. The impression made by the
Zasulich affair gradually faded away in society and in the press, while
the harsh repressive measures adopted by the government in answer to
the naïve endeavours of Populist youth provoked embittered anger.
The movement began to turn on to the path of an isolated struggle by
the revolutionary intelligentsia, on to the path of terror.

Vera Zasulich was not a terrorist in the plain sense of the word. Her
action had been a spontaneous impulse, and perhaps for that reason had
evoked such general sympathy. She herself remained opposed in
principle to terror for the rest of her life. Soon after the Zasulich affair,
however, Kravchinsky's[5] brochure appeared. In it he enthusiastically
acclaimed her action and called for its extension.

There was not long to wait. On 4 August 1878 Mezentsev, Chief of
the Gendarmes, was killed. During his usual walk accompanied by
General Makarov he had met two immaculately dressed young men on
Mikhaylov Street, who separated him from his companion. One of
these men held Makarov to the wall, while the other struck Mezentsev
with a dagger. A cab had been following a pace or so behind the
strangers, who got into it and disappeared without trace. This had
happened in broad daylight in one of the central streets of the capital.

The terrorist act had been carried out by Kravchinsky himself and
Barannikov. Adrian Mikhaylov had driven the cab. The proclamation[6]
issued in connection with this act gave a reason very close to that given

[5] Sergey Mikhaylovich Kravchinsky (1851–95), a member of 'Land and Liberty'.
After the assassination of Mezentsev he emigrated and lived in London. As a
writer, he is best remembered for his *Underground Russia* (*Podnol'naya Rossiya*),
1882, which is a somewhat oversensationalized picture of the revolutionary movement. In 1889 he wrote a novel in English, *The Career of a Nihilist*. He translated
Korolenko's story 'The blind musician' ('*Slepoy musykant*') into English. Korolenko
met him in London in 1893. The 'brochure' was, in fact, an article by Kravchinsky
that appeared in the emigré organ *Obschchina* 1878, No. 3–4.

[6] The proclamation was written by Kravchinsky and entitled 'A death for a
death'. A revolutionary, Kovalsky, had been shot in Odessa on 2 August.

by Vera Zasulich: vengeance for dead comrades. As well as this, in a poem by A. A. Olkhin,[7] the best he ever wrote, mention was made of Chernyshevsky. By law, Chernyshevsky, who had finished his term of hard labour, was to have been released. Instead, however, he had been imprisoned again in a special prison in Vilyuysk. It was said that this was thanks to Mezentsev.

The evening of the day of the assassination I stayed late in the printing-shop. Coming home (we were living at the time at the corner of Podolsk Street and Klinsk Prospect), I was amazed to see the whole apartment lit up. Suspecting something bad, I ran up the stairs feeling very concerned about my mother. She was suffering from a complicated nervous complaint which gave rise to nasty fits. The door was unlocked, and the apartment was full of police and witnesses. The first person I cast eyes on was the completely calm figure of my mother. I rushed to her and, as I embraced her, I heard her whisper: 'Pyankov is called so-and-so. He rented a room here today.'

Pyankov had been in 'the big trial': he had been acquitted by the court, but exiled by Imperial order to Archangel Province. He had just fled from there with Pavlovsky, who subsequently became Yakovlev the famous correspondent of *New Time* in France. It had been known in 'unreliable' circles that something was going to be undertaken this particular day, and both fugitives had that morning asked us for shelter, considering our place to be safe. Pavlovsky had not appeared, but I immediately caught sight of Pyankov sitting on the window-seat.

The search revealed nothing incriminating, but all the same my younger brother and I were arrested. The others—that is my brother-in-law, who'd recently married my elder sister, his foster-father, who'd just arrived from Petrozavodsk to meet his son's wife, and, finally, Pyankov—all had their papers taken away and were told to appear without fail the next day at the Third Section. My brother and I were taken to the building by the Chain Bridge, which, despite the late hour, was brilliantly lit and full of movement and bustle. I was taken to a corridor on the top floor, put into a cell, ordered to strip and had my clothes taken away. Even so, I'd managed to hide a pencil, wrapped in half a sheet of writing paper, in my thick hair. I later left it for my unknown successor in the cell. After five minutes they brought me underclothes, a thin cloth dressing gown, and hospital-type slippers. Ten minutes after that I was sleeping the sleep of the dead.

Early in the morning the attendant brought me a basin and washing

[7] The poem 'By the coffin' ('*U groba*') appeared in the underground *Land and Liberty*, 25 October 1878.

things. He was in a gendarme's jacket. At this time gendarmes were not yet volunteers, but recruits, who were appointed to the corps just as to other branches of the armed service. For this reason many plain and good-hearted men could be found among them—men who were without that special stamp that marked the volunteer gendarmes. When the attendant came into the cell for something, the sentry, also a gendarme, stood at the door with his back to the cell. When I'd washed and wiped my face, I asked the attendant the time. In answer there came a loud, coarse shout.

'Quiet. It's forbidden to talk.' But he immediately added in a whisper, 'Nine o'clock.'

I realized that I had no reason to be afraid either of the attendant or of the sentry standing at the door with sabre bared, and when he brought my breakfast in, I again asked him, 'Do you know if my brother is here?' There came an even more menacing shout and the quiet answer: 'In such and such cell, downstairs.'

The third time, when dinner appeared, the attendant himself winked to me to ask him something, and after his usual shout he said in a whisper, 'Your brother's been taken for an interrogation. Eat it quickly, they'll be sending for you now.'

My clothes were, indeed, soon brought to me and I was taken to the office. In the corridors and rooms of the Third Section there was an unbelievable bustle going on, the building was full of gendarmes, detectives, people arrested, and people summoned to appear. As I passed through the hall, I caught sight of Loshkarev, my brother-in-law, and his foster-father. Pyankov was well-known in the Third Section, and so he'd been advised not to appear.

My brother and I were interrogated quickly as to where we'd spent the first part of the previous day, and were then released. A young officer of the gendarmes came out into the hall with us and shouted:

'Those summoned from Podolsk Street, house no. such and such—are they here?'

'All present and correct, Your Excellency,' replied Loshkarev's foster-father, an old soldier of Nicholas's reign, and stood stiffly to attention.

This, evidently, saved the situation: the officer looked approvingly at this colourfully loyal figure and without calling out the names handed him all our passports. Thus Pyankov's non-appearance passed unnoticed. We walked out in a happy group into the narrow courtyard, where a tall, stout, handsome gendarme colonel in full dress uniform passed us. Much later we learned it had been the famous body-guard and personal friend of Alexander II, General Cherevin.

25

The Dilettante Revolutionary and the Free-lance Spy

THE EPISODE OF OUR ARREST IN CONNECTION WITH THE assassination of Mezentsev showed us clearly that we were now irrevocably deemed 'suspicious' and could expect similar surprises as a result of anything at all.

Now, looking back many years later, I ask myself whether there were proper grounds for this. Was I really a dangerous revolutionary? Of course, real criminals like Pyankov and Pavlovsky found refuge in my apartment. Later, as I've already said, Pavlovsky laboured in the most loyal of fields, decorating the columns of *New Time* with his articles. True, as an emigré, he had once written a story in French entitled *En cellule*, in which he had described the feelings of a political prisoner in solitary confinement. Turgenev had warmly recommended the story to the French editor, and this had brought down thunder and lightning on the famous writer in Katkov's paper. Later, however, this story appeared in Russian under the title *In solitary* in a little volume of Pavlovsky's, published in Tsarist Russia. Pyankov, as far as I know, acquired an inheritance after the death of his father, a rich Siberian wine-dealer, and later also became a big dealer on the Amur River. During the Russo-Japanese War he published a patriotic, even ultra-chauvinistic paper. So the fact that I had given shelter to those two fugitives did not have any pernicious consequences for the fatherland. I had already been in exile myself and was ready to shelter anyone evading extrajudicial punishment and naturally did not inquire whether he subsequently intended working for *New Time* or dealing in wine.

What else then? I formed plans for the reshaping of my life, linked with more or less misty plans for the reshaping of society as a whole. With these purposes in mind Grigoryev and I were learning shoe-making, and my younger brother had set up a small locksmith's work-shop. It is very likely that after a time my brother and I would have cast lots, and one of us would have set out 'to the people'—Grigoryev and I in the capacity of travelling shoemakers, my brother as a locksmith. This would have ended like hundreds of similar excursions, with the realization that the life of the people is a true ocean, the movements of which cannot be governed as easily as we imagined. For me personally this would have gone hand in hand with the amassing of artistic observations and I would probably soon have realized that I possessed the temperament not of an active revolutionary but rather of an observer and an artist. In a word, the extent of my criminality at that time, even in our country, from the point of view of our laws, remained for the most part in the realm of intentions and suppositions that were hardly punishable.

Was I nevertheless disloyal? Of course I was, and to the same extent that any representative of average Russian cultured society was disloyal at that time. 'Your Majesty,' Lavrov wrote to Alexander II in his paper *Forward*,[1] 'you sometimes walk through the streets. If you should happen to meet an educated young man with an intelligent face who looks at you straight, know that he is your enemy.' And that was very close to the truth.

The autocracy felt this. The authorities had to struggle with a widespread attitude of mind and, pursuing separate manifestations of it, became accustomed to using cannon to shoot at sparrows. The government began adapting the very laws to this mode of fire. However, seeing that it was not so easy to subject the courts to the temporary need to frighten society or make them into a sufficiently flexible instrument for combating not actions, but an attitude of mind, the government evolved a more obedient mechanism. A few brief decrees of the sovereign power created—or at least considerably extended—the mechanism of the so-called 'administrative order'.[2] These brief decrees could be called veritable 'laws for unlawfulness'. They soon acquired, besides, very wide interpretations; and with their appearance the reign of Alexander II, 'the author of the legal statutes', took to a road of asiatic despotism in respect of everything that even remotely touched political motives.

At this time (towards the end of 1878) we were living in a block of apartments with a communicating courtyard that opened on the one side to Nevsky Prospect opposite the Alexander Nevsky police station, and on the other side to Second Peskov Street. Two of the Ivanovskaya sisters (Aleksandra and Yevdokiya Semyonovna) were now living with us. This was one of the best periods in my life and, I am sure, in the life of my mother and our whole family too. We were all living together,

---

[1] I quote from memory. (Korolenko's note.)

[2] *Administrativniy poryadok*, the term used to denote the government's extrajudicial powers of arrest, detention and punishment.

except for my elder brother who came to see us once a week. The Ivanovskaya girls and Grigoryev became part of the family. We men (apart
from Grigoryev) all worked as proof-readers in various printing-houses
and got home late. It was usually after one o'clock in the morning when
the samovar was coming to the boil, and we would all gather round the
kitchen table. We would laugh and talk until my mother drove us to our
rooms. At this time even her nervous complaint passed and she had no
attacks.

By this time I had already given up the idea of the Mining Institute
and my brother had left the Building School. Only Loshkarev, my
brother-in-law, continued studying: he was in the Academy of Surgical
Medicine. In the mornings I had started going to the shoe-making work-
shop in Zagorodny Prospect. The young owner and all the workers
were Finns already affected by propaganda, and they all did their best
to teach me the secrets of their trade.

For some time now we had noticed that a systematic watch was
being kept on us by the secret police. 'Unreliable' people (the Murash-
kintsev family) were living next to us, and two spies had been put to
keep a watch on both apartments. Their faces soon became familiar to
us. One was a tall, fair-haired chap, quite presentable but somehow
lifeless-looking, with a permanently bandaged cheek. The other was
dark, short, and unpleasant-looking, with the face of an orang-utan, a
prominently protruding lower jaw, and grim, dark eyes. They would
stand one at each exit from our courtyard, and sometimes set up an
observation post on a landing of the house opposite, from where they
could see our windows. One of us had only to go out in the direction of
the Nevsky or Second Peskov Street for one of them to tail him. In
point of fact we amused ourselves cruelly at the expense of these poor
fellows. I, for example, didn't want them to know about my visits to the
shoe-making shop, and we resorted to a military ruse: my brother would
emerge from the doorway, look round anxiously and go to the gates. A
spy would immediately start tailing him. Illarion would walk a few
streets in the opposite direction to the one I was to take, go up staircases at random and then return home, while I was safely making my
way to Zagorodny Prospect. Our shadows were walking their feet off,
making useless notes of courtyards and staircases without being able
to find out anything of interest, and in their exasperation they naturally
came to harbour great animosity towards us.

However, much more serious consequences ensued from encounters with two detectives, of whom I shall need to speak in greater
detail. The first of them was a man called Glebov. He was a failed actor.

My elder brother Yulian, who was completely uninvolved in any kind of sedition, had picked him up in some amusement park at a time in his life when he didn't even have a place of his own to live. He was a young man who possessed a rather 'noble' stagey appearance. He was tall, quite well-built, with a splendidly artistic head of hair, but had no talent whatsoever and so was poverty-stricken. He moved into my brother's place with only a guitar, on which he accompanied himself singing romances. He sang in a sweet voice, trying to round his lips as pleasantly as possible. Like my father before him, my brother occasionally got unexpected bees in his bonnet, and when we asked him who his lodger was and why he was keeping him, he answered absolutely seriously, 'He's a gifted artist. He's teaching me music, and thinks that I show signs of talent.'

I should point out that our family was not distinguished by any particular musical abilities, and my elder brother, one might say, was the least musical of all of us. When, accompanied by the 'artist' on the guitar, he laboriously rendered 'On the midnight sky', we all roared with laughter, including him. The 'gifted artist', however, kept a very serious face.

One day this artist suddenly disappeared and didn't turn up for two weeks, which made my brother anxious. This happened shortly after Mrs. Goldschmidt, wife of the editor of *The Word*, had gone abroad. Many people knew that she was to take with her certain correspondence, which was to be handed to P. L. Lavrov in the editorial office of *Forward*. Glebov was among her acquaintances, and everybody noticed that he appeared for her send-off at the Warsaw Station out of breath just before the departure of the train and, saying good-bye to her, cast strange glances around. Two or three stops later Mrs. Goldschmidt was taken off the train and searched. It so happened that she had changed her mind about carrying the correspondence herself and had given it to a more 'reliable' person, so the search did not reveal anything incriminating. Mrs. Goldschmidt was issued with another ticket to Warsaw at the Third Section's expense, and Glebov had disappeared from our horizon for two or three weeks. It was later said that this had been his first volunteer undertaking and for false information the poor wretch had had to suffer a spell in jail himself. Be that as it may, after this mysterious absense my brother once more welcomed his 'artist' with open arms, the guitar played again; only instead of duets there were now trios: during Glebov's absence my brother had let in a new lodger, S-v. He had been in elementary adult education, but now gave private lessons and imagined himself a desperate revolutionary. He was a good-natured man, but not very bright. He was shortly going off to some estate in Kharkov Province with a young nobleman of sorts, and he asked my younger brother to get him some copies of illegal books that were then being published in Petersburg. My brother obliged.

On going to see my elder brother, I found S-v packing his things. He was being zealously assisted by Glebov, whom I watched tying up the illegal publications in a bundle with S-v's papers on top. They were talking about what they were doing in loud voices in spite of the fact that only a door separated the room from the next apartment, in which strangers lived. I must say I considered S-v a light-headed man and was against his propagandist ventures. When Glebov finished the packing, he quickly tidied himself up and ran off somewhere, saying that he'd come to say good-bye at the station. I suddenly remembered the stories about Mrs. Goldschmidt and started rebuking S-v for his unwariness.

'After all, we don't know this Glebov. Watch that you aren't stopped at the second or third station too. People are already talking about him.'

'Well, if that happened, it would be quite clear that Glebov is a spy.'

'But do you know,' I added, lowering my voice, 'who can hear us talking in the next room?'

S-v left for the station. The carriage he got into was crowded out. The porter put his large case in the first empty space in a luggage rack, and S-v had to sit at the other end of the carriage. Just before the train was due to leave, the panting Glebov came hurrying up again. He found S-v, thoughtfully inquired whether he was comfortable, and, coming out on to the platform at the last moment, managed to give him a few Judas kisses for the journey. At one of the next stations S-v was asked to take his things to the secret-police room. Needless to say, he only grabbed the little case lying beside him, and the other case continued the journey in safety. Thanks to this, nothing incriminating was found on him—just as with Mrs. Goldschmidt. The gendarme officer, a good-natured old man, shook his head in sympathy and said, 'Mr. S-v, you have a bad friend in Petersburg.'

Meanwhile, the case with the illegal publications and S-v's papers reached Moscow, where it was left unclaimed. Obviously, S-v had only to go to the Station Master and demand his 'forgotten things': the only chance of getting out of it safely. But he was a slow-witted and timid man. He therefore preferred to go off to Kharkov Province and wait passively until the unclaimed case (with his papers in it) was opened, whereupon he was arrested and brought to Petersburg.

Meanwhile, Glebov was again absent without trace from my brother's apartment, as after saying good-bye to Mrs. Goldschmidt. The failed actor was obviously not having any luck in his new career either, for every touching parting at a railway station only ended in his fresh arrest. When S-v was asked who had given him the illegal publications, he said straight out that he'd had them from Glebov. This was followed by a third mysterious disappearance on the part of Glebov, and S-v was released.

Talking with S-v about this incident, I told him that in his place I would never again embark upon any illegal venture whatsoever. After all we couldn't even be absolutely certain that it was actually Glebov who had given him away (however likely it seemed), and not our unknown neighbours in the adjoining room. S-v remained sitting in the corner for some time, then came up to me and said in a moved voice, 'You know, what you said has troubled my conscience. But what am I going to say tomorrow in the Third Section when I go to collect my papers ? If I'm to lift the blame from Glebov, I'll have to say I got the illegal books from your brother.'

I looked at him in surprise and said, 'Do me a favour. Say you got them from me.'

He was clearly very relieved, but a troubled look soon appeared on his face.

'But . . . but what will happen to you ?' he asked.

'Don't worry about me—I shall simply say that we all know S-v as an inveterate liar: first he lied about Glebov, and when we began shaming him for the lie, he tried to smear us.'

His face fell. He was a dilettante of a revolutionary, who considered himself bound to give frank answers to any questions the authorities might ask. Revolutionary activity he regarded as interesting and not particularly dangerous work: just distributing underground literature with a conspiratorial air to young men and, especially, girls. Should anything go wrong, he could propitiate the authorities with 'frank testimonies'. This would secure his release and he could take up the old work again in the role of a man who has suffered for the cause. The naïve man apparently saw nothing reprehensible in this.

'Listen, S-v,' I continued. 'My brother didn't force the illegal literature on you. You pestered him for it. If you think that after that you've got the right to inform on him, you should warn your friends beforehand. Still, don't worry about Glebov. Naturally, if he isn't a spy, you must lift the blame from him. But we'll soon clear that up.'

My brother and I had actually decided to clear the matter up at all costs. Some doubts still remained, and it seemed to us that in such circumstances we did not have the right to call Glebov a spy. So we called on 'the artist' and asked him to elucidate certain dubious circumstances. First of all he denied everything, but then got completely tangled up and, adopting a theatrical pose, said pathetically, 'Suppose it's true. But did S-v have the moral right to bring a false accusation against me?'

We cut short the talk about the moral right, and showed Glebov the door.

Later this gentleman appeared at searches in an official capacity, and shortly after our confrontation with him his name was included in the list of spies printed in an underground leaflet.

At the time of writing these memoirs, excerpts from documents relating to my biography are being published in *Russian Wealth*. In particular it is being said, regarding the reasons for my exile from Petersburg shortly after these events, that I was suspected of having made an attempt on the valuable life of a spy. Obviously, Glebov had over-dramatized his confrontation with us. Still, the story of the attempt on his life wasn't taken seriously in the Third Section (as I was later told even by gendarmes), since it was absolutely clear that in our dealings with him we had displayed a quixotic scrupulousness rather than ferocity of any kind. Even so, these little facts had the culminative effect of making ever thicker the atmosphere of 'unreliability' around our family and closest friends.

As for S-v, his revolutionary itch didn't leave him. Soon after, he was arrested again in connection with another case and made infamously frank depositions, which ended with the following pathetic appeal: 'If my comrades should chance to see these depositions, may they take into consideration the fact that, when I made them, I was languishing in a prison-cell.'

26
Caught in the Net

ONE FINE DAY A YOUNG MAN APPEARED AT OUR FLAT,
dressed in a splendid fur-coat with a sable collar and a hat of the same
description; he was very bright and prosperous-looking, with a fresh,
healthy glow on his well-fed face. It seemed rather strange when he
introduced himself as a plain workman from Moscow. He asked to be
provided with illegal Petersburg publications and sought direct dealings
with the editorial office most insistently. He had letters of recommenda-
tion from people we knew, but we were unable to meet his request
because we weren't in direct contact ourselves. He earnestly asked us
to make inquiries and let him know the next time he came. This, I suppose, we could have done, but we didn't particularly feel like putting
ourselves out for this strange workman, obviously proud of his expen-
sive coat, especially as one of the recommendations came from S-v,
described earlier. Reinstein came to Petersburg several times and
always came to us with his request. It so happened that once he did hit
upon a man in our flat who was close to the editorial office of an underground publication. This was A. A. Ostafev. After the large-scale wave
of arrests the people involved in revolutionary activity remaining in
Petersburg became completely transformed in their outward appearance. Ostafev (an acquaintance of my younger brother), who but a
short time before had been very unconcerned about his clothes, now
appeared in our house a real dandy, in a stylish coat and with a portfolio under his arm, exactly like a high-ranking civil servant. Without
the least embarrassment Reinstein again made his request: he was a
delegate from some Moscow workers who wanted direct dealings with
the editorial office of *Land and Liberty*.[1] Ostafev's prompt readiness to
meet this wish of a man he didn't know surprised us. He arranged to
see Reinstein the following day at the corner of a certain street. Reinstein departed, obviously very pleased. We asked Ostafev why he had
agreed so readily to the request of a man whose very name he didn't
know.

'What, in fact, is his name?' Ostafev asked, and when we told him

[1] The organ of the Populist revolutionary organization of the same name. It
came out in Petersburg from October 1878 to April 1879.

it was Reinstein he clasped his head: 'Heavens, a spy? We are printing his name in the list of police agents in the next issue.' And he left hurriedly.

The following day Reinstein came to see us grieved: he had waited in vain at the arranged place. Where could he now find the gentleman he had met yesterday?

My brother told him that we didn't know his address ourselves, as he conspiratorially concealed both his name and his address.

After this Reinstein went back to Moscow, and some days later it became known that he had been killed by revolutionaries. In Moscow he had run a 'secret flat', evidently for purposes of provocation, and in this flat at the time were hiding my good friend Pyotr Zosimovich Popov, S-v, and a Moscow workman with whom Petya Popov soon became very friendly. The workman was completely 'legal', but had recently come from the country and was living unregistered only because he had lost his passport and was awaiting another from his village.

This little company was peacefully asleep when the bell suddenly rang at the dead of night. S-v got up and asked who was there. The gate-keeper answered. When the door was opened, a tall man, whose face S-v couldn't make out in the dim light of the night-lamp, entered with the gate-keeper, handed S-v an envelope and left straight away. S-v went in a leisurely fashion into the bedroom, lit the lamp, and opened the envelope. When he'd read the note, he rushed into the hall and on to the stairs, shouting to the stranger to come back, but the stairs were deserted. S-v then threw himself on to his bed, burying his head in the pillow, and all Popov's questions he merely waved aside despairingly: 'Don't ask, for God's sake, don't ask . . .'. Popov took the paper from his hand and read it. On it in disguised handwriting was more or less the following message:

You are informed that your landlord N. V. Reinstein, having proved to be a traitor, has been executed in accordance with the sentence of the Executive Committee of the party 'The People's Will'.[2] You may take measures for your own safety, but are bound to preserve complete silence about this on pain of death.

[2] The notification could not have been from the Executive Committee of 'The People's Will', since Reinstein was murdered before 'Land and Liberty' split in August 1879 into 'The People's Will' and 'Black Partition'. The notification was probably only signed 'The Executive Committee' or 'The Executive Committee of the Social-Revolutionary Party', which was the usual way 'Land and Liberty' signed its notifications of terrorist acts.

It is easy to imagine what sort of night the tenants of the secret apartment spent after this. The next morning S-v hastened
to disappear. The workman could not disappear and decided to
wait for the registered letter with his passport. Petya Popov
didn't want to abandon him and so spent a further few days in the
flat.

I learned all these details from Popov's sister, who worked as my
assistant in *News* and was close to our family. She was handed a letter
from her brother at the time when the murder was still undiscovered
and Reinstein's body was lying in a locked hotel-room. Popov was
deeply convinced that in this particular case a terrible mistake had been
made. His sister shared this conviction and succeeded in instilling doubt
in me, though I still remembered the replete figure of that workman in
his sable hat. The thought that that prosperous young man was lying
murdered in a locked room made me shudder. I also felt that if Reinstein had in fact been a traitor, it meant there was yet another mesh in
the net of suspicion surrounding our family. Even before this, on
22 February if I'm not mistaken, our gate-keeper had come up to me
and said rather conspiratorially, 'Listen, sir: there wouldn't be anyone
unregistered in your flat, would there? Just so there won't be any
trouble . . .'

'What's the matter?' I asked.

'No, I'm just saying . . .'

We realized that this warning was not for nothing, and decided to
accelerate the departure of the Ivanovskaya sisters to Moscow. For me
it was a very sad day. A week before, I had taken my first story to the
editorial office of *Fatherland Notes*, and now Shchedrin had returned it.
I took this first literary failure rather to heart, and on top of it was this
saying good-bye.

We lived very near the Nicholas Station. Resorting to our usual
stratagem, we drew both detectives from the gates and then walked in
a group to the station. The whistle of the train was still ringing in my
ears when I returned to what now seemed an empty flat. That night,
when we were all home after work, the bell rang. It was the police
from the Alexander Nevsky district-station, who had come to make a
search: there was a tall, elderly Assistant Inspector, several constables
and witnesses, including, by the way, our two familiar shadows: the
cachectic fair-haired fellow with the bandaged cheek, and the dark-
haired chap who looked like an orang-utan. After the gate-keeper's
hint we were, of course, fully prepared for this visit, and the police
withdrew with absolutely nothing. But exactly a week later, on 29

February 1879,[3] there was another search, only this time the civil police were merely present and an officer of the secret police took charge of everything. The search was not particularly thorough (the gendarme behaved very correctly in a family home), but our two acquaintances were again at hand and were obviously concerned about something.

'Would you mind telling me who those gentlemen are ?' I asked the officer. 'From the Prosecutor's office, no doubt ?'

The captain understood the sneer, and, frowning with distaste, said to the detectives, 'What are you poking your noses in here for ? Stand by the hall door and don't move. Go on !' he shouted, when one of them tried to say something.

The two sleuths were forced to obey and stood like caryatids by the hall door. Some time later from the kitchen, which was next to the hall, came the indignant shouts of our cook Pelageya, 'What d'you want ? What are you badgering me for ? I'll use the poker on you'.

The detectives had obviously been pestering her with questions. She was a very simple soul, who had only recently come from the country. She had only been in one job before, where she had put up with quite a lot from her employers, and, coming to us, had grown very attached to everyone, like one of the family. After her indignant shouts the officer unceremoniously sent the detectives on to the stairs.

We later discovered that at that particular time a little spy drama had been going on in our flat: the next day, as Pelageya and my mother were tearfully making my empty bed, they found a note under the mattress. It informed me in the name of the compositors of The Slavonic Book Press that 'everything is ready' and that they were only waiting for my promised signal. The note was undersigned by Kuznetsov, the best and most educated compositor of *News*.

My mother was very alarmed and hurriedly destroyed the note: this I greatly regretted, as it was an obvious forgery. From whom it came I don't know. There can be no doubt, however, that the civil police had foreseen a search by the gendarmes, and the note had been left on the first occasion so as to be found on the second. I don't think the good-natured Assistant Inspector was a party to this frame-up, though, of course, I can't vouch for the other members of that police station. The most likely thing, however, is that the sleuths, incensed by our mocking tactics, had thought it up on their own. During the first search they had shoved the 'document' under the mattress and were to find it next time.

[3] A mistake, as 1879 was not a leap year. The first search was carried out on 28 February, the second on 4 March.

One can imagine their feelings when the officer deprived them of the opportunity. Ten years later, after my return from exile, passing the Anichkov Palace where Alexander III was residing, I unexpectedly noticed an old acquaintance: standing at the palace gates, observing the passing public as darkly as ever, was the memorable orang-utan. During those years, when I had been half-way round the world, his career had shifted him from the communicating courtyard of Second Peskov Street, where he had had to do with mischievous students, to the gates of the Tsar's palace.

Very late in the night, almost at dawn, the friendly gate-keeper, who had warned us of the possibility of a search, unlocked the gates on to the Nevsky, and a whole detachment of police drove us off to various stations. Loshkarev ended up near by—in the Alexander Nevsky station; I was taken to the Spassky station; my younger brother was taken somewhere else. As well as us three, that same night they arrested my elder brother in his flat, and also a younger cousin, absolutely uninvolved in any seditious activity, but, like the rest of us, working in a printing-house. The poor chap had failed in his studies and had chosen the career of a compositor. He was very impressionable, and his arrest upset his mental and emotional balance for a long time.

The fact that we had all been arrested compels me to suppose that in their searches for a secret printing-press the police had taken note of an unreliable family, all the male members of which were concerned with printing. The supposition arose that we were probably supplying type and could take charge of the technical side of a secret press. This hypothesis was enough for the police, although, I must say, it was a complete fantasy.

I was put in a cell on the second floor, the windows of which looked out on the courtyard. From my window I could see the wall of the registration office and the back stairs of the apartment of its chief. Climbing on to the table under the window I could, with a little effort, also see the gates, past which rumbled the horse-drawn tramcars.

That same morning I suddenly heard next door to me frenzied cries, interrupted by hysterical sobbing, and some time later two warders led past my cell a man, struggling in their arms and weeping. This naturally made a very strong impression on me. A deep silence ensued, eventually broken by a quiet tapping from the other side. I knew that prisoners conversed with one another in this way, and began listening. It was like the rapid click of a telegraph machine. I didn't know the conventional alphabet and couldn't decipher a thing. Therefore I simply started tapping out my name by numbers, beginning with the first

letter of the alphabet and stopping at the letter in question. My neighbour made allowances for my inexperience, and we engaged in a
difficult conversation, which yielded no results for a long time. The
tapping would somehow get confused and disconnected, and would
now be interrupted by impatient rapping, and then, finally, change
into a disorderly banging with the fists. I eventually made out that my
neighbour's name was Korolenko. I was overjoyed and laboriously
tapped out: 'Is it you, Illarion?' But the reply was unexpected: 'My
name is Dmitry.' In the end I became completely confused and simply
decided that a spy had been put next to me, who called himself by my
brother's surname but did not know his Christian name. Hence, I
should have to be on my guard, but still I did not stop tapping.

Finally I grasped the alphabet. My neighbour began scratching
sharply and insistently with something, making vertical and transverse
lines. Of the first sort I counted six each time, of the second seven. I
understood: it meant that you should draw squares and put a letter in
each square. In the end—the next day, I believe—I was tapping on a
new system. The alphabet consisted of twenty-eight letters.[4] First of all
you tapped out the row, then the letter in the row. For example, one
and three signified 'V',[5] two and five 'K', and so on. I thus discovered
that my neighbour's name was not Korolenko but Vinogradov, but his
attempt to pass himself off in the beginning as Korolenko continued to
make me very suspicious, until this too was cleared up: the tapping
came from two places; into my conversation with my immediate
neighbour there burst from time to time a less distinct tapping, which
seemed to come from below, and which occasionally turned into furious
drumming.

Eventually Vinogradov said to me, 'Try to come to an arrangement
with your brother, or he'll knock the wall down with his heels.'

It all became clear: this tapper really was my brother, only not my
younger brother, Illarion, but the elder, Yulian, of whose arrest I had
not known. He was in the middle corridor, directly beneath Vinogradov, and had utterly lost patience from the jumble of our conversations. He was an impatient and irascible man, and it proved absolutely
impossible to teach him the new alphabet. Moreover, his violent knocking on the wall attracted attention and he was threatened with solitary
confinement. After this I didn't manage to renew contact with him. The
other room—the one from which the sick man had been taken—was
empty, and so only Vinogradov remained to me.

[4] i.e. the basic—phonetic—alphabet.
[5] 'V', the third letter in the Russian alphabet.

Such contacts through a wall create an impression all their own: you can't see the person who's speaking, or hear his voice, or even see his writing, as with a letter. Sounds, as over the telegraph, are formed into dialogues, and the rest has to be filled in by the imagination. In time you learn to catch certain shades of mood in the person who's tapping, and you try to build up a picture of him—necessarily a pleasant one, inspired by a sympathy arising from common imprisonment and supposed harmony of thought.

'What do you usually do?' my neighbour once asked.

At that time I was already supplied with books, and planned my day strictly: a walk around my cell until the tea arrived, about two hours of serious reading, another walk, then a talk with Vinogradov, and lunch, after which I allowed myself to lie down with a book, but not for more than half an hour or an hour. Then more reading at the table, and so on. Men of experience had told me that when you are on your own in prison the most dangerous thing is to let yourself slide, get used to lolling on the bed, and lose a sense of system. When I said—or rather, tapped—this to Vinogradov, he replied: 'You're a lucky man. I let myself slide a long time ago. I sleep a lot, read little, and find amusement only at the window. Do you hear the accordion? That's the Assistant's son. He's playing just for me. Take a look out of the window.'

I opened the hopper-window and looked in the direction of the sound: at the very bottom opposite, in an open window, was the handsome face of a boy of about eight, who was playing the accordion. He was playing quietly and with feeling, his face raised, and his round child's eyes were looking with sympathy at Vinogradov's window.

'Well, what do you say?' asked Vinogradov, after someone had apparently driven the boy away. 'A real little angel, isn't he? You don't happen to have a coin?'

I had some change, which had been given me for food, and which I had not spent, as my younger sister and friends used to bring me lunch. Vinogradov told me to hide a coin in the lavatory. He went after me and collected it so as to give it to the angel.

He had devised a system for transmitting coins and wanted me to see the operation. He pulled a piece of wire out of the window-grille, bent it into a ring at one end, pulled a long strand from the bed-sheet and tied the coin to it. We watched it dangling in the air, the three of us together: Vinogradov from his window, I from mine, and the boy from below. Unfortunately, there was a fourth observer too: a sparrow on the nearest protuberance of the roof. Vinogradov had hardly let go the thread when the roguish sparrow took to the air, caught it in flight, and disappeared on to the roof. A desperate knocking on the wall: 'Did you see, did you see?' Vinogradov was utterly disconsolate.

The window seemed to be the sole source of joy and sorrow for him. Every now and then he would signal me to look out of the window. Once after such a signal I saw on the landing of a staircase a rather pleasant-looking, plump young woman, apparently a cook or a maid. She was standing at the window, making eyes in my neighbour's direction and blowing kisses. This was repeated at certain times every day, and Vinogradov naïvely informed me that he was in love and that the feeling was mutual. This, naturally, greatly shortened the long prison days for him, but alas, the platonic romance ended sadly. At a signal to look out of the window, I saw a sight that must have really shaken my neighbour: a fireman was demonstratively embracing his beloved. A tapping on the wall: 'Did you see? That was on purpose! Oh, women!' I tapped back a few joking words of consolation. My neighbour took them just as jokingly, but he was obviously grieved.

From the very first days of my arrest I had written to the Prosecutor, demanding an interrogation and release. For some time there was no answer at all, and Denisyuk, through whom these applications had to be sent, shrugged and said: 'It's no good. You're not the only one. They're all arrested like you and held without interrogation.'

But two or three days later I was summoned to the office. There a secret-police officer was waiting for me and declared that he had come to conduct an interrogation. After the initial formalities, he took out a fairly small oblong envelope, on which was written in a rough hand: 'To General Drenteln, Chief of the Gendarmes. The Third Section of His Majesty's Chancellery. Local.'

'Do you admit that this is your writing?' the officer asked.

I had already given written answers to the first formal questions and instead of a direct answer I suggested he compare the handwriting. There was not the slightest similarity.

I was disappointed. I had expected an explanation of my arrest, but instead I was being shown some fantastic envelope. I said this with such bitter indignation that the officer became somewhat disconcerted. He dug into his portfolio and took out a piece of paper. It contained the conclusion of a commission of experts who had compared the writing on the envelope with one of my letters taken during the search. The Commission had consisted of some government clerks and teachers of calligraphy. These calligraphic sages had admitted that the writing on the envelope had been carefully disguised, but, even so, the formation of certain separate letters and the overall character of my letter 'furnish grounds for concluding without any doubt that the address on the envelope and the letter presented to the Commission', signed in my name, 'were written by the same hand'.

I well imagined the way these calligraphists had tried to gratify their superiors with their expertise, and said 'I don't suppose you've tried giving somebody else's letters to another collection of experts like these?'

Obviously, I had guessed right, for the officer gave a queer smile and the interrogation was over. He could not satisfy my demands for an explanation of the reason for my arrest. I remember that the officer's name was Nozhin. He seemed rather embarrassed and soon left, and I returned to my cell.

Needless to say, there was an immediate knocking on the wall: Vinogradov wanted to know the result of the interrogation. When I'd tapped out the answer, he replied, 'That must mean that Drenteln has been threatened by the Revolutionary Committee, and that they suspect you of addressing the envelope.'

This seemed pretty likely. Drenteln had been appointed Chief of the Gendarmes in Mezentsev's place. His appointment had given rise to a lot of talk and a lot of expectations, based, among other things, on the fact that Drenteln was an army general, who until then had had nothing to do with the police service. In *Russian Truth*, the organ of young liberals with a radical flavour, there appeared an article by Girs, the editor, in the form of an address to Drenteln. The writer drew attention to the absence of police traditions in Drenteln's past career, and expressed the hope that he would be able to give a new direction to the activity of that unpopular institution. 'Go forward, upright and honourable soldier, on your new road. Society, weary of this struggle with our youth, expects much from you'—such, more or less, was the end of the address. There was a great deal of talk about it. However conventional and 'Byzantine' the style in which it was written, for those times it could only be considered bold because of the statement about the extreme unpopularity of the Third Section. Everybody waited to see what the reaction of the government would be to this address from a journalist. I recall that the first few days passed without anything happening. The censorship was, as it were, puzzled and hesitated. But after a few days an answer came: punishment descended on the paper. It was likely that there would be a reply from the other side too.

Then, on 13 or 14 March, Vinogradov started drumming excitedly on the wall after lunch. He had just come back from seeing someone or other and reported a sensational piece of news: an attempt had been made on the life of the Chief of the Gendarmes, General Drenteln. A young man on horseback had overtaken his carriage, fired two or three shots at him, and disappeared. This had happened in broad daylight on a busy street and the whole city was talking about it, amazed at the boldness of the unknown horseman.

So, our supposition had proved correct. Clearly, Drenteln had received notice, but had thought that nothing could possibly occur in such a brazen way. Furthermore, it became obvious that some sort of part in this attempt was ascribed to me. There were no further interrogations, in spite of my persistent demands. At this time, as, indeed, for a long time afterwards and in changed circumstances, such things were considered a superfluous luxury for us Russians.

Early one morning I was notified that my imprisonment in the Spassky station was ending that day and that I should get ready. The next few hours I spent in a painful state of impatience. I can say quite flatly that those hours of waiting for freedom were equivalent to several days of imprisonment. Finally, a carriage entered the courtyard, I was summoned to the office, given the articles and money belonging to me, and then I got into the carriage. Denisyuk got in with me. As we drove along he sighed continually. I asked him where we were going. In reply he gave an even deeper sigh.

'What are you sighing for?' I asked. 'I ought to be sighing, not you.'

'Who can say?' he replied sadly. 'Today I'm taking you, and in a month, perhaps, you'll be taking me.'

I couldn't help laughing. They say the Turks have a sort of collective national presentiment that one day they will be driven out of Europe. The same sort of mass presentiment was not unknown to our old régime. Later I many times recalled Denisyuk's melancholy observation.

Meanwhile, the carriage had travelled on, out across the Fontanka and round the Bolshoy Theatre. I started to guess: in front to the right, beyond a little bridge was the Lithuanian Castle. The gates opened. Before me for a moment I glimpsed the grieved face of my mother, who had obviously learned in some way that we were being moved, and half an hour later, dressed in prison clothes with the letters L.T.Z.[6] on my back, I entered a noisy, crowded corridor of the Lithuanian Castle.

A stranger met me right at the entrance to the corridor where the political prisoners were, with the joyful exclamation, 'And here's the third! Welcome. Both your brothers are waiting for you.'

[6] *Litovsky tyuremniy zamok*, the Lithuanian Prison-Castle.

True enough, I immediately found myself in my brothers' arms, and then began to make the acquaintance of the other people there. After a while we were taken to our cells. My brothers had already installed themselves in one of them, and an empty bed was waiting for me. Besides the three of us, there was also a middle-aged prisoner with the appearance of a 'man of the sixties', with long, greying, curly hair, thrown back, an intelligent face, and mocking smile. The short prisoners' pea-jacket and grey trousers looked really smart on him, as if they'd been made specially for him. When I came in, he got up from the bed, gave me a firm hand-shake and said: 'Griboyedov. And this,' he pointed to a tall youth sitting alongside him, 'is Tsybulsky, otherwise called Kid. He was arrested for his suspicious appearance.' I couldn't help laughing: the young man could hardly have looked less suspicious. He was very young, with the faintest beginnings of a moustache. There was a delicate flush and an almost childlike down on his cheeks, and he had ingenuous, protruding blue eyes.

I soon learned his story. Tsybulsky really had no idea why he had been arrested. He had been walking past the Summer Garden about midday; a stranger had come up to him and asked him to go into the building by the Chain Bridge, where he had been searched and sent to the Lithuanian Castle. The young man was completely bewildered, swore that he had only come that year from the country and, entering some higher educational institution, had not known about any revolution and had made friends only with people from his home locality. But . . . he had long hair, and being short-sighted he wore glasses. One day Griboyedov, lying on the bed and watching Tsybulsky walking round the cell, suddenly said, 'Listen, Tsybulsky! Did you wear a plaid when you were outside ?'

'Yes, I did,' answered Tsybulsky.

'And high boots ?'

'Yes, high boots too.'

'I see,' drawled Griboyedov, expelling a stream of smoke. 'A plaid . . . high boots . . . long hair . . . glasses. You were obviously arrested for your suspicious appearance. The Tsar must have been walking in the Summer Garden at the time . . .'

Everyone in the cell burst out laughing, so improbable did this supposition appear. Tsybulsky was nothing but a child. In our corridor one of the warders, a grumbling but very good-hearted old man, had taken him under his wing, considering it his duty to look after him like a nurse with a child.

'The others can do as they please,' he would say. 'They're a hardened lot. But you, Tsybulsky, are still a kid. Your mother is likely crying about you. Go and put your jacket on. It's chilly even in the sun: if you go for a walk, you'll catch cold.'

After this Tsybulsky was called Kid. Yet, Griboyedov proved to be right. When Tsybulsky's father eventually arrived—he was, seemingly, a landowner from Kovno Province—and went to the Third Section to discover the reasons for his son's arrest, they reassured him. When he'd looked through the file, the old official said, 'It's nothing at all. . . . Don't worry.'

The landowner flared up. 'What do you mean, nothing at all? My wife heard about it after she'd had a baby, and almost frightened herself to death. I've had to leave her ill at home and have come racing to Petersburg, and you tell me it's nothing at all!'

'A little misunderstanding, that's all,' the official said blandly. 'These are troubled times, you know, and we haven't managed to make full inquiries. You see, your son was arrested for his suspicious appearance.'

A few days after his father's arrival Tsybulsky was in fact released, having spent about two months in prison. His infuriated father immediately took him from Petersburg.

But I have forestalled events. Let me return to the other inmates of the Lithuanian Castle and their interesting experiences. In our cell there was also a first-year student whose name, if my memory serves me correctly, was Yakimov. His father was a court-broker[7] on the Petersburg Exchange. He was a man of conservative views and extremely severe character. His son admitted to Griboyedov that he was very afraid of his father.

'But you say you aren't guilty of anything,' they reassured him.

'He won't believe it,' moaned the young man. 'He thinks people aren't arrested for nothing: "If they've got arrested, it means they've been up to something. I'm telling you straight, if they arrest you, I'll give you a flogging."'

'He'll give you a flogging to celebrate your release, I suppose?' said Griboyedov with a smirk.

'He probably will,' the youth agreed sadly.

At this time, after the attempt on Drenteln's life, there was a decree stating that, in view of the fact that sedition was spreading, extreme measures had to be taken, and the police were called upon to search and arrest 'without regard to the rank or wealth of suspected persons'.

[7] *Hofmakler*, an official who supervised the activity of the brokers on the exchange.

One fine morning, when the occupants of cell no. 5 had just finished their morning tea, the door opened and the solid figure of an elderly gentleman in prison uniform appeared. He stopped on the threshold with some hesitation, and at that moment Yakimov exclaimed tragically, 'Father!'

It really was the court-broker, who'd been arrested to show that there would now be no regard paid to rank or wealth. There was silence in the cell for several minutes after this family reunion. Father and son just looked at each other, while Griboyedov, smoking his perpetual cigarette, lay on his bed watching them with intelligent, mocking eyes.

'Father,' the son finally said, 'do you remember telling me that if people are arrested, it means they've been up to something?'

'Mm, mm . . . I see now,' the court-broker answered morosely, and the merciless Griboyedov added:

'Apparently, your father also said something else, didn't he?'

'Yes, father. You also said they ought to be flogged.'

'Will you be quiet!' the poor court-broker shouted.

The father, it is true, did not stay long, and I only saw the son. But in the few days before the 'misunderstanding' was cleared up, Griboyedov, who had held quite a high position in the Red Cross, managed to torment him quite a bit. Each time the cell door was locked, he would lie down on his bed and, puffing away at a cigarette, would start an interrogation.

'Now come along, sir, just remember: you must have been up to something, mustn't you? I don't think it would come amiss if you and I "without regard to rank or wealth" had a little chat.'

There was indeed a virtual orgy of denunciations, searches, arrests, and exiles. The autocracy was experiencing a paroxysm of violent insanity, and the whole of Russian society 'without distinction of rank or wealth' was declared seditious and placed outside the law. All the Petersburg police stations were filled to overflowing with such criminals as myself and my brothers, and the stories of the other prisoners in the Lithuanian Castle were almost all similar to Tsybulsky's and Yakimov's. I also met there a whole bunch of Gordons and Kayranskys, who in most cases had not known one another at all before their arrest. At the head, as the prime bloom, so to speak, was Gordon, the Secretary of the Jewish Charitable Society. For the first few days his children—a boy and a very young little girl—were put in his cell with him (they had gone when I arrived).

It soon became clear to me what had happened. At one time in Petersburg there was talk of the escape abroad of one of the two participants in the so-called Chirigin Affair,[8] either Deych or Stefano-vich. I had even heard in this connection that there were plans to apply to Glebov, who had already said he was willing in return for payment to take out in his own name a passport for travel abroad. At that time we already suspected him and managed to forewarn the man who was trying to obtain the passport, so that the search for a passport was made elsewhere. A certain Gordon agreed to take out a passport, also in return for money. The passport was obtained, handed over, and Stefanovich (or Deych) left the country safely. In order to remove any possible accountability from Gordon an announcement of the loss of the pass-port was made. Everything would have passed off all right, had they not been too clever. The announcement requested the finder to deliver it to Kayransky of such and such an address. A completely fictitious address was given, and the name of Kayransky was invented, since the announcers naturally knew that nobody would find the passport. For some reason the announcement attracted the attention of the police. Perhaps the police had been informed by Glebov of the efforts to get hold of a passport. They made inquiries about Kayransky, couldn't find him at the address and, without further ado, arrested all the Gordons and Kayranskys in Petersburg. A three-day watch was kept on the apartments of those arrested. It was just at this time that the Jewish Society issued the usual grants to students at the Conservatory. The grants were handed out from the apartment of the Society Secretary, Gordon, and all those who came for their grants on the day of his arrest were also arrested and dispatched to the Lithuanian Castle, while watch was kept on their rooms, so that more and more people were continually being taken into custody.

All in all, I came across dozens of such chance victims of police high-handedness in the Lithuanian Castle. The most interesting thing, perhaps, is that, without wasting much time investigating the mass of arrested people, they simply sent them in administrative exile to various towns. Though it was absolutely clear that, for example, in the case of the passport only one Gordon and one Kayransky was involved, all the Gordons and all the Kayranskys were sent from Petersburg to various places. The Secretary of the Jewish Society landed in Olenets Province, if I'm not mistaken—in Pudozh.

[8] The Chirigin Affair was an attempt to incite an armed uprising of the pea-sants of the Chirigin District, Kiev Province, which was made in 1877 by the Populists Stefanovich, Deych, and Bokhanovsky. The police were informed by a peasant of what was going on, and, together with many peasants, the three leaders were arrested. On the night of 27 May 1878 the three of them escaped from a Kiev prison with the help of M. F. Frolenko, who had become a warder in the prison in order to organize the escape.

Of us three only my elder brother avoided this fate, and it came about in a wonderfully simple way. His landlady declared that he was her fiancé and was to marry her shortly. 'Well, if he's your fiancé, take him home.' And my brother was released.

As regards my younger brother and myself, no approaches were of any avail. After our arrest Grigoryev, the two Popova sisters, and other people we knew were arrested. They had been arrested for knowing us, and Grigoryev was told so straight out. When one respectable man (I think it was my uncle, Yevgraf Maksimovich Korolenko) applied to the City Prefect's to find out about us, he was simply told, 'Heavens! Just knowing them is enough: all their friends are in prison.' This was a fact which, of course, it was impossible to refute.

We were still in the Lithuanian Castle when, on 21 April, Solovyov made his attempt on Alexander's life.[9] This naturally made a very strong impression, but it can be said that the sense of shock was not genuine, except among the common people. Among the educated classes affection for the former Tsar-Liberator had long been undermined by his obvious sympathy for savage reaction.

Among the prisoners, as far as we could tell, the impression was one of indifference, and was, furthermore, coloured by a small humorous accident. We heard of what had happened from the criminal prisoners during our walk. To avoid any 'harmful influence' we usually took our walk in a small square enclosure, fenced off from the courtyard proper with tall stakes. The criminals often came up to this fence, hurriedly exchanging notable items of news with us. This particular day they had just come out of the prison church, where they had gathered for a Thanksgiving Service. According to them, the prison priest had made an embarrassing rhetorical slip. Entering the pulpit to explain the reason for the thanksgiving, and tuning himself in advance for a pathetic delivery, he began loudly, in a high-flown style.

'Dear brothers! There has been a further sacred attempt on the criminal person of His Imperial Majesty.'

A sudden fit of coughing by a member of the prison staff interrupted his emotional speech, and he found it very hard to recapture the same tone.

On a clear day at the beginning of May two carriages appeared in the part of the courtyard that could be seen from our corridor. The inmates of the Political Wing became uneasy: was someone to be taken

---

[9] Aleksandr Konstantinovich Solovyov (1846–79) fired three shots at Alexander II on the Palace Square, but missed. He was sentenced to death and hanged on 28 May.

away? A few minutes later my younger brother and I were called. Our preparations didn't take long, but our departure turned out to be a very solemn one: two gendarmes sat with us in each carriage, three more rode alongside and behind, and a sixth sat on the coach-box. This was a whole detachment and the sight inspired panic in the passers-by. When we turned off the Morskaya and drove out on to a wide part of the Nevsky, opposite the Gostiniy Dvor, workmen repairing the road jumped up quickly and, running to one side, took off their caps and crossed themselves.

I remember this touched me. I thought of Denisyuk and his melancholy exclamation. Yes, indeed, when and how would we return? It seemed to me that I wouldn't have to wait all that long. And, of course, we would return in different circumstances. We would come back to the free capital of a free Russia.

At the railway-station the first thing I noticed was the tall figure of Fursov, the City Prefect's Assistant. He had obviously been waiting for us, and met and escorted us with a strange, hostile look, which I found quite puzzling. Further on, on the platform, stood my mother, her eyes red from weeping, and my sisters. We were only permitted to kiss them and receive some money, and soon afterwards the murky haze over Petersburg had disappeared behind the horizon.[10]

---

[10] Korolenko and his brother Illarion were exiled initially to Glazov, Vyatsk Province on 13 May 1879. In the accompanying letter from the City Prefect (10 May, No. 6154) addressed to the Vyatsk Governor it was said:

The Third Section of His Imperial Majesty's Chancellery has reached the conclusion, in the light of the information it possesses about the noblemen Vladimir and Illarion Korolenko, that these persons, among others, are undoubtedly guilty of associating with the chief revolutionaries, and equally of participating in the printing and distribution of the revolutionary publications of the Free printing-press. However, despite such important indications, based on a thorough examination of the actions and relations of the persons named, they cannot in respect of legal evidence for prosecution be brought to account in a court, nor even before the inquiry about their chief accomplices, since they managed in their resource-fulness to conceal all traces of their criminal actions. The Third Section, in view of what has been stated, put the above-named Korolenko brothers at my disposal and added that, as well as the aforesaid general charge, there were also indications that they had conspired together to kill a secret agent, but had been unable to commit the crime, as information about it was received in time and the agent was protected from the danger threatening him. On receiving a report of this the temporary Governor-General of St. Petersburg, on the basis of the authority vested in him by the Emperor, has decreed: 'The Korolenkos are to be exiled to Vyatsk Province under the surveillance of the police.'

Thus began Korolenko's five years of exile.

Appendix

A NOTE ON POPULISM

Populism as an active revolutionary movement developed out of the ferment of radical thought of the 1860s. The new radicals of the 1860s saw liberal and constitutional ideals as irrelevant to the problems facing Russia. The Tsar would never be persuaded voluntarily to relinquish his autocratic power, and therefore if a just social order were to exist in Russia, it would have to come through revolution, which it was the individual's duty to help to prepare.

Initially, at least, the Populists pinned all their hopes on the Russian peasantry. They regarded such native peasant institutions as the commune (*obshchina*) and the village council (*mir*) as rudimentary socialist institutions, proof of the fact that the Russian peasant was a natural socialist. By developing such native institutions Russia could pass quickly and painlessly to socialism. She could develop into an agrarian socialist society without having to suffer the evils of capitalist industrialization which Europe was undergoing. Russia's economic backwardness was her great advantage. However, the Reforms of Alexander II had had as their purpose to transform the Russian economy into a modern capitalist economy. Therefore, it was necessary to act quickly, before capitalism had had time to put down firm roots in Russia. Revolution would be successful only if the Russian intelligentsia acted as the unifying and directing force which the peasantry needed. The socialist intelligentsia had only to open the peasants' eyes to the injustices they were suffering and inspire them with revolutionary socialist fervour (an easy task, since the peasants were already socialists without knowing it), and the peasants would rise *en masse* and overthrow the Tsarist régime.

Such (more or less) were the naïve beliefs and aspirations that impelled young people to 'go to the people' during the years 1873–6 (the high-water mark was 1874). Their attempts to spread socialist and revolutionary ideals among the peasants inevitably resulted in complete failure. The peasants hardly understood what the young students and intellectuals were talking about, and were deeply suspicious of them anyway. In many cases they handed them over to the police. The authorities, however, were alarmed by the proportions which the 'movement' had assumed, and over-reacted to the situation. In this way they helped to bring the more extreme elements to the surface—men now well aware of the need for organization and conspiracy.

Towards the end of 1876 the nucleus of a real organization, called 'Land and Liberty', had been formed in Petersburg. It was a very small organization: never at any time did it have more than 200 affiliated members. The 'mass' movement (even this had not involved more than a few thousand people) had been essentially spontaneous and really quite harmless. Most of those who had taken part in it were not prepared to accept party discipline or conspiratorial terrorism, and had been utterly disillusioned anyway by the way in which their socialist ideals had, in the words of Kravchinsky, bounced off the peasants 'like peas off a wall'. From the very beginning 'Land and Liberty' was split on the question of terrorism, and in the summer of 1879, it finally broke up into two parties—the weak, propagandist 'Black Partition' and a party now dedicated to political revolution, 'The People's Will'. In the third number of its paper it proclaimed that it was fighting for political democracy. In other words, though revolution would obviously not come through the peasantry, it would at least be on behalf of the Russian people as a whole. As one of its first acts the new party passed a formal sentence of death on Alexander II, and devoted all its energies to achieving this initial goal.

The dramatic assassination of the Tsar on 1 (13) March 1881 also marked the end of 'The People's Will', for within a few weeks of the assassination nearly all its members were either under arrest or abroad, and the regicides—five in all—were publicly hanged after a short trial. The demise of 'The People's Will' marks the end of Populism as an active revolutionary movement.